DESIGNA

Bloomsbury USA
An imprint of Bloomsbury Publishing Plc

1385 Broadway   50 Bedford Square
New York   London
NY 10018   WC1B 3DP
USA   UK

www.bloomsbury.com

Pages 350-353 from *Ancient British Rock Art* © 2007 by Chris Mansell. Pages 354–355 from *Mazes and Labyrinths* © 1996 by John Martineau. Pages 356-359 from *Weaving* © 2005 by Christina Martin. Pages 369–373 from *The Alchemist's Kitchen* © 2006 by Guy Ogilvy. Pages 388–391 from *Li* © 2003 by David Wade. Page 392 © 2014 by Tom Perkins. Pages 394–395 © 2014 by Dmytro Kostrzycki. Pages 396–397 from *Ruler and Compass* © 2009 by Daud Sutton. Pages 398–401 © 2014 by Adam Tetlow. Pages 402–403 © 2014 by John Martineau

ISBN: 978-1-62040-659-5

Library of Congress Cataloging-in-Publication Data is available.

4 6 8 10 9 7 5

Designed and typeset by Wooden Books Ltd, Glastonbury, UK
Printed and bound in China by C & C Offset Printing Co., Ltd.

To find out more about our authors and books visit www.bloomsbury.com. Here you will find extracts, author interviews, details of forthcoming events, and the option to sign up for our newsletters.

Bloomsbury books may be purchased for business or promotional use. For information on bulk purchases please contact Macmillan Corporate and Premium Sales Department at specialmarkets@macmillan.com.

DESIGNA

TECHNICAL SECRETS OF THE
TRADITIONAL VISUAL ARTS

BLOOMSBURY
NEW YORK · LONDON · OXFORD · NEW DELHI · SYDNEY

WⅢDⅢN
BⅢKS

Above: Analysis of ceramic panel from Sheikh Lotfullah mosque, Isfahan, by Simon Trethewey. The central medallion is a third of the width of the square. Two systems of spirals, major and minor, are shown separated top right and combined in the final design. Overleaf: General view of the Hypostyle Hall, Karnak, Temple of Amun-Ra, from Description de l'Égypte, *Paris 1809-1829.*

CONTENTS

Editor's Preface   1

Book I   Celtic Pattern   3
Adam Tetlow

Book II   Islamic Design   57
Daud Sutton

Book III   Curves   113
Lisa DeLong

Book IV   Perspective   171
Phoebe McNaughton

Book V   Symmetry   233
David Wade

Book VI   The Golden Section   293
Scott Olsen

Appendices & Index   349

EDITOR'S PREFACE

This book is a collection of six Wooden Books titles, with appendices drawn from other relevant books in the series. Artists, craftsfolk, and designers should all find some useful material here.

We begin with Adam Tetlow's breathtaking exposition of *Celtic Pattern*, packed with beautiful drawings, top tips and innovative insights. Next up, in Book II, Daud Sutton elegantly reveals the secret principles and constructions behind the genius of *Islamic Design*. Following on, in Book III, Lisa DeLong explores the techniques used for centuries to construct artisans' *Curves*, from formal foliates to floral flourishes. In Book IV, Phoebe McNaughton opens the strange artist-conjuror's box-of-tricks which is *Perspective and Other Optical Illusions*. Then, in Book V, David Wade invites us to explore *Symmetry*, one of the most pervasive yet elusive subjects of them all. Finally, in Book VI, Professor Scott Olsen masterfully presents the extraordinary fact of the *Golden Section*, showing how it operates in nature and is used in the arts.

Appendices have been drawn from *Ancient British Rock Art* by Chris Mansell, my own *Mazes and Labyrinths*, *Weaving* by Christina Martin, *The Alchemist's Kitchen* by Guy Ogilvy, and *Li* by David Wade. Fresh appendix material has also been contributed by Tom Perkins, Dmytro Kostrzycki, and Adam Tetlow. Further references and credits appear at the end of the book. Special thanks to George Gibson at Bloomsbury.

Apologies to purists but a mix of both UK and US spelling and punctuation has been used throughout this jointly printed edition.

Thanks to all involved, and happy reading.

John Martineau

BOOK I

Bronze shield mount found in the River Thames at Wandsworth, London. Lithograph by Orlando Jewitt in Horae Ferales, *1863.*

CELTIC PATTERN

VISUAL RHYTHMS OF THE ANCIENT MIND

Adam Tetlow

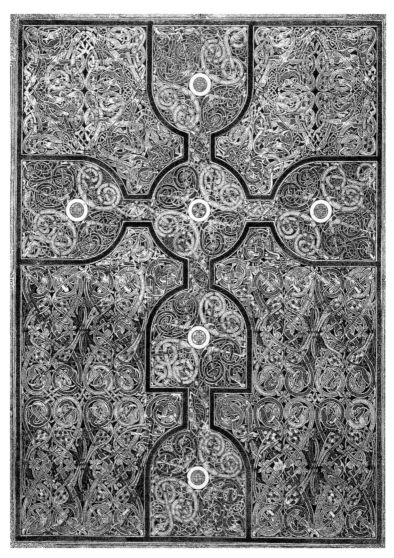

*Above: Matthew Cross; carpet page from the Lindisfarne Gospels, c.700*AD.

INTRODUCTION

The line has always been at our service. Tool and companion on our journey into being, it has measured, mapped, woven, and wriggled its way through our lives, its quicksilver flexibility fueling our discoveries.

We harness lines to make our world, to bind language into time, to connect and protect, surround and select. They are our means for bringing our imagination into existence, our will manifested.

Ancient societies were fascinated by the magic and poetry of the line, for within the patterns it described they saw the face of eternity, those qualities we name numbers. To study number is to study permanence—numbers are forever, they do not change, they are change. Traditional geometry studies the quality of number in space using cord, compass, and straight edge. It is rooted in the idea of a cosmos embroidered with number by causal intelligence.

As true philosophers, Celts, both Druid and Christian, lived in a world of vision, seeing nature as both living presence and vast book, written in a language of symbolic analogy (sometimes known as 'the language of the birds" or "the green language"). This vision of meaning in nature is nowhere better expressed than in the flowing ornament and rigorous geometry of Celtic art.

So join us as we follow the adventures of line through the Celtic world, as it winds its way from prehistory to the first books. Tracing its path we will see into the minds of the Celtic artists, unfolding their intent and imaginings, reconstructing their technical mastery and its strictures, and learning through practice to join the action of hand, eye, and heart, and see a glimpse of an immanent reality.

PRIMORDIAL SYMBOLS
a deep history of pattern

The essential motifs of indigenous art emerge from the mists of prehistory fully formed. Symbols found in the earliest examples of human mark-making (*opposite, in black*) dance through the artifacts of the pre-Celtic world. Marija Gimbutas tracked these early marks across central Europe and found them universally linked to the Bird Goddess (moon, mother, matrix, soul, imagination), our oldest image of deity, passed down to us some say from the Neanderthals. As we shall see later, forms such as nets, grids, rhombs, knots, 'S'- and 'C'- shapes, and mushrooms, and others like chevrons, zigzags, meanders, cup and rings, spirals, crosses, arrows, axes, butterflies, squares, and circles, resurface in every phase of Celtic art.

These geometric glyphs are stylised models of processes, ways to map the world and its cycles (*e.g. below center, lunar counts on stones from Newgrange*). They arise first from within, as symbols, dreams, and visions, as well as through physiological entoptic phenomena (*opposite, in white*), where patterns seen by carefully pressing the eyes, or in prolonged darkness and certain altered states of consciousness, are sent by the visual cortex to the retina, reversing the normal flow of signals and allowing us to actually see the structure of our own brains.

MEASURING HEAVEN & EARTH
the neolithic roots of celtic art

The Celtic peoples inherited a Neolithic network of tracks, monumental earthworks, and standing stones that form accurate geometrical structures over huge distances. Megalithic sites such as Stonehenge, Avebury, or Maes Howe on Orkney (*where large numbers of carved polyhedra have been found, see page 362*) also take advantage of geometrical aspects of the swing of risings and settings of the Sun and Moon. For example, at the latitude of Carnac in Brittany, any square drawn on a level surface produces the full swing of moonrises, and a 3:4 rectangle gives the swing of the Sun (*see the 3300 BC Crucuno Rectangle, below*).

The ancient builders of these star temples studied the science of measure—ancient metrology. Using a scale of measures related by simple fractions, they expressed the dimensions of their monuments purely in whole numbers, tied to the unit of the English foot (itself linking the proportions of the body to the dimensions of the Earth).

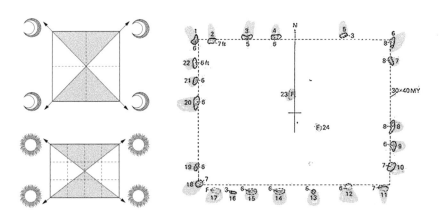

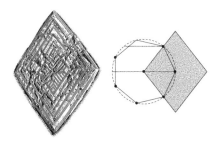

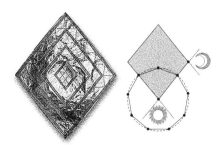

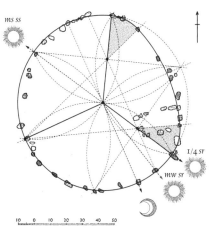

Above left: Gold rhomb found in Clarendon Barrow near Stonehenge, based on a 7-fold polygon (Avebury is 3/7's of the way between the pole and equator). Above right: The 100° and 80° angles of the 9-fold Stonehenge Bush Barrow lozenge define the extreme positions of the Sun and Moon at Stonehenge.

Left and below: Castlerigg stone circle, Cumbria, is based on a six-fold division of a circle laid out on the axis of midwinter sunrise and midsummer sunset. This method for drawing flattened curves appears in later spiral work.

CELTIC CONSTRUCTIONS
simple standing waves

Gal (Old Irish) or *Gallu* (Welsh), meaning ferocity, power or boldness is an appropriate term for the tribal group that emerged in the late Bronze Age from the Urnfield culture [1300–700 BC] of central Europe. The later Hallstatt [800–600 BC] and La Tène [400–100 BC] cultures, named for sites in Austria and Switzerland, spread and took the Celts into the Iron Age and as far as Turkey and Ireland.

Fierce protectors of their freedoms, brave warriors, lovers, scholars, and poets, the Celts were forward thinking: women and men held equal status in society, nature was treated with reverence, learning with relish. Celtic arts were equally advanced; they wrestled with fire to reach a deep understanding of metallurgy, learning to smelt iron and fuse glass to metal as enamel. Travelling artisans carried this knowledge to Britain and Ireland. Early Celtic art is woven with serpentine curves, leaves, mushrooms, teardrops, trumpets, and triskeles, derived from the geometry of intersecting circles and arcs.

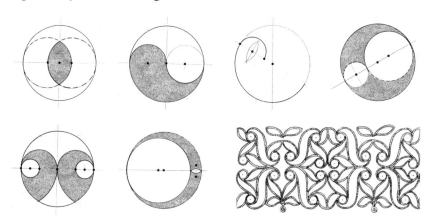

Above: Bronze French helmet, 450 BC, showing incised leaves and spirals.

Above: A circle divided into nine generates mushrooms, 'S'-curves, and hooked trumpets. All Celtic art motifs derive from tangenting circles and arcs.

Above: A three-fold division of the circle, 'master grid' for much Celtic compass work.

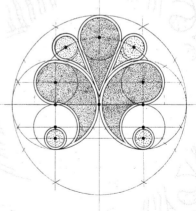

Above: A paisley-like palmette constructed by regular divisions of a circle, determining the size of smaller circles and arcs.

LIVING LINES
miniature metallurgical marvels

Using the compass as their primary tool the La Tène metalsmiths laid out complex vegetal patterns on a grid of underlying geometry. The drawing below shows two repeat patterns and a joining unit sharing the same grid, which has been proportioned by circles and triangles (*from Marne, France, 400 BC*).

Miniturization is fundamental to much of Celtic art, with pieces such as this gold disk (*facing page*) measuring just over 2 inches wide. Drawing accurately at this scale takes practice. The Celtic tradition is unparalleled in its use of curved geometry. The key to their method is learning to draw freehand with a compass until an understanding of what happens when a radius is changed or a center shifted becomes rooted over hundreds of hours in the muscle memory of the hands.

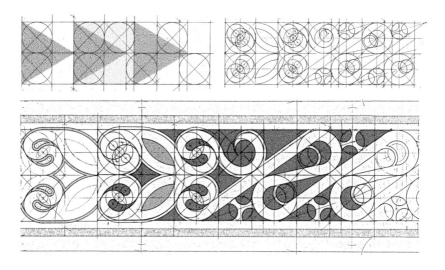

Above: Engraved 2½-inch diameter gold disc from Germany, late 5th century BC. The three-fold triskele forms spin around the edge of the disc, with eight pairs arranged radially. To construct: divide the circumference into sixteen and take half the radius to proportion the outer band; next, regularly space the circular centers and join them by parallel tangenting arcs.

TOTEMIC VISIONS
compass caricatures of animal ancestors

For the Celts, nature was a wild and living world, as aware of us as we of it. Each fold of the landscape, every mountain, river, spring, forest, plant, and animal were ensouled numinous presences with their own spark and character; gods, faeries, and ancestors, to be appeased or implored. Today, folk tales and place names still hold memory of them. Animals were ambassadors to the gods, symbols, and auguries of their qualities, points of reference in an integrated system of thought and experience. Significant trees and rocks became centers of focus, cosmological poles, places of worship and arbitration, where worlds met and laws were ratified.

This vision clothed in myth shaped Celtic imagery. Artists chose not to represent animals naturalistically, instead using stylization formed on underlying arcs and circles to bring forth the spirit of their subject. Surviving ceremonial, martial, and domestic metalwork (most wood has perished) depicts horses, bulls, dogs, boars, owls, swans, ravens, eagles, not forgetting bees and the odd centaur and sphinx, using the same undulating geometric curves found in plant ornament (*below, 'S'-curve dragons, Austria 500 BC*).

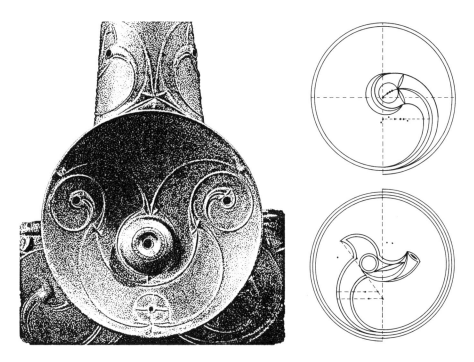

Above: The Petrie crown (detail), 100 BC, an Irish ritual crown with birds-head single spirals (drawn with compass as above right, see page 24; after Meehan). Below, left to right: La Tène brooch with horse and ram's heads from Austria, mid-4th C. BC; Bronze boar, Romania, 1st C. BC; Bronze cauldron mount in 'plastic' style shaped as owl, Denmark, 3rd C. BC.

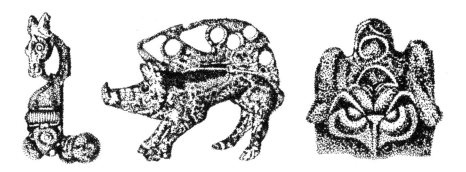

EARLY INSULAR
the land dreams the king

Between the 4th and 2nd centuries BC the La Tène style became established in Ireland and Britain and began to take on its own distinctive flavour, characterized by its ambiguous spiral plant and animal lines. The Irish Triads tell us of *"three things that constitute a carpenter: joining together without warping; agility with the compass; a well-measured stroke."* This agility is seen (and rarely equalled since) in the stunning and precise metalwork of the period.

Ornamented scabbards popular with warrior elites in the 1st century BC (*opposite, from Ireland, a, b, c, d, and England, e*) were decorated with 'S'-curve spirals (*b, c, d*), rotated single spirals (*a*) and openwork compass ornament (*e*), similar to bronze-backed mirrors (*see page 21*).

Some of the finest artifacts (*e.g. the Battersea Shield, below*) are found in lakes thought to be votive sites—remains of wooden piers suggest a liminal space for the supplicant to cast rich offerings into the water.

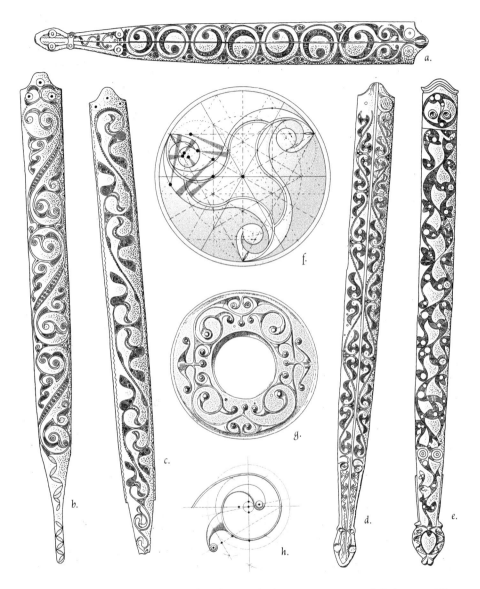

Above: (f): Triskele shield mount, Wales, 5th C. BC; the design is an expansion of the 'master grid' on page 13 (inner dashed circle); already petal and trumpet forms are established motifs. (g): Four-fold shield mount from Ireland made of single spirals (construction h); (swords after Harding).

FACES OF THE OTHER
moving forward gazing backward

The phenomenal degree of skill possessed by the British insular artists is no better expressed than in the geometrical ornament on the backs of their bronze and iron mirrors, the earliest dating to 150 BC. The style, likely started by a single master, features the use of slightly skewed bilateral symmetry, basket-hatching and La Tène compass curves, describing a multitude of human and animal faces at varying scales. The quality of the ornament varies, peaking in the supreme subtlety of the Desborough mirror (*opposite, bottom left*).

About thirty mirrors have been found, several in high status female graves. Perhaps these women were seeresses, the mirrors used for ritual rather than reflection; mages and artists have long scried shining surfaces to stimulate vision. Animal faces may be guardian spirits, their not-quite-symmetry a crafty device to befuddle malevolent forces (as a scattered box of pins is said to confuse a faerie).

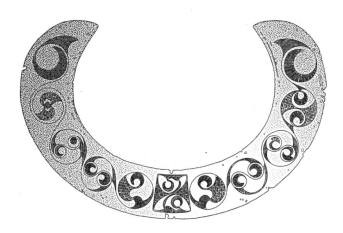

Left: Mirrors found at (a) Nijmegen, Holland, (b) Desborough, Northampton-shire, and (c) Holcombe, Devon. All are thought to come from a single studio in south west England, as is the Balmaclellan collar (facing page) from Scotland. They all display the use of three-line basket hatching and small crescent curves flowing into long 'peltae' or trumpets. Adapted from Harding 2007.

DIFFERENT TONSURES

bible in one hand, lump of quartz in the other

By the 5th century, Celtic Christianity had spread through Britain and Ireland, taking on a character that drew much from existing native traditions. On the remote island of Iona, St. Columba (Collumcille) spearheaded a renaissance of art and learning after founding a monastery in 563. Columba's respect for the bards—*"If poets' verses be but stories; So be food and raiment stories; So all the world a story; So is man of dust a story"*—and the druids—*"Christ is my druid"*—suggests how close the old ways still were.

Celtic Christianity, distinct from the Roman church, followed the teachings of St. John over St. Peter, and was monastic with no governing body. Men and women lived and worked together. Like the druids, they shaved their tonsures across the front and blued their eyes. In this magical time when the gods were people's inspiration, the Christian message needed inspiring works of art that surpassed the old tradition. New patterns were developed, and carved stones, deft metalwork and illuminated manuscripts poured out of the monasteries to demonstrate the power of the new faith.

*This page and opposite: Plates from the Spalding Club's 1856
Sculptured Stones of Scotland. Top left & center: The complex
Nigg Stone with raised hemispheres covered in knotwork.*

ASSORTED SPIRAL CENTERS
spotting magic mushrooms

Our line's adventure takes a twist with the three basic forms of Christian Celtic art: spirals, keys, and knots. Each will be studied in turn over the following pages. The elements were honed by the monks into a universal system of ornament that married patterns from Lombardic wrought iron knotwork, Greek meander keywork (*see page 364*), Saxon animal zoomorphics, and native spiral compass work. These ancient forms were revised and harnessed, preserving much of the old craft tradition's method and expanding artists' repertoires as the vocabulary of the style developed.

Accurate geometrical spirals can be drawn using the method below. The number of arms determines the radial symmetry of the spiral and the type of central polygon that defines the important centers, starts and ends of the arcs (the degrees of turn for each arc = 360°/no. of arms). Alternatively, it can be more practical to tangent curves by eye, laying out only the axes and arc centers.

The key to planning a page such as that facing is to think in terms of what archaeologists and historians call "mushrooms", made from bisecting spiral centers with smoothly meeting arcs or straight lines.

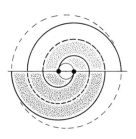 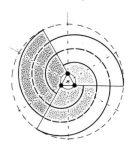 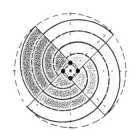

thin crescent keeps colour order

petals meet

two petal variant

petals align to subgrid

thin petals use wide radius

fat petals use narrow radius

terminated trumpet

trumpets meet halfway

large arc center at x.

petals meet at circle centers

fit circle by eye

tweak triangle to fit

enclosed 'S'

triangle drawn from three dots

one petal & one triangle variant

triangle arcs have diameter of dashed circle

joined 'S'

Above: Snapshot of a dynamic system. Position spiral centers on a grid of circles (dashed, top), then draw spiral arms and mushroom 'caps' before finishing with petals & triangles. Tweak centers so joins and nodes align (see also appendices, page 364).

RECURSIVE ROUNDELS

wheels within wheels

Our line winds ever tighter in complex manuscript panels consisting of roundels of densely packed spirals (*see opposite*). These were drawn entirely by compass—when magnified, both vellum pages and metalwork still show the compass points for circles as small as 1mm, and carpet pages also reveal the distinctive 'feathered one side' line of a Japanese brush compass (*see page 368*).

Notice how the roundels are arranged on a hexagonal grid. This is the same one as on the previous page (*dashed circles top and bottom, opposite, and see page 363*). Based on the close-packing properties of circles, these spiral forms repeat at different scales; they are self similar (spirals within spirals), like quarks in atomic nuclei, a window into the advanced fractal thinking of the Celts.

New permutations can be made using different centers, or whole roundels within (*e.g. hand-drawn spiral borders by George Bain, below*).

SELECTED
ROUNDELS

chip-carved

two → three

repeat unit

short fat arcs

touching petals

self-similar

contrary motion

threes & twos

arcs share axes

subtle shading

redrawn
from various
sources

four & threes

A PALEOLITHIC MEANDER

technical tips from the ice age

The practice of an art reveals its logic. Drawing a pattern reveals the line of its structure. The artist who carved the spirals onto a mammoth tusk armband (*opposite top and right*) embedded the secrets of its construction for us to decipher 20,000 years later, contradicting the stereotype of a savage caveman, and revealing instead a patient hand with a high level of geometrical imagination.

Here, as with Celtic key patterns, the spirals are rotated 45° so that the corners fall on the vertical and horizontal axes, giving them more dynamism than a Greek meander whose paths remain parallel to their boundaries (*see page 364*). To construct this, squares are split into paired chevrons, one side moved up by a unit, and the ends then rejoined to form the spiral (*opposite, bottom right*).

The culture of the craftsman is lost to time, but patterns persevere. Diagonally-oriented straight-lined spirals were to emerge again millennia later in the art of the Celtic Christian communities.

Double spirals became the route to the inner secrets of the Goddess, for example on the portable shrine from 5000 BC (*opposite center left*). Below, ceramic ritual bread loaves from Çatal Hüyük, 6500 BC, demonstrate some interesting proto-key patterns.

Above and top: Mammoth ivory bracelet 20,000 BC, Mezin, Ukraine. *Left:* Clay shrine, Vinça culture 5000 BC.

Right: Construction method for Mezin bracelet meander. 1. Paired chevrons or rectangles are drawn on a vertical axis. 2. Chevrons are split along axis and moved diagonally 1 unit width. 3. Diagonals re-join units making a vertical row of double spirals. The maker carved instances of each stage.

Unlocking Key Panels

secrets of square spirals

Key patterns (so named by George Romilly Allen in 1898), may be inspired by earlier Coptic spiral work (the recently discovered *Irish Bog Psalter* is bound with Egyptian papyrus). The Celtic scribes made one significant change. Turning the spirals 45° meant pattern edges now had a series of triangular spaces, and these the monks filled with great ingenuity, devising the 'key'-form and an entire graphic style. Our line has locked into shape.

The trick to drawing keys is the grid. The Celts used a grid of diagonal lines to fill their spaces with diamond squares (*or rhombs, see page 360*), their path lines being drawn along the diamonds' edges and later thickened by ¼ of a unit either side. Key panels are framed by edges drawn through the diagonals of the squares.

Below and opposite we can see that the root forms of Celtic keys are square spirals made of 'S'- and 'C'-shapes. These are counted by the number of grid units the line travels before making a 90° turn. So, for example, the 'S' below left (*and opposite top left*) is counted 1-2-3-7-3-2-1 (*for more on key-counting see page 364*).

*Interlocked opposing 'S'-shapes lay the path.
Thicken by ¼ unit each side of line.*

*'C'-shapes with a central bar make the
path. Unfilled triangular edges.*

*'C'- and 'S'-forms are here combined into
a single panel.*

*Back-to-back 'C'-shapes are rotated 90°
to make a fylfot design.*

Sawtooths and Arrowheads
stacking reflected edges

Key patterns simplify to a space-filling algorithm which follows a single rule: the line moves along a path of diagonals turning +/− 45° when encountering itself and 90° when encountering a framing boundary.

The pattern family on this page uses the key shape which solved the triangular border spaces on the previous page. This is now developed as a unit in its own right. These units can be recognized by their 'foot' branches and small triangle 'sawtooth' shapes.

Patterns of this type can be expressed as a single triangular unit alternating with a vertical reflection of itself and assembled into bands, frames, and panels (*below and opposite*). Further variations can be made by mirroring units (*opposite, f and g*) to make 'arrowheads', or by changing the orientation of a pattern within a panel (*opposite, h*). Some of these building blocks are so simple that they were once learned as calligraphic formulae (perhaps without even knowing the construction method), allowing complex areas of pattern to be rendered from units drawn with as few as six quill strokes.

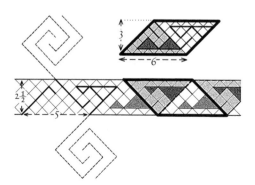

a. *The smallest of the key units (2½ × 5) can be used for bands of any length; it can be mitred, used in rings (see page 31), or as a square panel (right).*

b. *Increasing the height to 3 units lengthens the 'foot' shape and makes the small triangles equal in size (like a). Bands cannot end without a mitre.*

c. *A height of 3½ units makes the smallest key pattern that can terminate in a single strip, also the smallest possible panel (doubled to a square, right).*

d. *A 4-unit-high key. Expansion creates the distinctive fold in the line, the branched 'foot' shape, and 3 small triangles. Square unit shown right.*

e. *Stacked strips of 2½ × 5 units.*

f. and g. *Stacked bands can be mirrored to create 'arrowhead' shapes.*

h. *Top rotated 90° to give bottom.*

FOLDING SOLUTIONS
mitred and slabbed cavities

Some families of key patterns can be developed by spacing adjacent units further apart (*opposite top*), to make a rectangular gap with diagonally-opposed openings that can be joined in a number of ways.

The gap can be left as a small panel to be treated with a different pattern, but the simplest solution is to join the openings with a bar, making the distinctive 'Z'-shape mitre or 'diaper' (as it is known in medieval heraldry). The bar's thickness is set by taking the path through grid nodes (*opposite, a*). Further variations can be made using different sized units, for example in (*d*) the bar has been drawn across two squares to make a 108° angle (*also used on the border on page 5*).

Paths can also be given a curved effect by trimming the diagonal line's corners (*c*), or they can be 'slabbed', as though the diaper's diagonal is folded like a paper fan (*f*).

Below are shown two variants where the path is forced to move within triangles, rather than rectangles as on the facing page. Essentially the central part of the patterns opposite have their edge 'feet' and triangles removed. The pattern below right squeezes into less space by using a dot to terminate the line instead of a 'foot'.

a. A 2½ × 5 key is pulled apart vertically to make rectangular gaps. Horizontal bars can then be drawn to make triangles as shown, or other solutions and spacings can be used.

b. Spaces are filled with vertical bars; notice the strange gap required to finish this panel.

c. Curves can soften the vertical bars. Draw freehand or with compass.

d. From the Rosemarkie stone; bars are drawn from diagonals of a double square.

Diagonals in 3 squares make an angle just over 108° (internal angle of a pentagon).

Above: A useful way to make a pentagonal angle using only three squares.

e. Expansion of Rosemarkie pattern, with bars now drawn across the diagonal of a 3×2 rectangle; the 'foot' has grown by 1 unit.

f. Rectangular gaps are filled with a folded path, giving this pattern its 'slabbed' center and intestinal quality.

TURNING KEYS
some rings to bind them

Key patterns are incredibly versatile space-filling devices. Not only can they be drawn in squares and rectangles, but a pattern's subgrid of rhombs can be altered to fit all manner of shapes, to which any key unit can be applied.

Key patterns set out on ring-shaped grids can look more African than Celtic but they are found in many of the illuminated gospels, often in arches surrounding ecclesiastical tables.

To construct a ring-shaped key, a grid is made using a number of arcs that are a multiple of the units of the key (*see page 361*), otherwise the units will not meet up (this is not such a concern with semi-circles as a terminating end can be made to fill a gap). Key units can be applied to the grid concentrically (*below left and opposite*) or radially (*below right*). This grid of curved diamonds is a canny method for devising circular patterns, and is useful for many applications.

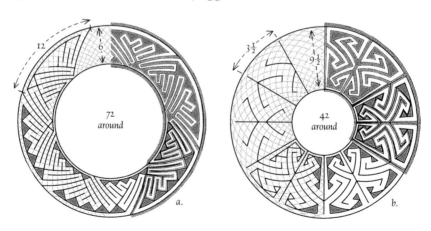

a.   *b.*

Keys in circular grids: (a): 6 repeats of a 12 radial × 6 concentric key fit in a grid 72 radial units around. (b): 'Arrowhead' pattern of 3½r × 9½c repeats 12 times around a 42 unit ring. (c): A 6r × 10½c unit tiles a ring whose radial divisions are a multiple of 6. (d): 'S'-spirals repeat every 5 radial units.

c.

6

10½

e.

5

10

60
around

d.

7½

5

60

18

g.

5

f.

(e): Unit width and radial grid divisions of repeat are the same as (d) but a concentric measure of 18 units makes this ring fatter. (f): Unit of 5r × 2½c requires a ring divided into multiples of 5, as does (g), here two patterns layered on a single grid.

5

2½

A BRAIDED LINE

to weave or knot

A simple rule brings a twist to the adventures of our line as we move onto another class of patterns where the path displays a new and useful ability, that of weaving over and under itself. Our line now metamorphs into knotwork.

Knots are laid out on a grid made of three layers: a primary and secondary grid of dots, and a tertiary grid of diagonal lines (*opposite, a*). The knot path moves around the dots following the diagonals (*b*); knots are then drawn as freehand curves on this tertiary line (*c*). Knots can either be 'open' with the path leaving the corners (*j,k*), or 'closed' (*c–i*), and made of one or more loops. The minimum closed knot is 2 × 2 units, the minimum open knot 1½ × 2 units (all knots using half-space units are open, others are closed).

The knot's path, once drawn, is now woven alternately under and over (the only rule in all of Celtic art that is never broken). The path's thickness alters the size of the knot within its frame, and once determined the knot may be shaded and filled. A split path divides a thickened path along its original center line before it is rewoven.

Slicing a knot allows you to count its bands. Since each band needs half a grid unit, this is a useful way to reckon a knot's subgrid.

Left (b): Path as straight lines, corners meeting mid-diagonals (circled). Right (c): Curved path. Below right (d): Left-hand weave is added.

Above (a): 4 units (2×2) of dot grid, made of 3 layers: Primary (corner dots), Secondary (center dots), and Tertiary (dynamic squares).

Left (e, f, g): Path thickened by varying amounts. Width alters knot size in frame. (g): Max. path width is size of the smallest gap.

Right (h): Path split with central line and woven (draw crosses at junctions first). (i): Path split, separated into 2, and woven.

Below: (j): As above but ½ space removed from base; path will leave adjacent corners if one edge has a ½ unit. (k): Path will leave opposite corners if both edges have ½ unit. (l): Trefoil knot.

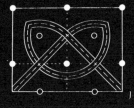
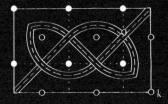
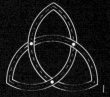

ROOTS OF KNOTS

threading a net of gems

Although knots can appear complex, they are all simply variants of each other made with break lines on the three-layered dot grid.

On the previous page, knots were drawn with just one boundary: the outside edge. 'Stops' or 'breaks' are now placed on the subgrid to change the knot's appearance and flow. Breaks on the secondary grid affect the internal shape of a knot, while on the primary grid they create gaps in the knot's outside edge (*below*).

If the knot has $n + \frac{1}{2}$ units on one axis, then the primary grid will be on one edge and the secondary on the facing edge. Knots of this type can have internal stops on both primary and secondary grids. With practice, one learns to spot break arrangements from the shape of the gaps around the knot's path (*below and right, shaded*). The facing page shows grids of $2 \times n$ (outer) and $1\frac{1}{2} \times n$ (inner) units, with asymmetrical, radial, or bilateral symmetries. For open knots, with $n + \frac{1}{2}$ units on one edge, the path leaves by adjacent corners, whereas with $n + \frac{1}{2}$ units on both edges, paths leave by opposite corners.

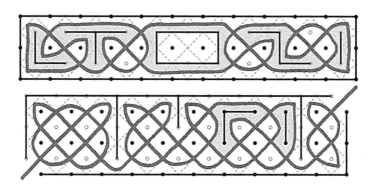

Above: Unwoven knot units made from a simple border grid, outer 2 units wide, inner 1½ units. Corners often need breaks to avoid isolated loops.

Variations on a Theme
songs upon a single knot

The graphic systems of Celtic art are akin to the imagination itself in their ability to generate endless possibilities from an initial seed.

All the patterns shown here are made from a single master unit (*below, top center*) that is asymmetrical in structure. A knot's symmetry affects the number of ways it can be arranged: asymmetrical units have more possibilities than those with bilateral symmetry, while radially symmetrical knots have very few. Permutations can be alternated, stacked, interwoven with extra cords, or laid on different shaped grids (*see opposite*), to create a dizzying variety of knot borders and panels which can then be further altered by splitting or thickening the path (*see page 39*) and by shading choices.

Knots can be extended by expanding them by half a unit on one side, or on both if adding two bands (*below*). Remember, for every half unit of grid there is one band.

Master Unit, 2×4

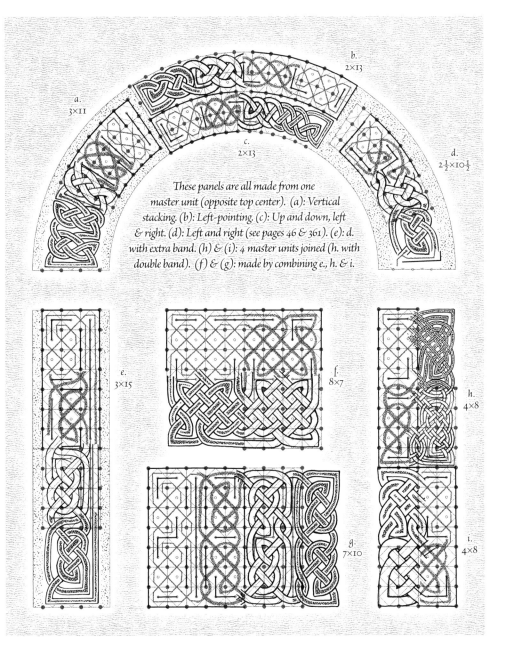

a.
3×11

b.
2×13

c.
2×13

d.
2½×10½

These panels are all made from one
master unit (opposite top center). (a): Vertical
stacking. (b): Left-pointing. (c): Up and down, left
& right. (d): Left and right (see pages 46 & 361). (e): d.
with extra band. (h) & (i): 4 master units joined (h. with
double band). (f) & (g): made by combining e., h. & i.

e.
3×15

f.
8×7

g.
7×10

h.
4×8

i.
4×8

KNOTS OF ROOTS
slicing squares

Square units are both practical and harmonious. Easily manipulated, they can function as master units in panels or borders, or as 'spacers' to join two bands together, e.g. when filling a corner.

The knots opposite resonate with the relation between the side of a square and its diagonal, 1:√2. An 'irrational number' (like π or φ), √2 cannot be defined using integers. To construct such knots, use breaks along the squares' diagonals to create four triangles. Notice how the same basic forms we saw earlier (*page 41*) are now squeezed into these triangles, which can then be used as units on their own or be tessellated in many ways. As the grid dimensions increase, extra bands build the knot and are 'held' between long breaks.

The patterns below do not use diagonal breaks, their paths instead curve around the unit emphasizing rings rather than crosses. Sometimes grid dimensions are not equal, and one edge is scaled to fit within the square (*e.g. below, rightmost, a 5×6 grid drawn to fit within a square*).

Woven Labyrinths

drawing rainbow serpents

Knotwork works beautifully within rings and circles, in a similar way to keys. Again the circumference must be divided into a multiple of the knot's unit size (e.g. for a unit three spaces wide the circle should be divided into a multiple of three). Polygons nested within the circles can be used to proportion the width of the rings. Initial straight-line diagrams may look clumsy, but the path will soon be smoothed when the curves and weaves are rendered.

Any number of units may be radially arranged to make the subgrid. An odd number of unit repeats will give a continuous path, while an even number will produce two paths.

Additional linked rings of knots can be placed inside or outside the original ring (*e.g. opposite top right*). When doing this, the grid divisions do not have to be the same, but the number of paths leaving each ring (and joining them) must always be equal.

ANIMATED CREATURES

when is a duck not a duck

John Scotus Erugenia (d. after 877), whom W. B. Yeats called *"the singing master of the soul"*, was scholar supreme of the Celtic church. A student of the seven Liberal Arts, he said that true philosophy and true religion were the same, that reality was reflexive, our inner states shaping our outward world. Like Celts through the ages, he believed in reincarnation and saw nature symbolically as theophany, a revelation of the qualities of the divine.

Given the Celtic love for and responsibility toward nature, it is no wonder they used their pattern systems to draw the fantastic ornamented animal forms known as zoomorphics.

Zoomorphic ornament is an adaptation of the methods used for constructing knotwork. A unit is developed from a freehand knot-like gesture, before heads and limbs are added and the path thickened and woven (*below*). Units can be arranged on a grid, just as knots and keys.

The intricacy and harmony of these patterns demonstrates a high level of artistic ability. Zoomorphic techniques were probably the final stage of a long apprenticeship, showing just how important visual improvisation was to the life of these patterns.

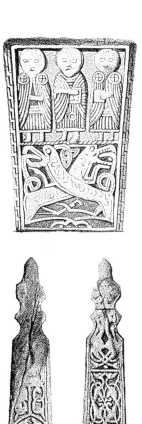

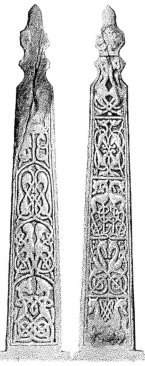

Above: The Hilton Cadboll Stone. Notice the similarity between the rotating spirals through which the birds weave and the sword at the top of page 19. Left: The Thornill Stone, with animals made entirely of knotwork and topped with an unusual finial (from Spalding).

ENTANGLED NATURE
line becomes life

The animal ornament found in the illuminated gospels is painted in extreme miniature. Freehand curves are layered and woven creating a field of complex interaction which can only be deciphered by redrawing. Three improvised layers of line are often employed, creating complex ornament from simple knots (*see below*). The underlying 'gestures' can become very complex (*small circles, opposite*).

In this sublime interweaving of the kingdoms of nature and number we see the ultimate meaning of Celtic art, that we live in a choir of inter-sustaining life, an ecology of souls, governed by the qualities of number. Our line has become woven with life itself.

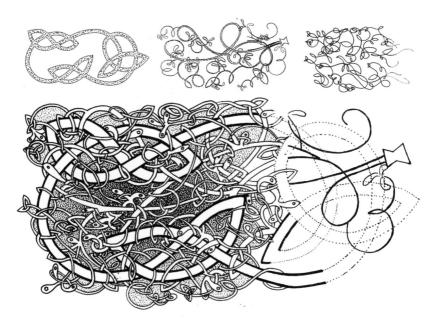

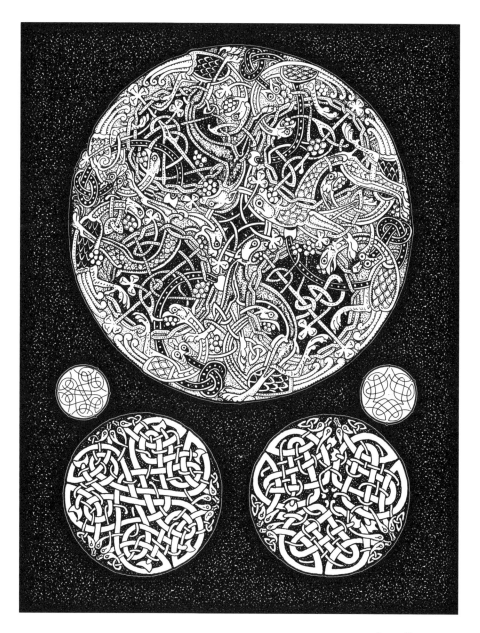

Region of the Summer Stars
illuminating manuscripts

Celtic manuscript pages often display strange and striking rectilinear shapes. The Celts 'grew' their ratios from a developed square using only ruler and compass (*see below*), and analysis has shown that carpet pages are often constructed using many of the same fundamental irrational numbers we have seen before: √2, φ, √3, and π, as well as 3-4-5 triangles (*e.g. in stone circles, see page 10*).

Early carpet pages such as those from the *Book of Durrow* use these proportions directly, their crystalline clarity and inevitability showing incredible geometrical acumen. Some forms are developed from simple square and hexagon constructions (*e.g. opposite top*), with the frame rectangles emerging from points inherent in the underlying grids. However, as the style matured increasingly complex schemes were used to explore the interplay of these presences of the infinite (*lower opposite*).

Arithmetic proportion and musical harmony were also used to arrange such pages (*see page 368*). Robert Stevick has discovered that Celtic literature was also laid out by similar methods, using geometrical devices to set line breaks in epic poems such as *Elene* and *The Phoenix*. The Celts were not the first to do this—recent discoveries indicate Plato also used geometry to structure his dialogues.

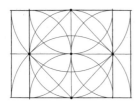 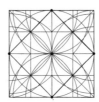 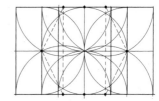

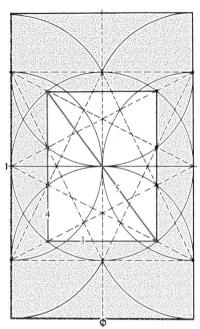

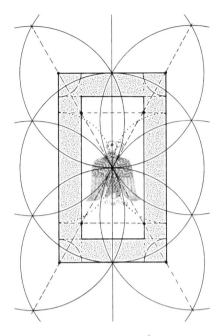

Book of Durrow, folio 1v. Outer 'golden' rectangle 1:φ; inner 3×4, diagonal 5.

Book of Durrow f. 24v. 2:(2-√2) rectangle; Eagle's heart at center of figure.

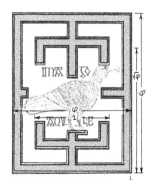

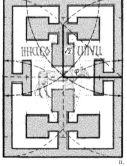

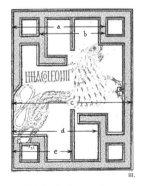

Above: Panels from the Effenbach Gospels. Later books used very sophisticated geometry. (i) f.126v φ proportions; (ii) f.115v √2 set against φ using triangle; (iii) f.75v a:b, c:d, e:f = 1:√2.

A Multitude of Shapes
metaphysical mentors and linear legacies

After a brief and beautiful flowering, Celtic Christianity was suppressed by the Roman Church. In 664, druidic tonsure and St. John-as-founder were both outlawed at the Synod of Whitby, but the mystical insight of the druids had already changed Christianity forever. Merovingian Kings, Cathars, and the School of Chartres (initiator of the Gothic style and the geometrical temples of the great cathedrals whose soaring vaults recall the druids' sacred groves) were all permeated with Ionian thought.

Here the journey of our line ends. We have traced its path from a point within, through the worlds and patterns of the Celts. Like the poet Taliesin, it has taken many forms yet always remained itself.

The Celtic vision of conscious nature and love of geometry has shaped the ideas of poets and artists ever since: Dürer, Vermeer, the Romantic poets, Blake, Mackintosh, Tolkien, and others. We even see its resonance in scientific thought. Physicists now delve into nature's secrets, revealing that we are woven together by paradoxical particles at a quantum level, that our very atoms were forged in the hearts of stars, echoing the words of Eriugena: "All that is is light."

Left: Carved wood panels showing legends of Sigurd, from 12th C. Hylestad stave church, Norway. Above: Wood carvings of interlaced deer from late 12th C. Urnes stave church, Norway.

Above: Gothic labyrinth from Chartres and turf maze cut by the medieval shoemakers' guild in Shrewsbury, both reminiscent of Celtic key patterns.

Right: Hedel Stave Church, Norway, 1160. Zoomorphic woodcarving taken to the limit of the material. Curling dragons interlace with animals and knotwork above the north portal.

BOOK II

ISLAMIC DESIGN

A GENIUS FOR GEOMETRY

Daud Sutton

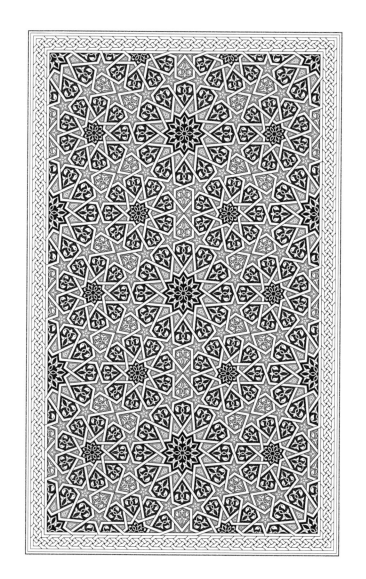

INTRODUCTION

The role of sacred art is to support the spiritual life of those whom it surrounds, to instill a way of perceiving the world and the subtle realities behind it. The challenge thus facing the traditional artisan is how to build with matter so as to best embody spirit. The great temples, churches and mosques of the world are the legacy of our attempts to do just this, each determined by the spiritual perspective in question.

Throughout their long history the craft traditions of the Islamic world evolved a multitude of styles applied to a great variety of media, but always with unifying factors that make them instantly recognizable. It is perhaps no surprise that an art form that seeks explicitly to explore the relationship between Unity and multiplicity should be at the same time unified yet diverse. Harmony is central.

The visual structure of Islamic design has two key aspects: calligraphy using Arabic script—one of the world's great scribal traditions—and abstract ornamentation using a varied but remarkably integrated visual language. This art of pure ornament revolves around two poles: geometric pattern, the harmonic and symmetrical subdivision of the plane giving rise to intricately interwoven designs that speak of infinity and the omnipresent center; and idealized plant form or arabesque, spiraling tendrils, leaves, buds and flowers embodying organic life and rhythm. The following pages focus on Islamic geometric patterns, exploring their structure and meaning.

First Things First

unfolding from unity

Consider a point, dimensionless position in space. Extending the point defines a line (*below left*). Turning the span of this line about the first point traces a circle, the first and the simplest geometric plane figure and Unity's perfect symbol. Mark a second circle, centered on the circumference of the first and passing through its center. Continue by placing circles at each new intersection to fit six identical circles cycling around a central one, the ideal representation of the Quranic six days of creation. This beautifully simple construction can be continued indefinitely (*opposite*), defining a tessellation of regular hexagons perfectly filling the plane.

The mid-points of a regular hexagon's sides join to form a double triangle (*top right opposite*), known in the Islamic world as *The Seal of Solomon*—it is said that the ring by which he commanded the *jinn* bore this crest. Repeating the outline of this six-pointed star within each hexagon gives a pattern of stars and hexagons.

The final stage opposite shows the pattern as it is found in the Ibn Tulun Mosque in Cairo [879 CE], carved in plaster. The pattern's lines are rendered as interlacing bands, passing over and under each other where they cross, and the remaining spaces filled with arabesque motifs.

SIXES EXTRAPOLATED
some more basics

Many different techniques of geometric construction have been used throughout the Islamic world, adding aids such as set squares, stencils and grids to the fundamental tools of compasses and straight edge. The illustrations in this book emphasize the structure of the patterns rather than construction methods. When constructions are given they use a philosophical method relying solely on compasses and straight edge.

Simple patterns lend themselves to adaptation in many ways and the constructions shown opposite develop two variations on the star-and-hexagon pattern from the previous page. The points of intersection in the patterns' paths remain fixed at the midpoints of the hexagonal subgrid's edges, while the stars expand and contract respectively. The same equilateral three-fold hexagons occur in both of these adaptations, yet the two patterns give remarkably different overall impressions.

Below is another example of how simple patterns can extrapolate into more complex ones. Starting again with the star-and-hexagon design, cut four points off some stars to form rhombs (*center*) and remove small hexagons to create a pattern that reads as both individual shapes and large overlapping hexagons (*right*).

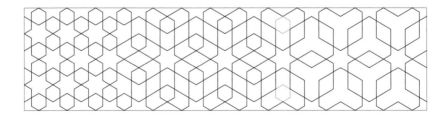

Starting with six circles
around one, add six more
at the outer vertices.

Join the marked points. The
hexagonal repeat (shaded)
contains the first circle.

The basic star-and-hexagon
pattern can be traced on
this substructure.

The substructure's vertices give
a section of an alternative
pattern (repeated below)

Add lines joining the points
marked to define a small
proportioning circle

The vertices now defined give a
section of the second alternative
pattern (repeated below).

Transforming a Subgrid
and framing the infinite

The construction on the previous page also defines a semiregular tiling of equilateral triangles, squares, and regular hexagons (*opposite top left*). Notice that this design, when repeated (*top right*), is itself underpinned by the regular tiling of hexagons (*dotted line*).

Picture the triangles in the pattern inflating as the white hexagons are pinched, the squares giving exactly as much as they take. When the triangles have become the same equilateral three-fold hexagons as on the previous page, a beautiful pattern of overlapping regular dodecagons is defined (*center left*). Continuing this expansion and contraction until the triangles form regular hexagons gives a second frequently encountered pattern (*right, middle row*).

Conceptually a repeating pattern can continue forever, but in practical applications Islamic patterns are generally cropped to form rectangular sections. The corners of these sections are normally located at the center of key pieces, often stars (*bottom row, opposite*). Framing a pattern this way maintains a geometric elegance at the same time as clearly implying that it could repeat indefinitely, as it were, under its borders—the perfect visual solution to calling to mind the idea of infinity, and hence the Infinite, without any pretence of being able to truly capture such an enigmatic concept visually.

This framing also usually gives a single central piece which ensures that the total number of pieces in the rectangle is odd—a numerical quality traditionally said to invoke, and find favor with, Divine Unity.

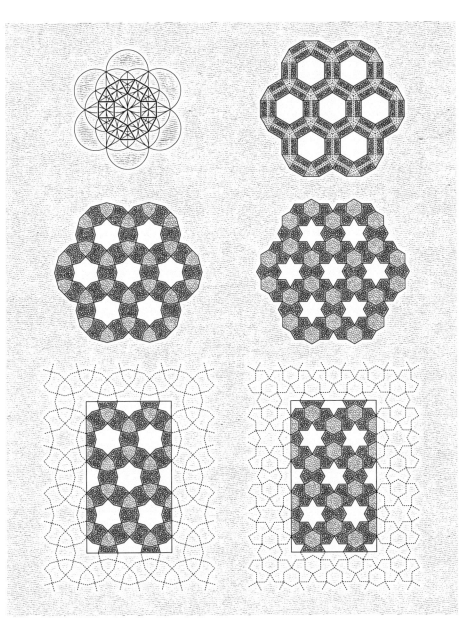

GIVE AND TAKE
the breath of the compassionate

Start with a circle set on a horizontal line and trace arcs centered on and passing through the intersections to define a vertical (*below left*). Repeating this on the new intersections defines diagonals on which four circles, identical to the first, can be drawn. Add four more circles to produce an array of eight around one. As with the pattern on page 62 this circular matrix can be continued indefinitely to define a tessellation, this time of squares (*opposite*).

Combining a horizontal square with a diagonal one produces an eight-pointed star (*top right opposite*). Like the double triangle this double square is also known as *The Seal* (*khātam* in Arabic) *of Solomon*, for the legends vary. It is the starting point of a vast family of patterns (*see page 86*), and repeating them in each square makes the fundamental pattern of stars and crosses opposite.

This pattern can also be seen as a tiling of smaller diagonal squares, half of which expand and the other half of which contract. For this reason it has, in recent times, been referred to as *The Breath of The Compassionate*, a name referring to the teachings of the Great Master Ibn al-'Arabi which expound the Divine Breath as the basis of creation, liberating the possibilities of the four Elements; Fire, Air, Water and Earth.

 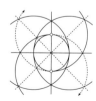 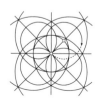 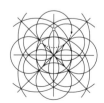

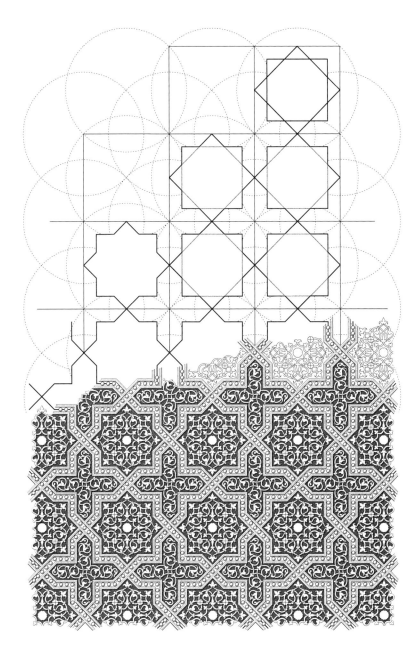

EIGHT-FOLD ROSETTES
and some construction principles

A prevalent device in Islamic geometric patterns is the distinctive geometric rosette, with its petals arranged around a central star like an archetypal crystalline flower. Rosette patterns such as these can also be seen as a network of stellar motifs, inverting perception to picture the petals as negative space. Shown here are eight-fold rosettes rendered in a style based on carpentry panels.

Two methods of construction are shown. Below is a simple one based on a square grid; here the large regular octagon is defined by diagonals and a circle, and partitioned into the geometric rosette with petals one quarter the width of the whole square repeat. Opposite is another that ensures the points of the five-pointed stars, two halves of which are set on each side of the square, all lie on the same circle. This makes the four short edges of the hexagonal petals identical in length, a geometric subtlety particularly common in carpentry applications.

The other patterns opposite show some of the ways that the shapes generated in the simple rosette can be rearranged, giving rise to new shapes in the process. Repeating sections are not restricted to squares only, but include carefully proportioned rectangles.

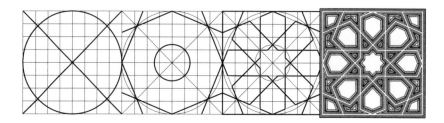

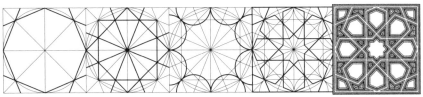

Place a circle and both diagonals within a quartered square to define an octagon.

Adding a double square octagram defines one sixteenth radial divisions.

Trace arcs as shown centered where the one sixteenth division radii cut the square.

These arcs intersect the radii to define the rosette's petals and central star

A single repeat unit rendered as it might appear as a simple carpentry panel.

A variation in a rectangle with sides in the ratio 1:√2.

Rotated one sixteenth of a turn and set in a larger square.

A curious variation using the petals and small octagons.

A large composition showing the harmonious interaction of the small octagons and the eight-fold rosettes.

The central vertical section of the pattern to the left tiled as a repeat unit, two shown here.

CALLIGRAPHY
the proportioned alphabet

Quran literally means *recitation*, for initially the Holy Book was memorized by heart. Soon, however, it became necessary to record it in written form and the hitherto rudimentary Arabic script became the focus for generations of devoted scribes striving to develop the most suitable hands for the scripture.

The first truly Quranic script to be used [*ca.* 9th c. CE] is termed Kufic, after the town of Kufa in Iraq. Predominantly horizontal in movement, its commanding presence conveys majesty and austerity (*below*). Many ornamental scripts were derived from Kufic (*see page 379*) and remained in use long after the original hand.

The most well-known styles of Arabic calligraphy today are the cursive scripts. Their refined form originated in the inspired system of proportioning developed by Ibn Muqla [d. 940 CE], prior to which they held a relatively low profile in relation to the majestic Kufic. Here the fundamental starting points of geometry also underpin calligraphic form—every letter is carefully proportioned in relation to the circle, its diameter, and the point, or *nuqta*, marked as a rhombic dot with the reed pen. The first and most fundamental letter is the *alif*, traced as an elegant vertical stroke within the circle. Different systems of proportioning the *alif* exist, using six, seven, or eight vertically spaced *nuqāt*.

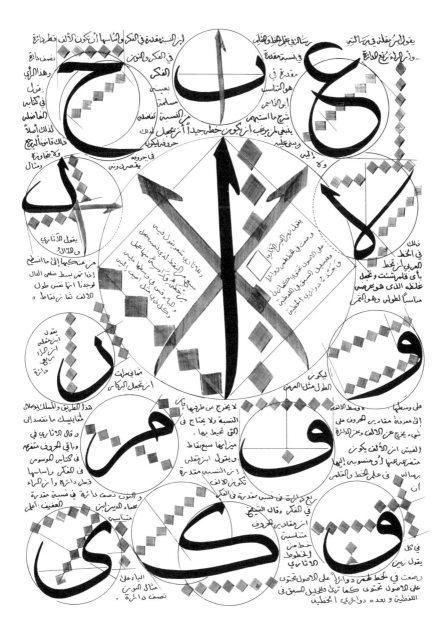

ARABESQUE
the gardens of paradise

Arabesque designs, *islimi* in Persian, are the complement of geometric patterns. They aim not to imitate the plant kingdom naturalistically but to distill visually the essence of rhythm and growth it manifests, recalling the archetypal Gardens of Paradise. Varied arabesque styles (*opposite*) are one of the more obvious differences between regions and eras of Islamic design.

Spirals are primordial and universal symbols, intimately related to life and its cycles. They embody the eddying process of Creation's expansion and contraction and find their application in Islamic design as the basis for many arabesque motifs. Designs such as the one below are often found winding behind Quranic text, in friezes and the title panels of illuminated books. When used this way the vine continues behind the letters while the leaves and flowers fill the remaining spaces.

The spiral is associated worldwide with the sun and its yearly cycle. The sun unwinds from its rebirth at the winter solstice, loops ever more widely in the sky, past the balance points of the equinox to the summer solstice, when it is sky borne for the longest period in its cycle, before winding back up to its midwinter demise.

A 9th century arabesque design in marble relief, from the great mosque in Kairouan, Tunisia.

A repeating arabesque design in carved plaster from Alhambra in a typically Andalusian style.

Ottoman arabesque from underglaze Iznik tiles in rich dark blue, turquoise, green, and red.

A highly geometric arabesque design from Cairo, trellised by the pattern on page 96.

SIX OF ONE
half a dozen of the other

Start with the basic star-and-hexagon pattern (*below left*) and rotate each star through one twelfth of a full turn (*below center*). Extend the lines of these stars' corners to form small triangles to create a basic pattern of twelve-fold stars (*below right*).

Illustrated opposite is the generation of a pattern based on the semiregular tiling of regular dodecagons, hexagons, and squares. Stars are set within the subgrid's shapes, with 60° crossings at midpoints of each edge. As below, the twelve-pointed star is made from two overlapping six-fold stars. The star points of Islamic patterns often touch to form two intersecting line segments making over-under interlacing, as used opposite, an easily applied articulation. Appropriately, geometric patterns are known in Persian as *girih*, literally knots, calling to mind weaving and the talismanic effect of knots and braids. A pattern with interlacing strap work no longer has mirror symmetry; reflecting it turns all the 'overs' into 'unders' and vice versa.

The world's spiritual traditions are in agreement that what we see of the world rests on an unseen, subtle and meaningful order. Likewise, the subgrid and implicit circles of patterns like that opposite are openly concealed in the finished design, hidden in plain view by the clothing through which they can be perceived.

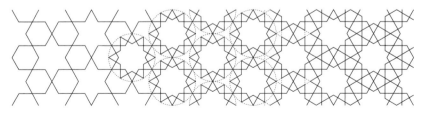

THREE TIMES FOUR
and four times three

From the disciples of Christ to the months of the canonical lunar year the number twelve has many associations in Islam. Twelve is the first *abundant number*, its factors summing to more than itself: 1+2+3+4+6=16. These factors also all occur in either the hexagonal or square repeat systems, making twelve-fold motifs particularly useful in pattern making.

The diagrams opposite explore the family of patterns introduced on the previous page. The basic pattern of twelve-fold stars is shown unfolding from the semiregular tiling of regular dodecagons and triangles (*opposite top*). Notice the way that the finished pattern can be seen as overlapping large hexagons and interwoven zigzags.

Arranging dodecagons edge to edge on a square repeat gives the second subgrid opposite. The star pattern created from this subgrid can be seen as overlapping octagons with interlaced paths.

Take the arrangement of four triangles around a square from the second subgrid and use it to space dodecagons in a triangular repeat to create the third subgrid opposite. The spaces left form the same triangular hexagons as on page 65 (*below, fourth shape*).

This third subgrid can be extrapolated into a fourth, arranged in a square repeat. Adding the relevant stars creates a particularly sophisticated pattern. Note the dodecagonal paths around the twelve-pointed stars in both the third and fourth patterns.

Further Twelves

and some rosette constructions

Generating patterns by the interplay of square and hexagonal repeat structures with twelve-fold motifs is not limited to the previous examples. For example, shown opposite are a pattern from a door panel in the Christian quarter of Damascus and a variation on this by Paul Marchant. Their underlying structures are shown below; groups of three squares forming twelve-fold stars are set respectively on square (*left*) and triangular (*right*) grids—the dotted lines show the sections used in the illustrations. Dedicated geometers will note that the corners of the squares (*marked opposite as black dots*) define lines that give the rest of the points needed to develop the full pattern (*white dots*). These lines also extend to give the proportion of the central stars within the rosettes.

The same rosette proportions can be established independently of the pattern, as depicted opposite with two more rosette constructions. All three constructions start from a double hexagon set within a regular dodecagon with radial lines added. Black dots mark key points that are found in the initial structure, gray dots mark any intermediary points needed, and white dots mark the points that give the final proportions of the star.

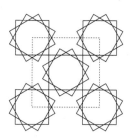
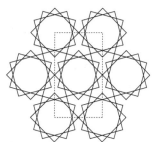

Source pattern from Damascus with square repeat above. Triangular repeat variation opposite.

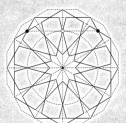

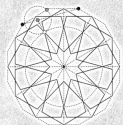

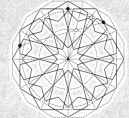

The rosette used above, proportioned from its outer structure.

A rosette constructed to make the petals' four short edges equal.

Narrow petals with an additional harmonious star added.

The rosettes above, plus a fourth variation, placed within a square repeat framework from Alhambra.

THREE-FOLD PERMUTATIONS
multiples from the matrix

Most of the patterns covered so far repeat on either a regular hexagonal or square grid, and a more systematic look at the hexagonal grid is shown below. Joining the centers of the hexagons defines a regular tiling of equilateral triangles—these two grids are each other's duals. Any pattern that can be repeated with regular hexagons can also be repeated with equilateral triangles.

The smallest section needed to define an entire hexagonal repeat pattern is one of the light gray or white triangles below. These triangles have sides in the ratio 1:√3:2 (√3 is approximately 1.732) and this structure is sometimes called the √3 system. By rotating, reflecting, and translating (sliding) one of these triangles it is possible to generate the entire pattern. Some traditional methods construct a stencil of such a triangle and apply these three symmetry movements to complete the pattern.

The points where three hexagonal repeats meet have shapes with rotational symmetry in multiples of three, and the points where six triangular repeats meet have shapes with rotational symmetry in multiples of six (*opposite top left*). These multiples permute to give different numbers at these key points. Each illustration opposite shows the same portion of a pattern in relation to the subgrid.

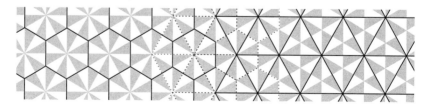

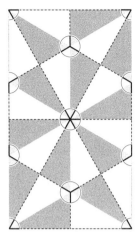

A 1:√3 rectangular section made of 1 hexagon and 4 quarter hexagons, or, 2 triangles and 4 half triangles.

A Seljuk design with wide strap work. Threes and sixes, in this case triangles and six-pointed stars, lie on the key points.

Twelve-fold rosettes with three-fold equilateral hexagons. All the petal shapes, in the rosettes and between them, are identical.

A Maghribi, or western, pattern, based on the semiregular grid at the top of page 77, with twelve and six at the key points.

A sophisticated Mamluk design, three times three gives nine at the three-fold key points, with six on the others.

A pattern combining fifteen, five times three, with twelve, two times six. For nine and twelve see page 60.

Four-Fold Permutations
quadruples in quadrangles

Joining the centers of squares set in a regular tiling defines another square tiling—the square grid is its own dual. The smallest section needed to define a whole square repeat pattern is one of the light gray or white triangles below. These triangles have sides in the ratio 1:1:√2 (√2 is approximately equal to 1.414) and this structure is sometimes known as the √2 system. As with the hexagonal system, rotating, reflecting, and translating this minimum section can generate an entire pattern.

Two minimum triangles, long edge to long edge, form a square and with so many squares to choose from it can sometimes be tricky to distinguish the two dual grids and the minimum section triangles in a square repeat pattern. In addition, the size of a pattern's pieces relative to the repeat can vary considerably. However, with a little practice these structures can be discerned quite easily.

In square repeat patterns the points where four squares meet have shapes with rotational symmetry in multiples of four, but, as there are two dual square grids to consider, different multiples can be combined (*opposite top left*). Opposite are some of the ways these multiples permute, each illustration showing the same portion of a pattern in relation to the subgrid.

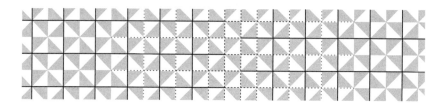

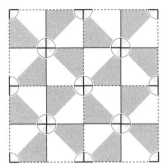

Dual square grids, dotted and solid, and the key four-fold points.

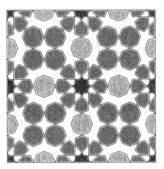

Eight, two times four, and four, in a pattern related to those on page 71.

Another elegant pattern combining eight and four, at the key points, with six.

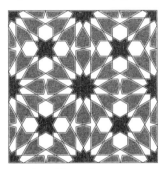

Twelve and four in the square repeat version of a fundamental pattern.

Twelve and eight, the petals are the same shape as on page 83, top right.

Sixteen and four at the key points, with eights in between.

Pieces of Eight
barbary brilliance

Over the centuries artisans in the Maghrib, the West of the Islamic world, explored a remarkable form-language based on the square repeat and, in particular, the possibilities inherent in the eight-fold *khātam*. The *Breath of the Compassionate* is shown below unfolding from the semiregular tiling of octagons and squares. Tracing octagram stars by joining every third corner within each *khātam* creates a simple pattern using this set of shapes.

Opposite is an example of the way simple geometric relationships build upon each other from an initial square grid to generate a whole series of different square repeat patterns. The shapes that arise from generating these patterns are collected in the central panel. Together with many other related shapes they are cut to this day in Morocco in brightly colored friable tiles to create a vast puzzle set with countless solutions. The double-square hexagon found third down in the left-hand column of the central panel opposite, known as a *ṣaft*, is a particularly important shape in this system. The *ṣaft* plays a fundamental role in the generation of more complex *zillīj* patterns such as the one covered on the following page.

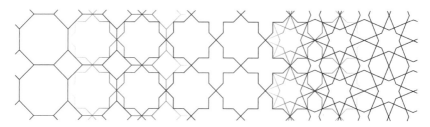

ZILLĪJ DESIGN
eight-fold extravaganzas

The cut tile work of the Maghrib is known as *zillīj*. The medieval glaze palette for this work was limited to only a few colours; black, white, dark green, turquoise, blue, and a warm yellow ochre. Nowadays many other colours are also used. Vast compositions can be made with *zillīj*, compiled in a modular technique that alternates *khātam* with *ṣaft* to make a framework of sections to fill (*black pieces opposite*). Rings of colour are arranged within these sections to create designs that read well to the eye from far away, when geometric detail can no longer be seen, and close up, where individual shapes are clear. Note the way that the same shape occurs in different tones in the design.

The rosettes used opposite have twenty-four and sixteen petals, requiring the construction of pieces that interface with the eight-fold geometry. Although asymmetric these pieces read comfortably in context, perhaps because of their geometric necessity.

Zillīj can be composed on paper using a simple square grid (*below*), sketching approximations of the forms before assembling the final work with correctly cut tile pieces. This method works by replacing the √2 ratio of a square's diagonal to its side, found in the correct shapes, with the fractions ³⁄₂ (1.5) and ⁷⁄₅ (1.4).

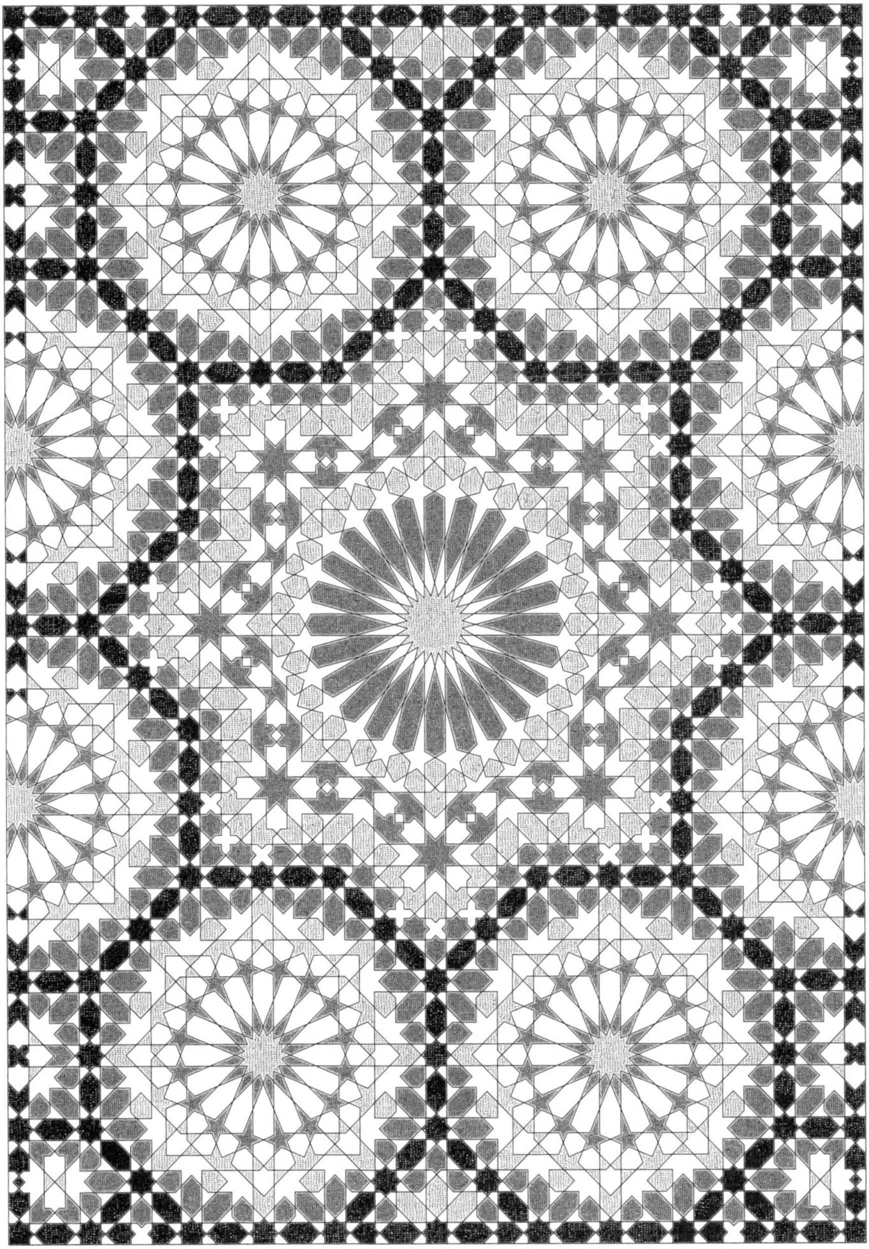

SELF-SIMILARITY
the same at different scales

Self-similarity is the occurrence of the same forms and patterns at many different scales in a design. It embodies infinity through the endless recurrence of similar structures, rather than the unbounded continuation of repeating pattern. Nowadays, it is perhaps best known as a property of the mathematical objects known as *fractals*, but it has also long been used in some aspects of Islamic design.

The panel opposite is based on *zillīj*, found in the Alcázar in Seville. A complex web of interlaced white strap work contains the familiar *zillīj* shapes in blue, green, ochre and black. Remarkably, these shapes then form large versions of themselves, outlined in black. This design also contains a third level of implicit self-similarity—the white interlacing strap work is proportioned exactly as if it too rested on even smaller *zillīj* pieces (*opposite below*). It seems the designers of this pattern were well aware of the possibility of this subdivision continuing indefinitely.

Self-similar designs such as this are not limited to eight-fold *zillīj*; the families of forms derived from ten-fold geometry (*pages 94–97*) are also eminently suited to this type of composition. Self-similarity also occurs in arabesque designs, with leaf forms composed of interconnected smaller leaves and vines (*below*).

ARCING PATTERNS
the balance of line and curve

Not all Islamic patterns leave circles hidden within their implicit construction. Geometric designs that combine arcs and straight lines in their final forms have been a feature of the art form since its beginning. They are usually found rendered in materials that are relatively easy to form into curved shapes, such as the painted arts of the book, metalwork, and carved stone. Patterns using arcs have a distinctly softer appeal, on occasion giving the impression of merging with the arabesque designs their pieces may contain.

The pattern below is from a carved stone window grille in the great Umayyad mosque of Damascus [715 CE]. Straight bands form the semiregular tiling of regular hexagons and equilateral triangles. Interlaced with these are sections of circles centered on the triangles' vertices and passing two thirds of the way along their sides.

The design opposite is based on a pattern given to Professor Keith Critchlow. The arabesque motifs filling the spaces are in the style of Ilkhanid Quran illumination. These two patterns are an excellent example of the way that the subgrids used, often quite obvious in early patterns, are more fully concealed in later work.

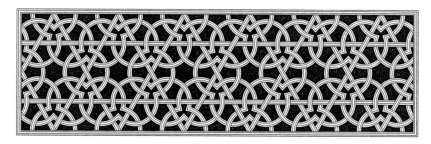

Ten-Fold Tiling
a family of forms

Unlike triangles, squares and hexagons, regular pentagons cannot be arranged to fill a flat surface without leaving gaps. As the art of geometric patterns developed in the Islamic world, artisans inevitably turned their attention to this challenge and discovered ingenious ways of creating designs using five–and ten–fold symmetries.

The diagram below shows a pattern unfolding from a subgrid of repeating regular decagons, placed edge to edge to leave curious bowtie-shaped hexagons. Stars are traced from the midpoints of the decagons' edges forming pentagons at the decagons' corners. The lines of the stars extend into the spaces between decagons to complete the pattern. This pattern is known in Persian as *Umm al-Girih*, the mother of patterns (knots), and its component shapes are the first generation in a whole family of forms (*see page 376*).

The constructions shown opposite are based on an Iranian method. Radial lines marking every eighteen degrees (*dotted*) are intersected by additional lines (*solid*) to give proportioning circles. These circles intersect the radial lines in delicate webs that give the vertices of the final pattern. The arabesque motifs used opposite are in the style of Mamluk Quran illumination.

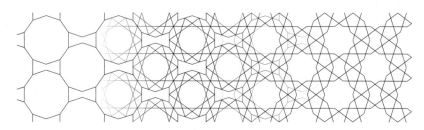

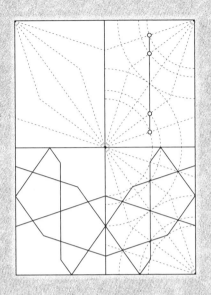

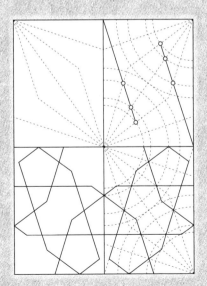

PENTAGRAMMATON
a second ten-fold family

Replace every regular pentagon in the *Umm al-Girih*, including the two overlapping pentagons of the large ten-pointed stars, with five-pointed stars to generate the fundamental pattern of a second ten-fold set of shapes. As with the *Umm al-Girih* this pattern's components are the first generation in a whole family of forms, some of which are shown opposite. Both of the ten-fold shape-sets can be used to make a countless variety of patterns. For example, the wooden window shutters in the great Ottoman mosques of Istanbul bear a multitude of ten-fold designs, in some buildings seemingly without repetition. Two designs from the Sokullu Mehmet Pasha mosque are illustrated opposite with an example of the symbolism sometimes concealed in the number of a pattern's pieces.

Five-fold and ten-fold geometry embody the elegant golden section, the proportion formed when a line is cut such that the shorter section is to the longer as the longer is to the whole line (approximately 1.618). In the pattern below each distance that can be measured between corners or intersections on a line forms a golden section with the next smallest or next largest distance.

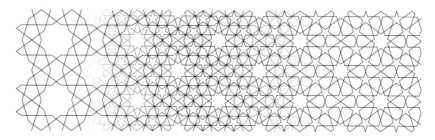

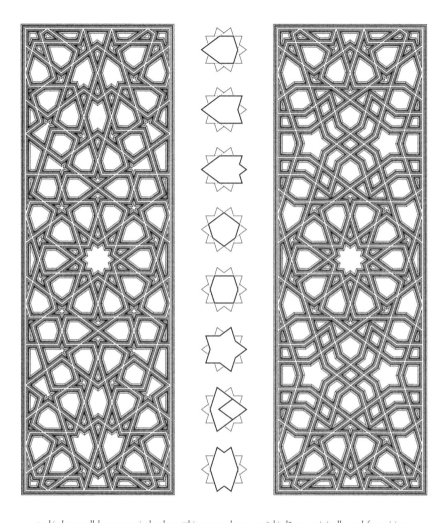

Arabic letters all have numerical values. This system, known as "abjad", was originally used for writing numbers before Indian decimal numerals were adopted. Nowadays it is used for its symbolic value. The pattern above right is composed of 165 pieces, the abjad total for "La ilaha illa Allah"– "There is no divinity but God" – the quintessential statement of Divine Unity in Islam. A related example is shown on page 58; 99 pieces correspond to the traditional number of Divine Names.

DECIMAL CONNECTIONS
between the two families

The basic ten-fold patterns on the previous pages can also be generated from a subgrid of regular decagons, pentagons and pentagon-based hexagons (*below left*). Placing pentagons and pentagram stars in this subgrid gives the two patterns (*below right*).

Arranging the two patterns this way suggests the possibility of varying the angles formed where paths cross at the subgrid's edge midpoints. The *Umm al-Girih* has angles of 108° at these fixed points, while the other basic ten-fold pattern has angles of 36°. A surprisingly floral design is given by 90° (*top left*), while 72° generates a pattern combining both families of ten-fold forms, an example of how successfully they can be integrated (*top right*). Finally, an angle of 54° produces particularly elegant petal shapes and a small central star the same shape as the first example's central star (*bottom left*).

The final example opposite takes the second variation (*dotted line*) and replaces its rosettes with those found on the previous page, showing just how beautifully harmonious the interrelationships between patterns in these ten-fold form-languages can be.

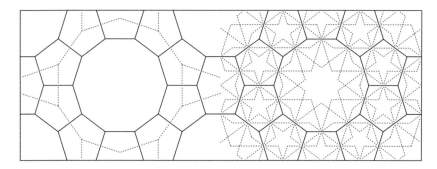

PERFECT FOURTEEN
number of the prophet

The patterns shown here are based on fourteen-fold rosettes, the petals of which fit within the central star in the same way that the petals on page 97 fit within their central ten-fold star. However, the proportions inherent to the heptagram and the tetradecagonal star are more complex than the unique golden section found in the pentagram and the decagonal star, and, as a result, they can easily combine to fall out of synchronization with each other. Patterns in this fourteen-fold family are thus much harder to design successfully and are consequently much rarer. Two basic patterns are shown below. The more intricate pattern shown opposite is rendered as it is found in a carpentry panel at the mausoleum of the Mamluk Sultan Qaytbay [d. 1496] in Cairo.

In the Islamic calendar the month begins on the evening of the new crescent's sighting, making the fourteenth of the month the night of the full moon, when the moon reflects the sun's light most fully on the Earth (the moon can also appear full on either the thirteenth or fifteenth). Accordingly the Prophet Muhammad, held to be the mirror of Divine Light within creation, is associated with both the full moon and the number fourteen.

Singular Stellations
working with odd numbers

With a few notable exceptions, such as five and seven in ten- and fourteen-fold patterns, or multiples of three, odd numbers, particular prime numbers, are tricky to create patterns with.

A frequently used technique for making patterns with odd numbers is to set the odd-numbered motif along the edges of a square or rectangular section, half on one side and half on the other. This section can then be repeatedly reflected on all sides. A simple example of this technique is shown below; heptagonal stars forming an elegant dancing pattern.

Opposite is a more sophisticated design using nine- and eleven-pointed stars in the style of Persian cut tile work, based on a pattern devised by Jay Bonner. The subgrid for this pattern uses hendecagons and enneagons (*opposite below left*). It can be understood as reflecting rectangular sections (*dotted center*), or, alternatively, an elongated hexagonal repeat joining the centers of six hendecagons (*shaded center*). A similar elongated repeat hexagon can be set on the centers of six enneagons. Two ninths of a full turn, 80°, plus three elevenths of a full turn, approximately 98.2°, is very close to 180°. This allows a rhombic arrangement of two enneagons and two hendecagons (*shaded right*), the nine- and eleven-fold symmetries being almost imperceptibly tweaked to fit together.

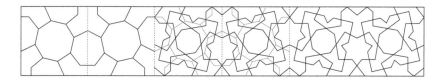

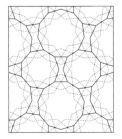 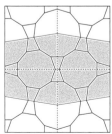 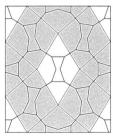

Making Things Fit
tweaking towards unification

The tweaking technique used on the previous page is not restricted to working with odd numbers—certain remarkable patterns aim to integrate many different numbers as accurately and beautifully as possible. Two examples of this type of pattern are shown opposite with their subgrids. A simpler combination of twelve-, eight-, and approximate five-fold geometry is shown below.

These patterns aspire to reintegrate the multiplicity of number in a harmonious unity, and the connection with harmony is more than just visual analogy. As with the previous pattern using nine- and eleven-fold stars these constructions rest on the fact that the sum of certain fractions is very close, but not equal, to other fractions. Similarly the very first challenge that the student of musical harmony faces in forming a scale is the small discrepancy between multiples and powers of the pure overtone wavelength fractions of ½, ⅓, ¼, ⅕ and so on. For example, six pure whole tones, $(⅛)^6$ (approximately 0.493), falls just short of one octave, ½.

The kite shapes in the pattern below, bridging the space between the stars and defining small quadrilaterals where they overlap, are an example of a frequently used device that occurs in both number-combining patterns and those with one key symmetry.

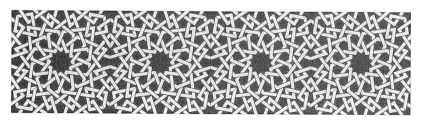

Regular octagons and regular hexagons make a framework into which approximate pentagons and heptagons fit to leave small squares, combining 4, 5, 6, 7, and 8 in one pattern. The important fractional approximations in this construction are $1/5 + 1/6 + 1/8 = 1/2$ (the triangle joining the centers of the 5-, 6-, and 8-gon), and $1/5 + 1/6 + 1/7 = 1/2$ (the triangle joining the centers of the 5-, 6-, and 7-gon).

Regular dodecagons and decagons combine with approximate enneagons to generate a rosette design using 9, 10, and 12. The important fractional approximation in this construction is $2/9 + 3/20 + 3/24 = 1/2$.

DOME GEOMETRY
the third dimension

Islamic architecture is well known for its domed structures. Many architects of these domes were content to present them unadorned, their engineering and elegant form proving sufficient for their goals. But on occasion domes were ornamented with geometric patterns. Well-known examples occur in the monuments of Mamluk Egypt and Safavid Iran—the dome illustrated opposite is from the mausoleum of Sultan Qaytbay in Cairo. The basic method used in the geometric ornamentation of domes is to repeat sections like the segments of an orange. Stars and interconnecting pieces are placed in these segments and tweaked to fit as the width narrows towards the top (*opposite top left*). Many such domes resolve at the top with petal- and kite-shapes that form rosettes when viewed from above (*opposite top right*).

The true spherical equivalents of the regular and semiregular tilings are the divisions of a sphere that arise from the Platonic and Archimedean solids. There is no well-known evidence of artisans in the Islamic world using these uniquely spherical tilings—they seem to remain a largely unexplored possibility in Islamic design. The example below shows a spherical pattern derived from the cube and regular octahedron, based on work by Craig Kaplan.

Muqarnas

celestial cascades

Surmounting a square or rectangular structure with a dome necessitates a transitional device, and in time a distinctive solution for this, known as *muqarnas*, arose in Islamic architecture. *Muqarnas* are structured on tiered horizontal layers joined by flat and curved surfaces which articulate their descent—echoing the idea of spiritual light cascading from the Heavens to condense as crystalline matter on Earth. They are also used in niches, for example the niche, or *mihrāb,* that marks the mosque wall facing Mecca.

Muqarnas' functions range from fulfilling structural necessity, for example transferring forces with carved stone in Egypt, Syria, or Turkey, to the purely ornamental articulation of space in the tile-clad structures assembled within the brick architecture of Iran, or the wood and plaster techniques of the Maghrib.

The design of *muqarnas* varies in different regions and eras. In the Maghrib a modular system based on eight-fold geometry proved perfectly at home (*below*). The east of the Islamic world employs *muqarnas* with concentric tiers around a central pole, some designs using different stars on each tier, others using stalactite forms within curved bays (*opposite*), and yet others emphasizing a triangular, prism-like articulation between tiers.

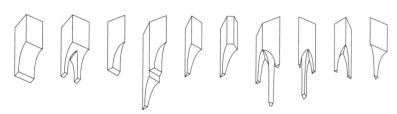

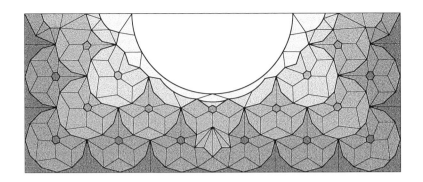

Closing Thoughts
and further possibilities

Traditional Islamic ornament is eminently functional—but its function is not utilitarian. It seeks to compensate for the spiritual losses of civilization by re-establishing something of the primordial beauty of virgin nature, and to transport the viewer from immersion in the mundane to serene contemplation. Islamic design can be thought of as a form of visual music; the repetition and rhythm of its motifs establish an inner sense of balance and act as a visual extension of the invocatory remembrance of the Divine.

The simplicity and apparent inevitability with which many Islamic geometric patterns unfold belie the effort involved in finding them. The anonymous artisans concerned must surely have regarded them as preexistent possibilities gifted from the Source to those who proved worthy. Not a few such craftsmen must have been well aware of the *abjad* equality between the words "point", *nuqta*, and "geometer", *muhandis*, and aspired to allow this transcendent relationship to shine through in their works.

The design opposite is based on a variation on a theme by Paul Marchant, marrying forms from the two interrelated ten-fold families. As we draw to a close, it is a fitting reminder that possibilities yet remain open for exploration in the art of making Islamic geometric patterns.

BOOK III

Above: Iznik dish decorated with an arrangement of leafed spirals composed with three-fold symmetry in the outer band and seven-fold symmetry in the central medallion. An example of the 'rumi' style of leafy ornament, with teardrop-shaped leaves composed of smaller leaves whose placement is structured by a framework of nested hexagons and triangles.

CURVES

FLOWERS, FOLIATES & FLOURISHES
IN THE FORMAL DECORATIVE ARTS

Lisa DeLong

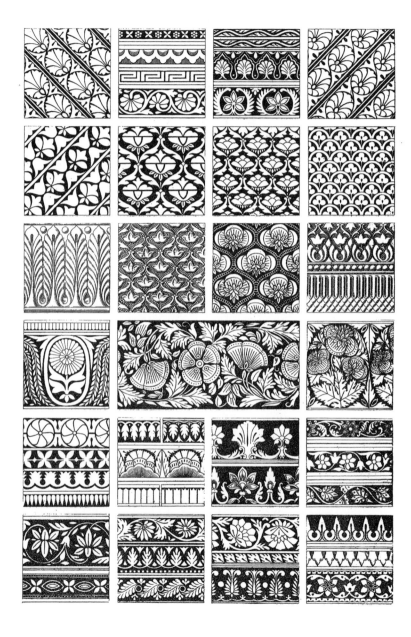

INTRODUCTION

The urge to adorn and beautify sacred things and ordinary objects is universal. Ancient myths worldwide hint at Nature's symbolism and ornamental significance. Trees of Life, leafy crowns, richly decorated robes, and even palaces and temples echo her fertile forms. In each case, the application of symbolic ornament endows an object with both aesthetic and metaphysical value. Our instinct to decorate is ancient.

Nature is complex. She is elegant and serene, turbulent and wild. Her forms can be beautiful, graceful, vicious, brutal, or delicate—but they are always fit for purpose. Owen Jones, author of *The Grammar of Ornament*, who drew the plate of Indian ornament opposite, wrote of Nature: "See how various the forms, and how unvarying the principles." These principles of generation, growth, symmetry, and order also govern the curvilinear ornamentation found in the art of every culture.

Principles do not constrain creativity; rather they inspire diverse and imaginative echoes of seeds, vines, leaves, flowers, and fruit. A designer who works with repetition, alternation, undulation, tesselation, spirals, and symmetry soon discovers the rich variety made possible by working with these simple generative processes. The designs opposite incorporate these principles in their microcosmic gardens of paradise, giving a glimpse of the abundant liveliness of curvilinear decoration found across the globe. It is hoped that readers will discover their own sources of inspiration in the echoes of Nature and the principles of design gathered here.

EARLY CURVES
primordial patterns

Ornament brings cosmology into our mundane world. What may initially appear to be superficial decoration can in fact represent transformational principles and deep structural insights. Ananda Coomaraswamy writes that "the human value of anything made is determined by the coincidence in it of beauty and utility."

The earliest surviving prehistoric clay vessels (*e.g. opposite*) embody this creative urge to participate in the transfiguration of the ordinary. Formless clay was centered on a wheel and spiralled upward in a potter's hands as it was shaped into a vessel. The meanings of the painted spirals, loops, folds, and clefts are lost to time, but the modern eye sees profound beauty in the lines of energy and flow.

The human desire to decorate knows no bounds. Traditional oceangoing Pacific cultures such as the Maori often decorated their entire bodies with tattoos, including their faces, using the same swirling patterns seen on their paddles and canoes *(see below)*.

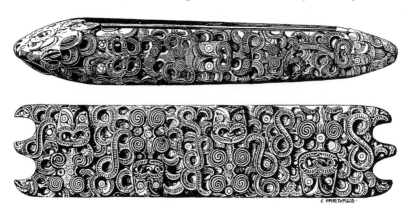

Jiangxi Prov., China, 8000 BC

Yangshao Culture, China, 4000 BC

Majiayao Culture, China, 3000 BC

Machiayao Culture, China, 3500 BC

Trypillian Culture, Romania, 4000 BC

In the Beginning
point, separation and reunification

The visual richness and complexity of biomorphic ornament often obscures the underlying principles of its design. A core matrix of simple forms regularly hides beneath the leaves and flowers.

A point origin • is the microcosmic germ of life, expressed macro-cosmically as a circle ○. The point slides to create a line ‒, rotation yields a circle ᴄ, the circle stretches into a drop shape ◯, the drop spins to introduce a form found in both the positive and negative spaces of many curved designs ℓ, and circles overlap to produce leaves and petals ◊.

Separation, convergence, and reunification recur as lines spring from points of generation, branch, flower, and return. C- and S-shaped curves are especially useful elements for building a compositional structure (*opposite*). The proportions can be stretched and squashed, drawn freehand, or geometrically regulated. Below are examples of curves from square and hexagonal circle grids—useful 'spines' for linear compositions and border designs.

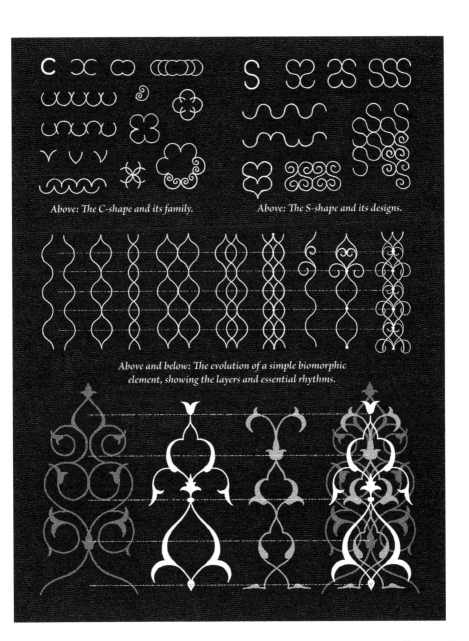

Above: The C-shape and its family.

Above: The S-shape and its designs.

Above and below: The evolution of a simple biomorphic
element, showing the layers and essential rhythms.

Structure and Movement
line and curve

Geometrical grids are highly useful to designers. They provide a formal linear trellis for curves to cling to and spring from, a structured counterpoise to curvilinear movement, growth, and fertile development. Straight-edged patterns with sharp corners can evolve into waves and ripples, whilst the softening of corners and edges can transfigure crystals into flowers and transpose staccato rhythms into melodic compositions.

Geometrical designs display strong visual repeats, from chessboard grids to simple brickwork and basic weaving patterns. However, many often have a lifeless quality, and it is only when the straight lines of the grids are brought to life like spreading ripples on a lake or the oscillating strings of a violin that they begin to pulse and transform toward the living forms of biomorphic designs.

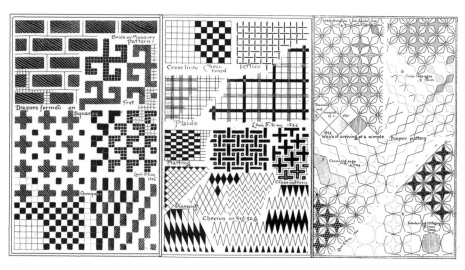

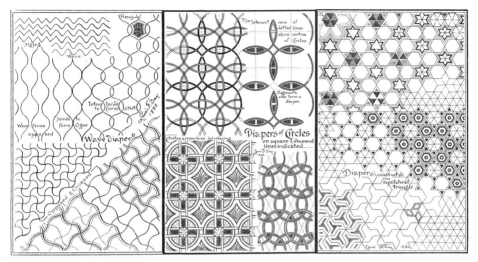

This page and opposite: Known as "diaper" patterns, these playful explorations of geometric and curvilinear pattern by Lewis F. Day (1898) offer a small glimpse of the design possibilities across the plane. Notice how curvilinear designs emerge from straight line grids. These examples are based on the three simple regular tilings: squares, triangles, and hexagons. However, other novel and intriguing possibilities quickly appear once semi-regular structures are employed, for example octagonal, rectangular, or rhomboid grids.

YIN AND YANG

opposition and complementarity

Curved forms embody the principle of 'give and take'—as one edge advances, another recedes. This relationship is beautifully illustrated in the 'yin-yang' motif which expresses the interdependence of opposites: female and male, black and white, active and receptive, manifest and mysterious. Each principle is incomplete without its partner; each is found at its partner's core.

In any design, positive and negative space are bound together as parts of a whole, mutually defining one other. A successful design often demands that the 'negative' background space that is *not*, be as beautiful as the 'positive' foreground space that *is*.

The single 'teardrop' shape itself is ubiquitous, and may manifest as a paisley (*see pages 166–7*), a single leaf or young flower bud, the open spaces of Gothic tracery (*lower, opposite*), or gilded rumi motif leaves twining around the margins of an illuminated Turkish Quran.

In the 19th-century Azeri jewelry piece shown below, spirals and teardrops are playfully combined.

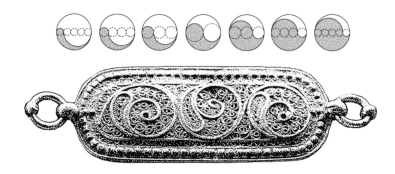

Above: A rumi motif is similar to the paisley or yin-yang shape, shown here with fractal infill.

Above: Designs which show exact complementarity of shape, where the white elements are the same shapes as the black ones. Below and right: A significant element of Gothic tracery is the graceful, tapering yin-yang shape. These playful German compositions illustrate just how flexible a system based on these forms can become.

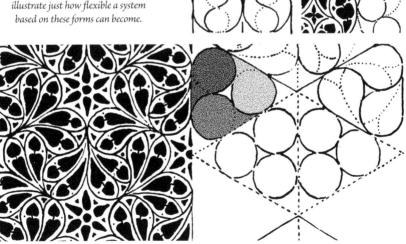

ELEMENTS
action, reaction, and interaction

Natural forces appear everywhere in the decorative arts—watery spirals, shoots forcing up through the earth to unfurl leaves, blossoms opening petals to the radiant sun; biomorphic decoration reflects Nature's fierceness, cyclical rhythms, and transformative power.

The freedom of movement found in curvaceous ornamentation is an interpretation of the order of Nature and her elemental principles and symmetries. Many cultures evolve designs which attempt to convey these often abstract and fluid concepts.

In Japanese art, echoing nature, designs depict the flow form interactions of elements over time—ripples in wet sand, eddies in a stream, arched rocks sculpted by wind, streams of molten lava, crack patterns, cloud formations, and crossing branches.

This page and opposite: In these classical Japanese textile designs (after Jeanne Allen), elemental forces combine and coalesce as blossoms drifting down a stream, metal shattering the air, radiant flame, windblown clouds, eddies of water, and bamboo thrusting upward from the earth. Each design is a piece of art which, in the words of Thomas Aquinas "imitates Nature in the manner of her operation."

SEEDS AND ORIGINS
the mystery of life

Life begins with a seed that swells, sprouts, and begins to grow, a process echoed in biomorphic ornamentation. The designer first establishes a point of origin from which all stems and branches spring. These then serve as generation points for more vines, branches, leaves, and flowers. Ultimately, each part of the composition is traceable to one source and maintains a consistent direction of growth.

The artist may choose to reveal the point of origin as a seed or a cluster of roots. In many cases, however, the mystery of the origin is hidden from direct view behind a veil of clouds, a knot or medallion, or concealed within a vase (*see Indian fabric, Iznik plate, and Persian wall tiling, opposite*). Any change in the direction of growth would break the continuity and logic of the design. In the rare cases when this becomes necessary, the designer obscures these inflection points in some way by a flower, a ring or knot, or some other sign that suggests a new node of origin.

The shape within which a composition grows needs to be handled sensitively, the artist responding to it with well-balanced, space-filling foliates (*as illustrated in the Mughal box lid, below*).

Spiral Mania

vines and spines

Pure spirals are ornaments in their own right, but they can also become the basis of structures from which leaves grow and flowers blossom. Glide, rotation, and reflection symmetries are used by designers to create borders or other ornamentations (*see below*).

A linear sequence of spirals can form a spine from which leaves and flowers may later sprout. Care should be taken to ensure that the spirals spring from one another smoothly and consistently. If floral and foliate elements are to be added, consider how they will respond to the spiral structure. Tessellated spirals produce lively compositions, while radial arrangements can become the basis of complex rosettes. By changing the type of spiral employed, designs can take on quite different appearances. Examples of various kinds of mathematical spirals are shown in the appendix (*see page 384*).

Above left: Egyptian spirals, 2000 BC with lotus motifs in a variety of compositions (after Glazier). Above right: Late Italian Renaissance stone spiral flourish. Below: Late Roman copper alloy with champlevé enamel vase, central France, 250–300 AD; Celtic spiral design from the 7th c. Book of Durrow; Modern handprinted Indian textile; Detail of Yuan dynasty vase (1300–50 AD), Jiangxi province, China.

IRONWORK
decorative and protective

Ironwork provides an exceptionally clear example of how simple curved elements can be combined into complex ornamentational objects. A quick glance at the examples below and opposite will show that C and S curves, combined with spirals and a few straight lines, constitute the primary visual vocabulary here.

The first people to smelt and purify iron were the Hittites, around 2000BC, but it was not until 17th-century France and Spain that form and function first truly met and the family of iron flourishes was explored. Blacksmiths forged together clusters of C- and S-shaped spirals to provide both security and beauty in the form of elaborate gates and grills. Needing to find a balance of strength and delicacy, they chose curves which were neither too tight nor too lax and openings not so large that they offered no security nor so tight that they blocked visibility.

The medieval hinges of vast wooden cathedral doors are another wonderful example of the use of iron (*e.g. the hinge from the Cathedral of Notre-Dame, opposite lower left*). In fine detail they often depict trees, evoking the Tree of Life, or Knowledge, thus designating the consecrated space within the church walls as paradisiacal Eden.

Above: A regal set of wrought iron gates from the 19th-century catalogue of the French Denonvilliers company. Notice the various motifs: spirals, C-shapes, S-shapes, and hearts. Below left: Medieval door hinge from the Cathedral of Notre-Dame, Paris. Below right and opposite page: More French wrought ironwork, fences, grills, brackets, and garden lunettes, all using the same simple elements.

LEARNING FROM LEAVES

structure and stylization

A leaf is a wondrous thing; it transforms light into nutrients for life. Each leaf, whilst essentially a repetition of every other leaf on a plant, is also completely unique, its veining often suggesting a microcosmic version of the whole of which it is a part.

Leaves come in many shapes and sizes, but the primary distinction is between simple leaves (e.g. aristate ◗, ovate ◗, or obcordate ◗) and compound forms (e.g. palmate ❦, pinnate ✺). There can also be different edges to a leaf (e.g. spiny ◗, serrated ◗, or lobed ◗), and there are various veining patterns. For the designer, learning to notice, study, and then stylize Nature's profound and varied forms requires a sensitivity to lines, curves, shapes, universal qualities, and individual quirks.

A widely-used leaf in the classical world was that of the acanthus plant, and it offers a case study of stylization principles in foliate ornamentation. Stylization can take many forms; each of the iterations shown (*below and opposite*) retains the essential character of the acanthus.

Stylization is a key part of successful biomorphic design. Other motifs throughout this book provide examples of the principle: the essence of form and energy of growth remain, whilst details are flattened, distilled, and organized to show an ideal form.

This page and opposite: The acanthus leaf has been an important motif since classical times and provides an example of how nature can be stylized. The characteristic principles and energy of its form can be turned into a scrolling border (opposite, two variations of one design), a 2nd-century Roman Corinthian capital (above), other variants (above), or a William Morris pattern (below).

ARABESQUES

a garden around every corner

The "arabesque" is a term used to describe interlaced foliate designs from Islamic art which later permeated the European Renaissance. C-curves, S-shapes, spirals, and undulations are choreographed to produce swooping, flowing, playful adornment for every surface. In these 1856 plates by Owen Jones, regulation and rhythm counterpoints and structures the riot of growth. Look for repetition, alternation, spirals, mirroring, rotation, glides, and the partnering of complementary opposites.

Plans and Elevations
looking at plants from different angles

In biomorphic ornament, plants and plant elements are typically shown either in plan (*from the top, e.g. below*) or in elevation (*from the side, e.g. opposite, top left*), rather than in perspective as in other arts.

The simplest form of elevation appears in palmettes (leaves or petals springing out from a generation point), often seen in Greek ornament. Calyx ornament employs another form of elevation (*see appendix, page 381*). Rosettes, meanwhile, are plan-projected flowers with petals or leaves radiating out from a center.

In some instances a fusion may be successfully employed, with the plant rising in elevation and the flowers shown in plan, emerging toward the viewer. Flowers are often stylized to show the eternal essence of flowerness, rather than an individual bloom.

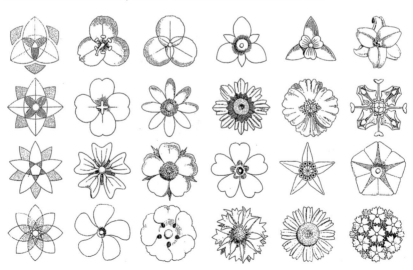

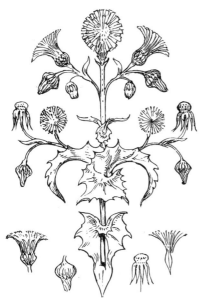

Above: Botanical illustrations need to show a lot of information about a plant, so often show flattened plants in both plan and elevation. Above right: Quarter of a Victorian elevational composition. Below left: Islimi flowers in elevation. Below right: Greek vase with elements in elevation. Opposite: Flowers in plan.

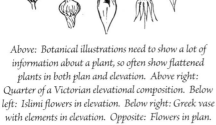

CENTERED COMPOSITIONS
the bee's-eye view

Medallions and rosettes find their way into most floriate decoration. From the grandeur of a cathedral's rose window to a biscuit or a child's shirt button, these motifs bloom everywhere. Compositions of this form are typically radially symmetric, often combining both rotational and reflective symmetry (*as in the carved stone bosses, below*). Some simply show a flower, while others are a complex arrangement of foliated spirals and curves interspersed with palmettes and calyx ornament (*opposite*).

Many designs appear surprisingly simple once their basic unit is identified, although the artisan must always ensure that the parts all come together in a beautiful whole. Experiment with some tracing paper, rotating and reflecting a design drawn in one-eighth of a circle. Notice too how the vines and leaves of elevation-style motifs, when arranged in a rosette, can unite to create the illusion of a blossom unfolding, petal by petal.

Planning with Geometry
foreground and background

When ornament adapts to inhabit a shape, the structuring form should contain rather than confine. It is thus often useful when preparing an area for ornamentation to use a proportional system to govern areas of emphasis and the arrangement of major shapes. Although smaller shapes may be intuitively in-filled with flourishes and scrolling ornament, more often the designer will again use an underlying structure (*see examples below*).

An appropriate balance should exist between foreground and background to allow the emptiness of the negative spaces to play a role at least as important as the positive. Designs are made more or less elaborate depending on factors such as the medium, intended use of the decorated object, viewing distance, scale, and style.

Above: The same essential triangular design with different levels of elaboration.

Above: Iznik design from a 1560 Ottoman table, ordered by a nest of sixfold stars.
Islamic artisans were particularly skilled in structuring their designs, always striving
for a balance between order and freedom.

EXTRAVAGANT ORNAMENT
the baby and the bathwater

In the 1600s, an exaggerated form of ornamentation became fashionable in Europe. The new style, known as the Baroque, was driven by a desire for elaborate and grandiose opulence, characterized by increasingly extravagant and floridly flamboyant forms, culminating in the almost cartoonlike 18th-century French Rococo style. Over this period ornamentation became bigger, more asymmetrical and voluptuously curvaceous. Huge cornucopias, shells, nymphs, scrolls, and neopagan and oriental fancies competed for space with old-fashioned foliate themes in houses, gardens (*opposite top*), furniture (*see page 115*), and everything else from picture frames to bathtubs, shoes, and fountains. In this period obsessed with flights of fancy and the impossibly bizarre, the seed principle (*page 128*) faded in importance.

As popular revolutions spread across Europe, the Baroque and Rococo styles eventually withered to be replaced by an austere classicism. Today, we live in a world dominated by unornamented rectangles, squares, and straight lines, although gilded encrustations are still a signifier of wealth and decadence.

Above: 18th-century Rococo ornament is based on the curves of seashells and parchment scrolls.
Below: Elizabethan strapwork balances positive and negative space. Although both styles often feature
foliate elements, neither generally obeys the traditional 'seed' principle (see page 128).

TILES

slide, drop, and rotation

A tile unit need not be elaborate or complicated to produce an interesting pattern. For some tiles, a simple slide may be the only action required to generate a sophisticated design.

In the same way, merely rotating a tile can generate surprisingly complex designs. Tiles intended for rotation usually involve careful consideration of diagonal movement since each 90° twist brings a new corner into play. Consider the examples shown (*opposite*): some motifs on the edges and corners are halved or quartered because they extend past the limits of the tile. When the tile is tessellated, these motifs are made whole. The 'missing' portions are cleverly designed to be completed by rotation, reflection, and glide.

A *drop pattern* is one in which the design is planned in such a way that the basic unit repeats when slid down by a set proportion, most commonly by one half its height. This type of repeat is typically used in wallpapers, since it allows horizontal seams to be offset (and thus disguised) when vertical strips are placed side by side. In each of the drawings below, rotation produces a continuous design, but a drop pattern is only possible with the right-hand one. Can you see why?

A selection of early tiles from Turkey and England which show the staggering complexity of design which can arise from the simple acts of rotation and translation of a unit.

BLOCK PRINTED REPEATS
thinking outside the box

Production methods often affect design. In printing, for example, although hand-carved wooden blocks of many shapes (e.g. rhombs or hexagons) are sometimes used, finished designs are most often rationalized into rectangles. This makes them easier to transfer onto rollers and facilitates the simple alignment of edges and corners as the inks are finally pressed onto the fabric or paper.

To help create designs that flow organically beyond such artificial limits, a designer can reconfigure a rectangle, removing corners and redistributing them to create a shape which tessellates and has the same area as the original rectangle. This technique has the virtue of allowing the artist to respond to a new shape and see new possibilities (*see below*).

A "turnover" is a design which uses reflection to generate a wider pattern. In many turnover designs, details along the central axis are deliberately asymmetrical to create visual interest.

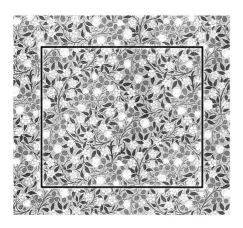

This page: Four 19th-century designs by William Morris, exhibiting a mastery of composition and colour. Above: A drop repeat. Below: Turnover design with underlying left-right symmetry disguised by asymmetry in the leafy detail. Top right: Spiral vines and a scattering of flowers make up a design with no obvious structure. Below right: Alternating boughs move in and out of the governing rectangle.

COMPOSITIONAL TECHNIQUES
inside the boxes

Whilst block printing helps the designer plan at large scales, additional techniques assist with the creation of a pattern.

When setting out a design, the area to be filled is often divided into a grid with certain boxes selected for emphasis. This strategy allows for the planning of open spaces or large motifs as well as the distribution of colour effects (particularly useful when the designer wishes to minimize unwanted linear effects).

Several useful 19th-century tricks are shown here. Below, a 6×6 grid is used to organize a scattering of leaves, to beautiful effect. Because only one square in each row or column is selected, the appearance of stripes is cleverly avoided. In the upper diagrams opposite, a similar grid system structures the placement of large motifs and open spaces.

It is impossible to demonstrate here the effects of colour, but it is worth remembering that, like so many things in nature, colours have opposites and friends, and two colours with the same gray value placed side by side can confuse the eye. Using only colour, a repeated unit can create a pattern all by itself (*opposite lower right*).

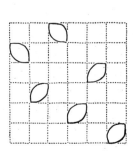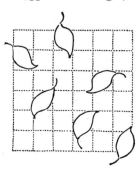

The flowers in this square block have been distributed using a 6×6 grid system. Notice how the flowers have been tilted in 6 different directions.

In this leafy composition, particular boxes in the 5×5 block were determined in advance to create a balanced set of spaces within the overall design.

Diamond units are the basis for this design, but by combining them as strips in a long zigzag, interesting new possibilities become available.

Colour introduces further variation and complexity into a design. New subtle lines and stripes can appear which may or may not be intentional.

PROVING A PATTERN
refining the design

It is vital to thoroughly test the basic unit of any new repeat pattern to ensure that when printed, no unexpected effects will emerge. For example, in the drop pattern below, no matter which corners or edges are joined, positive and negative areas remain balanced and all motifs are completed. To be confident about the final effect it is advisable to repeat the design several times. This allows the designer to see stripes or lines that might unintentionally emerge, or to strengthen motifs that may recede in visual strength when repeated in a pattern.

The example opposite shows how a design can extend beyond the limits of the printing block. Motifs that burst outside the frame on one side can be found creeping in on the opposite edge.

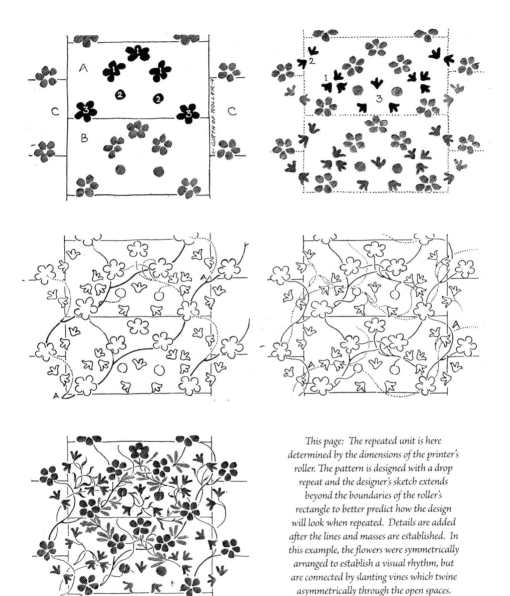

This page: The repeated unit is here determined by the dimensions of the printer's roller. The pattern is designed with a drop repeat and the designer's sketch extends beyond the boundaries of the roller's rectangle to better predict how the design will look when repeated. Details are added after the lines and masses are established. In this example, the flowers were symmetrically arranged to establish a visual rhythm, but are connected by slanting vines which twine asymmetrically through the open spaces.

Turning a Corner
bringing it all together

There are a number of different ways to turn a corner. In the medieval illuminated French manuscript borders below, a leafed vine design has been organically adapted to move around a corner, demonstrating how to build up a skeleton of curves populated with foliate elements using no repetition or reflection. This approach works well in a unique hand-painted design, but is obviously less suited to block printing.

When creating a system of units that can be slid, rotated, or reflected, corners must be considered carefully. A 45° mitred corner can require the enlarging or stretching of the border design, or even the composition of something entirely new. Sometimes, the designer may simply 'box off' the corner to avoid such labor.

With the inclusion of lengthening pieces and turnover units (*opposite lower right*), a basic square motif can be adapted to a variety of purposes by making it longer or wider. In the example shown, there are five unique units that constitute the central composition. These standard units have then been rotated and reflected as necessary to create the much larger composition.

 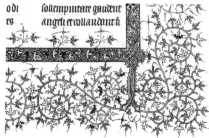

Above left: Corner detail from Sultan Baybars' 1304 Quran, with corner section derived from the edge border units. Above right: A border which is a continuous part of the central design.

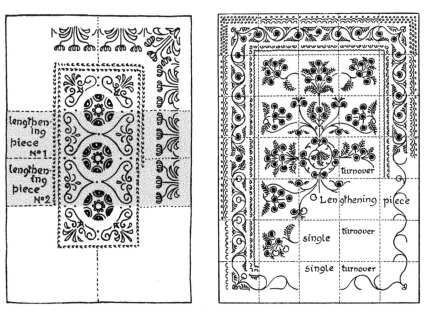

Above: Strategies for planning a bordered textile composition using turnovers and lengthening pieces. With this flexible approach, designs can be adapted to be as large or as small as necessary.

CONSTRUCTED CURVES

tracery, volutes, and moldings

Architects often soften their structures with curves in the form of arched windows, doorways, or other features. These are drawn with compasses from multiple centers (*e.g. below, trefoil and quatrefoil windows, arches, ellipses, and ovals*). Similarly, subtly moving the center allows an Ionic volute to be drawn using compasses and ruler (*opposite top left*). Wooden or plastic 'French' or 'Burmester' curves (*opposite top right*) are useful templates which allow a designer to find a portion of a required curve between two points.

Moldings in plaster, wood, or stone are decorative features perceived as straight lines of light and shadow. When viewed in profile they can reveal unexpected sophistication (*lower opposite*).

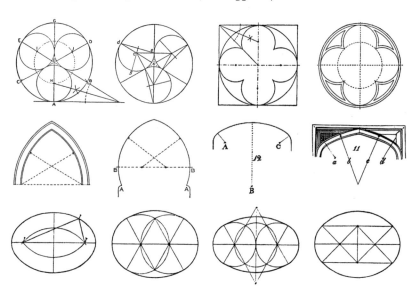

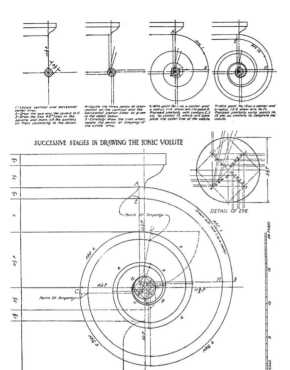

SUCCESSIVE STAGES IN DRAWING THE IONIC VOLUTE

DETAIL OF EYE

Points Of Tangency

Points Of Tangency

Left: The Ionic Volute by Wooster Bard Field, 1920. Above: French curves and garment rulers, very useful for drawing curves. Below: Moldings soften corners.

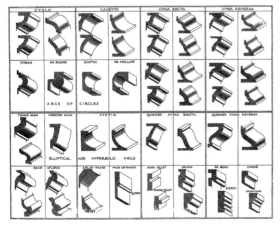

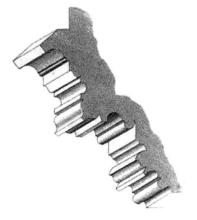

ARCHES AND DOMES
leafy forests of stone

Biomorphic ornamentation is not just limited to the plane. In the same way that flowing branches emerge from the confines of two-dimensional grids, structural arches and domes awaken the tedious cubes and straight lines of three-dimensional architectural spaces into forms more resembling those of living things.

The largest plants are trees, and it is the powerful form of the tree that is most evident in columns, arches, and fan vaulting (*opposite top right*). Leaf-like tracery suggests the play of branches, and colorful rose windows shine like flowers in a dark forest. Passing through a tall arch is similar to walking through a grove of trees, their magnificent branches vaulting overhead.

Domes, the quintessential symbol of heavenly perfection, are a curve spun around a central axis, and suggest emergent buds, shoots, or breasts, bursting full with the promise of life. They can be pointed, hemispherical, segmented, or onion, and are often covered, inside and outside, with cosmological ornamentation.

Above left: Arches constructed of interlocking circles and curves. Above right: English cathedral fan vaulting, echoing the branches of a forest arbor. Below: Decorated arches from a palace in Tanjore, India. Opposite page: Pointed Mamluk domes from Cairo.

THE ART OF THE BOOK
illuminating the word

Ornamentation has long been used to supplement a sacred text, such as the Bible or Quran. This labor-intensive and time-consuming process takes great skill. Frequently, the decoration responds to the written word, as gold and bright pigments reflect the physical light as a fitting complement to the spiritual illumination of the sacred writings. Sometimes this may take the form of an illustrated scene described in the text; in other cases the connection is more abstract.

By far the most frequent ornamentation is plant-based, with foliates and flowers climbing the margins, marking the beginnings of chapter and verse, or carpeting a double frontispiece in a lavish paradise garden of golden vines, leaves, and blossoms.

Book decoration enjoyed a resurgence during the 19th-century British Arts and Crafts movement (*see examples below*), often with a similar symbolic correlation between text and ornament.

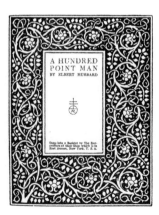

Left: Detail from a carpet page illumination in an 11th-century Persian Quran. Within the lovely 8-fold rosette, doubled spiralling branches perfectly fill the available space. Beyond the medallion, the spiral is complemented by curving clouds.

Below: Detail from an illuminated page in the 7th-century Lindisfarne gospels, a beautiful repository of Celtic Christian Art. Here the Greek letters chi and rho are decorated with intricate spirals, a veritable symphony of swirls.

PEN AND BRUSH
penmanship and flourishes

The art of pen or brush is perhaps the most ubiquitous form of curvilinear expression, available to everyone who has ever hand-written a note. It is an art form that emerges from the rhythms of the body, an internal state of mind revealed in curves, loops, and flourishes. It is possible that "handwriting, being a manifestation of one who writes, somehow reproduces something of its writer's temperament, personality, or character" (Camillo Baldi, 1621).

Clarity and fluidity, highly prized by artists and designers, can be refined by a careful study of the calligraphic arts. These demand both precision and spontaneity, regulation and rule-breaking, directness and circuitousness (*e.g. see flourishes by Ann Hechle, opposite*). Whether produced with a reed, steel nib, or brush as in the Norwegian acanthus rosmaling design below (note the seed principle, flowers in plan and elevation, and the teardrop-shaped brush strokes), the quality of line in a calligraphic composition can be a thing of beauty.

MARBLED PAPERS
dynamically fluid

Marbled paper provides an opportunity to see curved patterns of ebb and flow that normally are too transient to observe closely when in liquid form. The subtle chaos, captured as a one-time monotype on paper (or sometimes silk), is a microcosmic echo of the tides and currents, whirlwinds, and tsunamis, which have been induced by the artist. Ripples, vortices, striations, flourishes, and turbulences are all captured, frozen in time. Unlike most other decorative ornamentation, in marbling there is no difference between positive and negative space.

To marble, very finely ground colour oil pigments or inks are floated on the surface of water or a viscous solution. Various additives prevent the colours and solutions from mixing. The artist carefully manipulates the design using breath, brushes, feathers, or special combs, before a single sheet of paper or silk, quickly applied to the surface, receives the unique imprint of the composition.

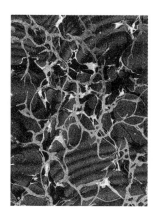  

PAISLEY

pregnant with possibility

The 'paisley' shape takes its name from the Scottish town which produced patterned shawls inspired by Kashmiri textiles in the 19th century. Incredibly elastic, the *boteh* can become short and squat, lean and elongated, or everything in between. It is variously thought to represent a mango, the new shoot of a date palm, a tadpole or fish, a pine tree, or the human form. Like its close cousin the yin-yang, the boteh is full of paradox. It is both watery and flamelike, simultaneously a single leaf and the archetypal Tree of Life, a body curled into a fetal position swelling with life and potential, and the infinite abundance of paradise reflected in a single drop of water.

THE TREE OF LIFE
and gardens of paradise

A cosmic tree is revered in some form in virtually every culture. It manifests variously as olive, date, fig, pomegranate, fir, almond, bo, oak, yew, mulberry, maize, or bamboo.

The essence of this archetypal tree is implicit within biomorphic decorations as both a visual pattern and a mythological matrix—its roots draw nourishment from the darkness of the earth, its trunk stretches upward against the pull of gravity, and its branches spiral across the heavens to leaf, flower, and bear fruit.

Nature's beauty and ingenuity perpetually inspire and direct human creativity. Echoes of her order and abundant variety are manifest in ornamentation and loved by her entire human family.

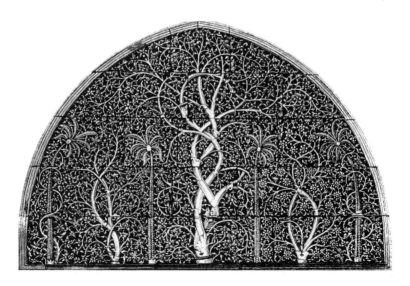

Top left: Gold oak leaf crown, Macedonia, 350 BC. Top right: Gold myrtle wreath, Greece, 150 BC.
Above: Traditional Sarawak painted world tree, Borneo. Opposite: Stone screen, Ahmedabad, India.
Below left: Detailed biomorphic woodcarving, Malaysia. Below right: Carved wooden doors, Thailand.

BOOK IV

Sandro Del Preté's impossible chessboard. However much you look at it, your brain will continually struggle to reconcile the paradoxes it contains.

PERSPECTIVE
AND OTHER OPTICAL
ILLUSIONS

from Kirby's Perspective of Architecture, London, 1761

Phoebe McNaugton

Although it looks like one at first, this is not, in fact, a normal caption. Indeed, it misdirects from the start. You will find no details concerning any pictures here. Try opposite instead.

INTRODUCTION

You're holding a book. Or you could be looking at a screen. Perhaps someone's reading this to you. Maybe you learned it by heart. By chance you're in a garden. In all cases you are experiencing a world with this word "now" in it which has been constructed for you by complex systems largely fed by data from your senses. Things you cannot sense you tend to be largely unaware of, and neither telling your senses to sense themselves, nor developing new ones, is going to be an easy task.

There are, right now, monks, bats, and ordinary people across the world who are accessing senses which other people, snails, and yucca plants can hardly dream of. The following pages use sight, the seen world, and the many ways of reproducing it, as an allegory for all our senses, although schematic systems, maps, printed circuits, technical diagrams, and other widely-used representational techniques are omitted here for lack of space.

Why question the way we look at the world? Look at William Hogarth's catalogue of errors opposite. All seems well at first, but then, studying it more closely, consistent impossibilities begin to emerge, one by one. Customs have been broken, we are in a strange world, we have been tricked by a master trickster.

Welcome to one of the few sane disciplines (excluding eye-popping shamanics and monotonous meditations) which can actually awaken your mind to some of its profound invisible biases and help it become more aware of the way it constructs the world.

Welcome to the world of perspective and optical illusions.

THE DEPTH ILLUSION
a short history of points of view

Perspective creates the illusion of depth on a flat surface, and its history is crudely shown here in three fundamental stages.

Firstly, an Egyptian wall-painting from the 1200 BC Tomb of Siptah (*below*) depicts a table seen in *elevation* (front-on), with Anubis standing behind it, reaching over with arms which *occlude*, or block out, the mummy. Front and side view orthographic (straight-on) and later oblique (slanting) projections form the backbone of world representational art from antiquity right up to the Renaissance.

The second picture *(top right, from Bettini, 1642)* shows a multi-pinhole *camera obscura* projecting perfect reversed images of the world onto a wall in a darkened room. The engraving is itself constructed in one-point perspective, with a revolutionary *vanishing point*.

Finally (*below right*), we have a modern stereogram. Gaze through the page, merging the white dots, and a 3-D figure will appear.

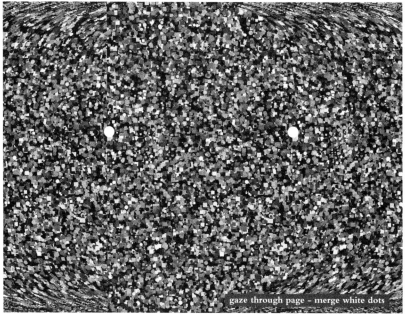

gaze through page – merge white dots

ORTHOGRAPHIC PROJECTIONS
top, front, and side views

Whether you are a caveman or an architect, a useful representation of an object or scene is often one of three simple drawings: the *plan* (top view), section (side view), or *elevation* (front view). That these three ancient views, correctly combined, completely define an object was only first understood in the Renaissance (by Uccello and Dürer). Later, in early 18th century France, Gaspard Monge developed the method of projective geometry where the object to be drawn is placed in a box and projected (by an infinitely distant light source) on to its faces. This gave rise to two systems, the back-thrown "first angle projection" (*below left*), used in Europe during the Industrial Revolution, and the forward-thrown "third angle projection" (*below right*), which was adopted in the US.

Most cave paintings are simple elevations, showing animals and hunters seen from the side. Early maps are rough plans. By contrast, in Andrea Pozzo's 1693 picture (*opposite top*), the careful use of plan and elevation has facilitated an accurate perspective drawing, and in the picture of block machinery from *Ree's Cyclopedia* of 1820 (*lower opposite*) all three projections are shown aligned, enabling a manufacturer to take measurements directly off the drawing.

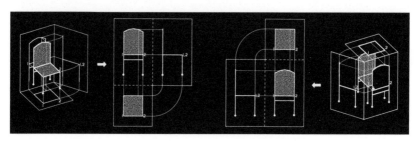

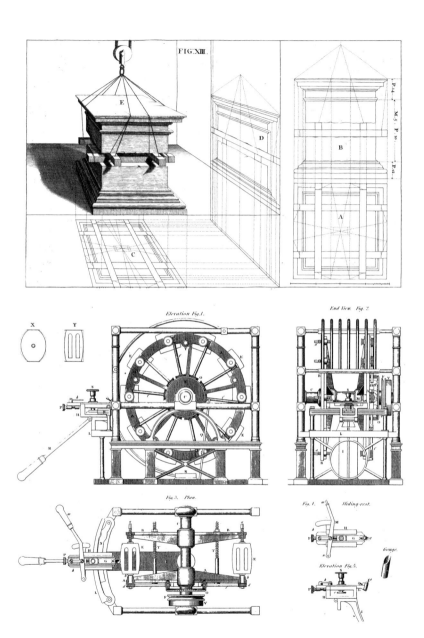

FIG. XIII.

Elevation Fig.1.

End View. Fig. 2.

Fig. 3. Plan.

Fig. 4. Sliding-rest.

Gouge.

Elevation Fig. 5.

OBLIQUE PROJECTIONS
slightly sideways glances

With the arrival of slanting oblique projections in ancient China, India, Greece, and Egypt, all sorts of artistic possibilities flowered which were impossible in the primitive perpendicular orthographic projections of early cave, pottery and temple paintings. Now, instead of seeing an object from merely one, infinitely distant (thus divine), point of view, further divine viewpoints were glued on to the drawing. So to the side view of a chair, the front, overhead, or both views were sewn on, as though 45° sunlight was striking the object and casting a shadow, either to the side, or down, or both.

Various methods of oblique projection are shown opposite (*after Dubery and Willats*) with illustrative examples. *Foreshortening* further enhances the illusion of depth (*below*). Fascinatingly, these ways of looking at the world were all but forgotten in the West during the scramble for 'real' scientific perspective until they were rediscovered by Cezanne, Bonnard, and other 'modern' painters.

In Asia, oblique projections have remained in use in various traditional painting styles for over 2,500 years.

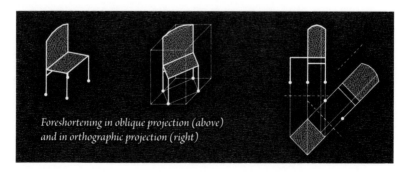

Foreshortening in oblique projection (above) and in orthographic projection (right)

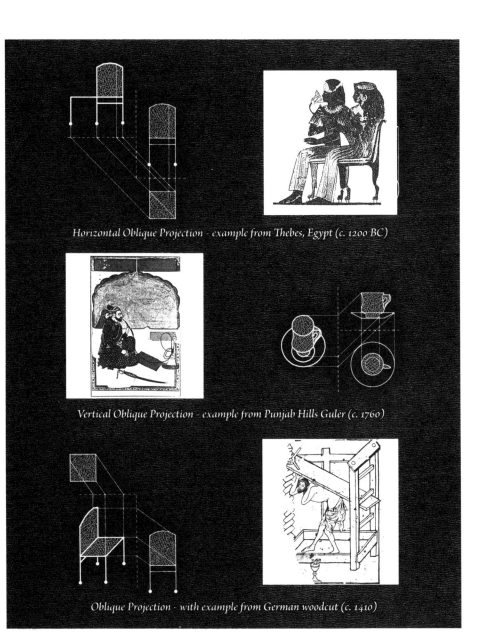

Horizontal Oblique Projection - example from Thebes, Egypt (c. 1200 BC)

Vertical Oblique Projection - example from Punjab Hills Guler (c. 1760)

Oblique Projection - with example from German woodcut (c. 1410)

THE ISOMETRIC SYSTEM
the all-in-one hexagonal projection

A special case of oblique projection is the isometric system, which combines plan, section, and elevation drawings in a simple hexagonal grid, each separated by 60° to give a remarkably authentic picture. Developed by Sir William Farish in the mid 18th century to make the complex drawings of the Industrial Revolution easier to read, isometric projections can be extended infinitely over any surface and accurate measurements taken off the drawing along all three axes. In Louis Bretex's famous 1730s' isometric map of Paris (*lower opposite*) the city extends for miles (or kilometers) in every direction, and roofs, doors and windows, and even individual trees can be seen, counted, and measured. The easily readable isometric system today survives only in popular home automobile manuals, mechanical journals, and a few other rare habitats.

Also shown (*below right*) is the related 45° *axonometric projection* with its pure plan. A few medieval and Byzantine examples exist, but this became most popular amongst 20th century designers.

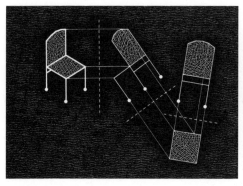 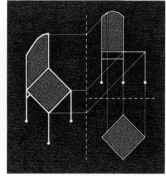

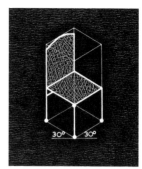

Left: R. B. Brook-Greave's 1928 exercise drawing of London's St Paul's Cathedral in isometric projection.

Above: The special isometric oblique viewing angle in which all sides appear equally foreshortened.

Below: A tiny fragment of Louis Bretex's vast isometric Turgot map of Paris, started in 1734.

Opposite: Isometric and axonometric systems.

ONE-POINT PERSPECTIVE
the dot on the horizon

If you stand in front of an avenue of trees, or look down a street, the objects in front of you seem to get smaller the farther away they are from you, converging on a *vanishing point* on the horizon (*opposite top*). A system of scientific perspective based on this perception first appeared around 1405 when Brunelleschi famously drew the octagonal Baptistry beside the Duomo in Florence, and noticed the way that the diagonal vanishing points framed his picture (*e.g., below*).

By 1436, in *Della Pitura*, Alberti was able to clearly describe the fundamental principles of perspective: the fixed observing point, the central vanishing point (*vpc*), and a picture plane with two further planes set at 45° which converge to left and right vanishing points (*vpl* and *vpr*), ideally both the same distance from the central vanishing point as the observer is from the canvas (the observer should stand in this special place for maximum effect). If the viewing angle in one-point perspective is too wide then distortions occur (*lower opposite*) and for this reason it is generally limited to 60°.

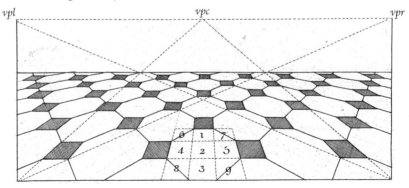

22

Two to Five Points

vanishing in every direction

The use of vanishing points was extended, in the centuries after their discovery, to represent space in a variety of novel ways.

Artists often employ two horizontally separated vanishing points (*shown below*), ideal for objects or views which are "corner-on". Verticals, instead of being parallel, can also be represented as converging on a point through the addition of a third vanishing point (*opposite top*), a projection often used in comic strips.

For an even more comprehensive, albeit distorted and fisheye, view of the world, try four, or even five, vanishing points, using curved space (*opposite lower left and right*).

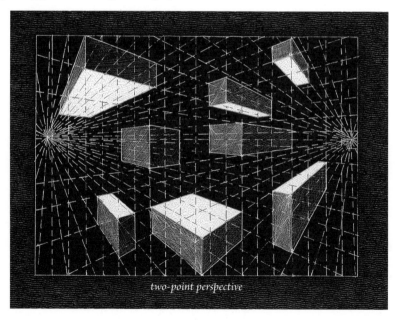

two-point perspective

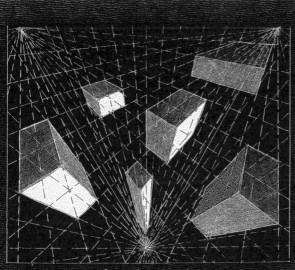

three-point perspective

The fascinating extension of the primary geometry of perspective into two-, three-, four-, and five-point systems is shown here. From the edge-on two-point system, to the lofty three-point, the floating curved verticals of the skyscrapers of four-point, or the global fisheye lens provided by five-point, each method has a specific character, place and function, and all are easily mastered with a small amount of practice.

four-point perspective

five-point perspective

DRAWING MACHINES
tricks of the trade

Today we are so used to the simple act of picking up a camera and pressing the button that we sometimes forget just how hard it was (and still is) for painters to capture the scene in front of them.

Not long after the invention of perspective all sorts of clever systems began to appear to help them ever better imitate perceived reality. By the early 16th century various methods and devices were appearing across Europe; shown here are those illustrated by Dürer in his *Underweysung der messung*. Sketches made in this way, whether by grid, or on glass, were then transferred to canvas.

Later in the century, another device, the *camera obscura*, became popular. This used a lens, pinhole, or mirror to dimly project the world onto a canvas in a dark space (often requiring the artist to put his head into a cloth blackout). Used widely by painters like Vermeer in the 17th century, it best suited high-contrast subjects.

Four pictures from Dürer's
Underweysung, 1525, 1538.

*Opposite: Carefully plotting points
to correctly foreshorten the image
of a lute.*

*Left: Creating a painting on glass
from a fixed eye position.*

*Below: A draftsman using a grid/
net to draw a foreshortened
nude figure.*

*Bottom: Employing a distant
viewpoint perspective device
invented by Jacob de Keyser.*

SOME PERSPECTIVE BASICS
diagonals and inclined planes

A few perspective primers are shown on this page, all of which make good exercises. Start (*opposite top center*) with the simple square in the center of the image. It is completely defined from its front line, as its back corners are the intersections of diagonal dashed lines from its front corners to the central and side vanishing points. The next square away from the viewer can be positioned by the same method, and so on.

The *perspective center* of an object is obtained by drawing its diagonals and noting where they cross (*opposite top left*). It is useful for correctly positioning doors, windows, roof arches, belly-buttons, belts, and noses in paintings and drawings.

Inclined planes, like shadows, use vanishing points exactly above or below the ordinary horizon vanishing points (*center opposite*).

Circles in simple perspective are always perfect ellipses (*lower, opposite*). To draw them, remember that a circle sits in a square, cuts the diagonals at just over ⅔, and touches the square at points which are given by the perspective center, and that the same is true for the ellipse.

Below is a helpful clue to using plan and elevation in perspective.

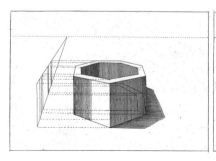
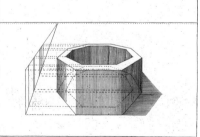

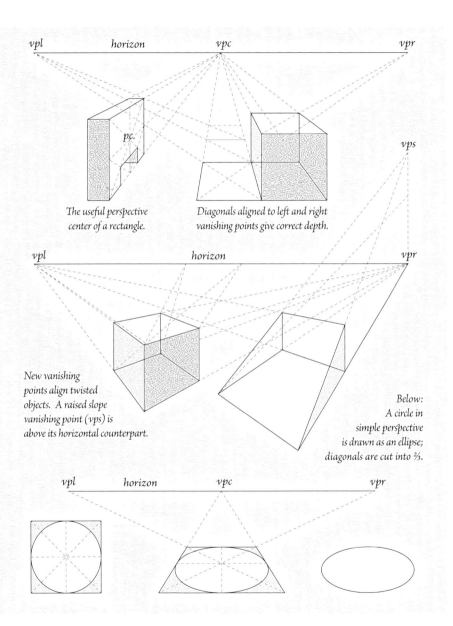

vpl   horizon   vpc   vpr

pc.

vps

The useful perspective
center of a rectangle.

Diagonals aligned to left and right
vanishing points give correct depth.

vpl   horizon   vpr

New vanishing
points align twisted
objects. A raised slope
vanishing point (vps) is
above its horizontal counterpart.

Below:
A circle in
simple perspective
is drawn as an ellipse;
diagonals are cut into ⅔.

vpl   horizon   vpc   vpr

PERSPECTIVE ILLUSIONS
when equal things seem unbalanced

The illusion created by perspective is so pervasive that it throws up all sorts of strange effects. If you hold your hands in front of you, with one at arm's length in front of one eye, and the other half arm's length in front of the other, they will still seem the same size. This is for the simple reason that your brain *knows* they are the same size. Similarly, yet conversely, in Roger Shepard's table (*opposite top left*) both tabletops are exactly the same rectangle, yet your brain distorts them based on perspectival clues in the picture.

Herringbone patterns (*opposite top right*) likewise bend perfectly parallel lines, and visible vanishing points bend the space around them causing all sorts of seeming inequalities between measurably perfectly equal elements (*below and opposite*).

Most of these illusions are noticeably weaker for traditional peoples unused to perspectival art or cityscapes, suggesting that perspective illusions are broadly brain-based hypotheses.

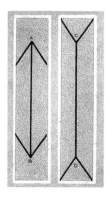  

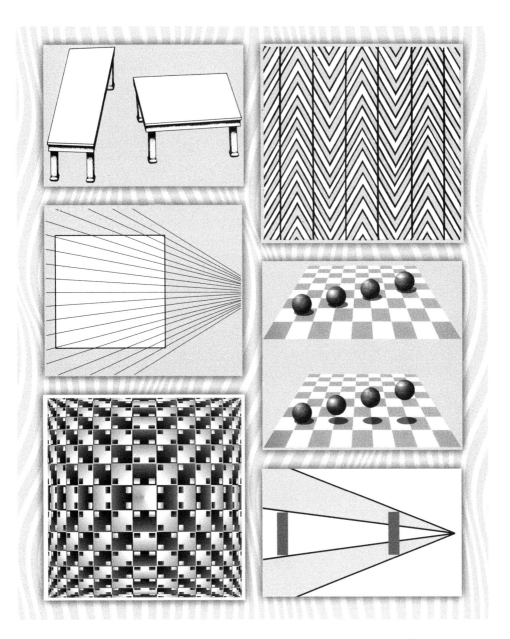

SHADOWS
and the absence of light

Accurate shadows are easy to draw in perspective and deepen the sense of realism in a drawing. Like stairways and other seemingly complex operations, if you have a go you will soon get the idea.

One of the most common forms of shadow-plotting is from orthographic projections (*see pages 178-9*). Take, for instance, the front of a house, where sunlight may be assumed to be obliquely striking the facade, casting shadows in the recesses of pillars, windows and ledges. Shadow termination lines are struck at 45° off the plan (and the side) and brought down (and across) to the elevation, enabling the correct shadows to be drawn (easier than it sounds!).

Working in scientific perspective it is important to establish whether the light source is near or far, and whether it is to the front, side, or rear of the viewer. The four basic types of situation are shown opposite, and mostly involve a small amount of study before they can be clearly grasped. Multiple light sources will obviously throw multiple shadows based along the same lines.

In a way, everything we ever see, or ever paint, or draw, is just some kind of shadow of that thing. It is never that thing itself.

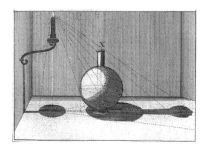
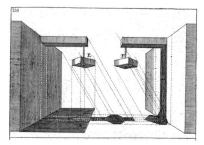

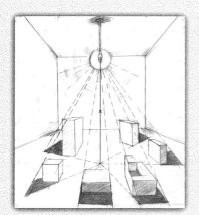
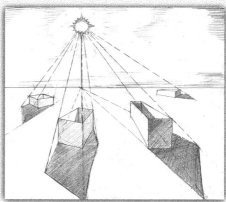

Above left: Lightbulb shadows. A nearby point-source of light casts shadows which recede along lines drawn both from the light itself and from the point on the floor directly beneath the light. Right: Sun in front of viewer. The vanishing point for shadows is on the horizon directly beneath the sun. Use lines from the sun to the corners of objects to determine where their shadows terminate.

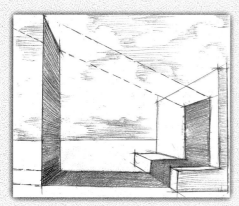
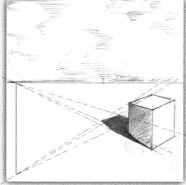

Above left: Sun to the side. With light parallel to the picture plane, use horizontal and vertical extensions, along with parallel angled sloping rays, to complete the various shadows. Right: Sun behind viewer. Determine a vanishing point for shadows on the horizon directly opposite to the sun, and a shadow termination point, directly below this.

REFLECTIONS
through the looking glass

Mirrors are fascinating things. Why, for instance, do they flip you left-to-right, but not turn you upside-down? They somehow hint at another world, a counterbalance to this one. Escher's beautiful 1950 study of ripples in a pond (*below*), hints at three worlds, the world of the trees themselves, the world of surfaces and reflections, and the world of fishes below. Why do we speak of "reflecting" on something? Is the mind some kind of surface? Are perceptions some kind of reflections?

The answer to the question above is that mirrors don't flip you—your right side is shown to the right, your left to the left, your top at the top and your feet at the bottom!

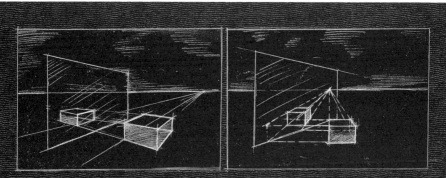

Above: A rectilinear object parallel to a mirror is easy to draw in reflection (left), as is the same object set at 45° to a mirror plane (right). Further mirror angles require the vanishing points to be carefully established. Below: Reflections in water. Drawing by Dan Goodfellow.

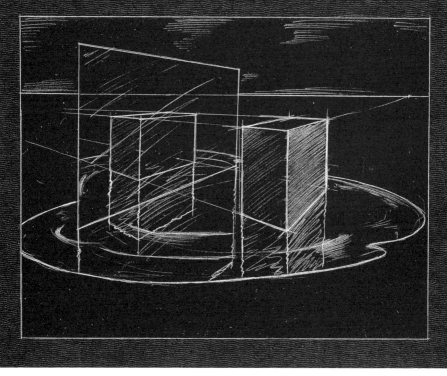

MIRAGES AND PROJECTIONS
nature working on a larger scale

Shadows and reflections occasionally reappear in nature in remarkable, almost magical circumstances. Mysterious and sometimes tempting reflections known as mirages have long been known to haunt the thirsty desert explorer, and a hot road surface likewise can take on a mirror-like appearance from a low angle on a dry day, with illusory puddles perfectly reflecting the sky and overhead bridges. Stratified layers of air function as an overhead mirror not only in deserts but sometimes show a city its own reflection in the sky (*see Paris opposite top left*), or reveal a hidden navy fleet to its enemy (*lower opposite*).

Standing on a hill-top at sunset under special conditions can give rise to a huge shadow cast on to the clouds, an effect known as the "Shadow of the Brokken" (*opposite top right, and below*). A related effect is the 'aura' or glow which can appear centered on the head of one's shadow when cast by moonlight on a misty or dewy night (*opposite center left*).

LIGHT ON FORM
tonal illusions of the third-dimensional kind

We glean information about the form of objects not only from the shadows that they cast (*below*), but also through the subtle shades that appear on their surfaces. All materials, whether glass, wood, metal or plastic, have different reflective properties and opacities which we instinctively read. The merest hint of graded shades gives the eyes subtle clues as to the form, depth and substance of an object, and, with the addition of reflections, can also indicate the positions of other light sources and nearby objects.

In the Victorian engineering engravings opposite, a 2-D outline has become 3-D by the use of shade, here as a textured tone. Tones may be scale illusory, as in fine cross-hatches (the engravers' preference) or printers' halftones (newspaper dots), or actual shades (in paintings or computer screens). Luminosity is a factor in colour (along with hue). When two colours, say red and green, are *equiluminescent* they appear the same in a black-and-white photograph. Artists sometimes use this to place 'wrong' colours of the 'right' luminosity in paintings, to confuse your colour-blind 'what' system while engaging your 'where' system.

ATMOSPHERIC PERSPECTIVE
and depth of focus

Another way the mind reads distance and depth is by the extent to which atmospheric or aerial perspective is brought into play. In the diagram below the trees are all drawn to the same scale, yet the fainter ones are perceived as being more distant. Particulate matter, whether water droplets (as in fog, mist or spray) or smoke or dust particles have the effect of washing out colour saturation and contrast, and on a clear day distant objects are less red, more green-blue-purple. In fog or smoke we may speak of a *vanishing plane*, as objects beyond a certain distance are invisible to the viewer.

Focus perspective, not shown here, is another trick in the illusionist's chest. Out-of-focus or blurry objects, relative to defined in-focus ones, are interpreted by the mind as either close foreground or deep background to the sharp objects depending on certain clues. Some modern artists play with this to great effect.

Atmospheric perspective is widely used in landscape painting. In these pictures by Chinese painters Wang Chien-chang (17th C) and Lou Guan (13th C) we can see the suggestion of distance by the washing out of contrasts and hues in the more distant objects by fog, mountain mists, or waterfall sprays. Again, the mind fills in what the eye cannot see.

RELATIVITY RULES

compared to what

Most perceptions are relative. Have you ever experienced a moment of panic, stuck in a car in heavy traffic, when a truck slowly passes by but gives the impression that *you* are rolling backwards? Likewise, if you place one hand in a bowl of hot water, and the other in a bowl of cold, then remove and plunge them into some tepid water, each will give you a response *relative* to its immediate past, not an objective impression. Then there is the strange case of large and small objects which weigh exactly the same—the larger ones feel considerably lighter than the smaller, just because we *expect* them to weigh more. In a related example (*below*) the two central circles are the same size.

In the powerful tone diagrams opposite, you can actually perceive yourself perceiving tones relative to their background as you struggle with changing tones where there are none. Try covering up the shaded backgrounds to remove the effects.

Likewise, personal wealth, morality, and happiness levels are all experienced as largely relative to those of your friends.

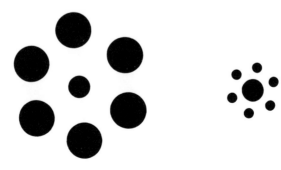

Lower rhombs appear lighter than high

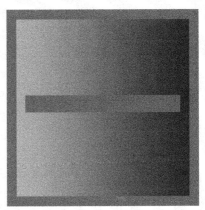

A solid tone bar appears lighter on the right.

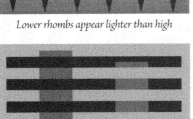

The small rectangles are all the same shade.

Identical squares seem lighter on the right.

The dark squares outside the shadow are the same shade as the light squares in the shadow.

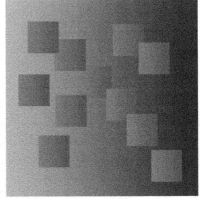

The squares are all the same shade but appear darker on the left, lighter on the right.

FIGURE AND GROUND

either or this not that

The illustrations on this page all show images that are simultaneously two things at once—not a state of affairs our brains enjoy much, so they flip between the two interpretations for us. It is almost impossible to see Napoleon (*opposite top left*) without the trees momentarily becoming a background, and once the trees are studied, Napoleon becomes thin air again. Likewise with the reversing boxes, 13-B puzzle, duck-rabbit, and old and young man and woman below; if your brain allows a second opinion it will try it out to the exclusion of the first. The dangers of alcohol (*opposite top right*) similarly take on a Jekyll/Hyde quality.

Fascinated by this flipping, Escher captured and time-slowed it in his 1938 engraving *Day and Night* (*opposite*), where the black and white points of view become each other's backgrounds.

IMPOSSIBLE OBJECTS
and a fable for the certain

A king, debating the nature of reality with a sage, decided to show him the objective nature of truth. He set up a gallows on the bridge into his castle, and stationed two guards to question people crossing it. If they told the truth they could pass, but if they lied they were to be hanged. In this way truth would be upheld. The following day, the sage approached the castle. The guards asked him his business. "I am on my way to be hanged" he said. They scratched their heads. "If we let him through, he will have lied!" said one. "But if we hang him, he will have been telling the truth!" said the other. Thus the paradoxical and relative nature of things was shown to the king.

Impossible objects similarly confound our certainty of the world by impossibly contradicting themselves. Some only work from one point of view. Like the paradoxical objects of the quantum realm, they neatly demonstrate that over-simplistic perceptions of the world are almost certainly too narrow, cartoon-like, and illusory, and that more subtle perceptions may be helpful.

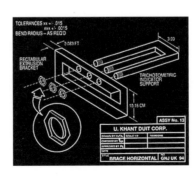

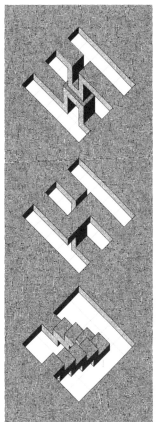

Above left: One of M.C. Escher's (1898-1972) famous impossible buildings, here his Belvedere lithograph from 1958. Above right: Three impossible figures based on the work of Swedish artist Oscar Reutersvard (1915-2002) who drew impossible objects throughout his life. Right: Shepard's elephant looks normal at first glance, but is it really okay? Why does the brain struggle so hard to make sense of it?

CONTEXTUAL CLUES

seeing what you're looking for

It is not easy to see things as they really are. The mind continually attempts to overlay the safe and predictable reality it expects. Take the words in the picture (*opposite top*); try and repeatedly read aloud the colours of the type, rather than the words. Confused? Look at the white triangles below, except there are no white triangles. Can you see a face in the rock (*opposite lower left*)? If you're not careful you could start seeing faces everywhere. How many interpretations of the archaeological survey (*opposite lower right*) can you find? And what about the image below (*center*)? Once you have seen what it is, your brain will never cease to remind you when you look at it. Why do we look for patterns quite so much?

From childhood, patterns of materials, shapes, and functions sink in, so that years later when we see a ceramic bowl, we know it will hold soup, smash if it is dropped, and can even imagine the side of it we cannot see. Our roles in life, choices of friends, enemies, partners, political parties, tastes and personal habits are all limited by illusory patterns we have reinforced with our experiences.

BLACK WHITE BLACK
WHITE BLACK WHITE
BLACK WHITE BLACK
WHITE BLACK WHITE
BLACK WHITE BLACK

Above: Quickly say aloud the colours of the words, not the words themselves. The automatic nature of pattern recognition gets in the way. Below left: This natural rock near Chermoog in Armenia shows the face of the 5th century Saint Vartan (from Simulacra, by John Michell). Below right: The brain continually hypothesizes about what the eyes see. Here various possible huts from one survey (after Richard Gregory).

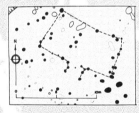

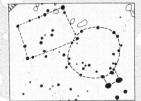

THE CARTOONING MIND

us and them—pressing the right buttons

Our brains have changed very little since the time we were cavemen. We like to think of ourselves as civilized, advanced kinds of folk, but the truth of the matter is that our attention is still easily grabbed by exactly the same basic things as thousands of years ago (*opposite*). These conceptual cartoons, "us/them", "this/that", "better/worse", or "sex/baby/danger", underlie many of our programmed biases, and are regularly accessed by storytellers, advertisers, and politicians. They are all essentially illusory, and it can be a valuable exercise to attempt to see them as such.

In particular, we evolved to respond to immediate personal crises, rather than slowly advancing global ones. This is one reason why, as a species, we find it so hard to stop our current destruction of Eden. A frog, placed in a pan of water slowly heated to boiling, will not jump out to save itself, instead boiling to death, because, like us, it is hard-wired to recognize only *sudden* changes as profoundly dangerous. Similarly, a hungry frog surrounded by sleeping flies will starve to death—the flies aren't buzzing about so it can't 'see' them.

Optical illusions are one of the easiest ways of getting your brain to realize just how clichéd and prejudiced it has probably become.

These headlines could apply to events in any period of history from primitive times to the present. All play on cartoon hopes and fears. Male and female minds fill in assumed details from limited information to an astonishing degree. Opposite: Washerwoman & pail (after Gregory); Mexican frying an egg.

UPSIDE DOWN
left to right and round about

Our brains construct an incredibly real world for us. Most people can navigate their homes in the dark, picturing a shelf and its objects. Even with the lights on, it may be said that the world basically exists *within* us, and probably very differently in each of us too. So to help the mind realize what it is doing, why not try turning the world inside out, back to front, or possibly upside down?

The pictures on this page all show a different take on things when simply rotated. The images below, and the two small faces opposite require a rotation of 180°. Escher's lithograph of staircases has three-fold rotational viewing possibilities (*opposite top left*), and Johann Martin Will's 1780 zoomorphic engraving displays a hidden animal when rotated clockwise by just 90° (*opposite below*).

The odd one out is Margaret Thatcher (*below*). Special areas of the brain that deal with eyes and mouths are much more interested in them alone than whether they are in the right place.

by Gustave Verbeck, 1904

created by Peter Thompson, 1980

MAKING SENSE OF THE LIGHT
centers, curves, and edges

Many people assume that their eyes resemble cameras, projecting the world into their heads for them to watch. The truth is, of course, much stranger, for what inner eyes could be watching anyway?

Human eyes are much more complex than cameras. If you hold red and blue balls out at 90° (to your side) you can see them but not tell their colours apart, as your peripheral vision is specialized for spotting motion, not colour. Your central vision, by contrast, is specialized for fine detail and colour (try reading something you are not looking at). Center-surround arrays of photoreceptors (*shown opposite*) only fire when unbalanced by an edge or point of light crossing them. These have their colour counterparts too, and combine to build curved edges and areas.

As we turn our heads or move our eyes the world stays remarkably stable outside us. Wear a pair of inverting spectacles that turn the world upside down, and lo! after a few days your brain will turn it the right way up again (until you take the glasses off). Our minds even kindly fill our blind spots with informed fiction (*lowest opposite*).

The world is an informed hypothesis.

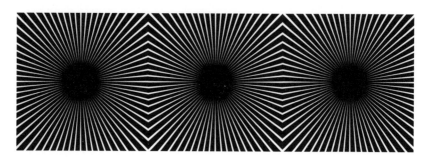

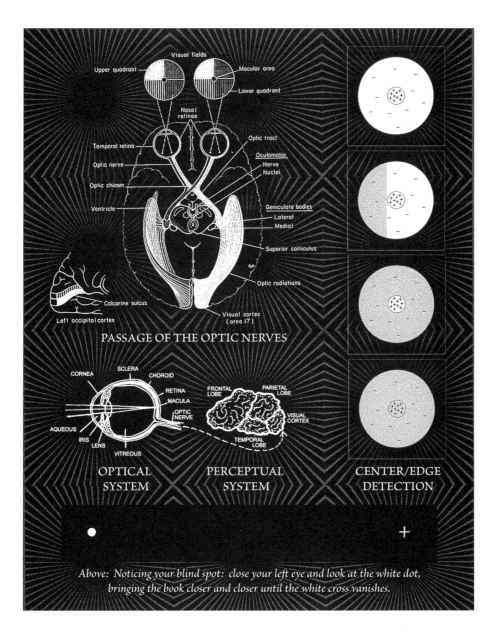

Visual fields

Upper quadrant
Macular area
Lower quadrant

Nasal retinae

Temporal retina
Optic tract

Optic nerve
Oculomotor
Nerve Nuclei

Optic chiasm

Ventricle
Geniculate bodies
Lateral
Medial

Superior colliculus

Optic radiations

Calcarine sulcus

Left occipital cortex
Visual cortex (area 17)

PASSAGE OF THE OPTIC NERVES

CORNEA SCLERA CHOROID
RETINA
MACULA
OPTIC NERVE

FRONTAL LOBE PARIETAL LOBE

VISUAL CORTEX

AQUEOUS

IRIS LENS
TEMPORAL LOBE

VITREOUS

OPTICAL SYSTEM

PERCEPTUAL SYSTEM

CENTER/EDGE DETECTION

Above: Noticing your blind spot: close your left eye and look at the white dot, bringing the book closer and closer until the white cross vanishes.

Perceptual Illusions
malfunctional clues to the system

There are some illusions that really show up the cracks and biases in our basic vision, and a few are presented here. You may need to bring the book a bit closer to your eyes for them to work.

Focus on the dot at the center of either one of the circles below and watch as your eyes grow bored of registering the subtle grays. Next observe the excitation and inhibition operation of your eyes' center-surround cells in the pictures on the top row opposite.

Separate areas of the brain deal with *what* things are and *where* they are. Your slow 'where' system is best at dealing with motion, depth, space and figure/ground perception, whereas your fast 'what' system is colour-blind and much more sensitive to high contrasts. Kitaoka's illusion (*center left*) uses this to great effect.

Center-surround cells are themselves grouped into oriented arrays, which detect curves and angles. The final three images opposite all play on this to create powerful illusions where circles seem like spirals, and straight lines appear warped, or broken.

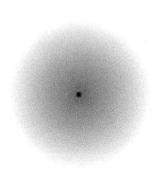 

The Hermann Grid illusion.

The Lingelbach scintillating grid illusion.

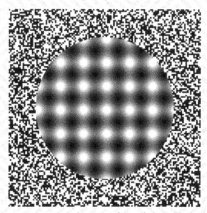

Kitaoka's two surfaces illusion

The Fraser Spiral illusion.

The Bristol Café Wall illusion.

The Poggendorf illusion.

Motion Illusions
the page appeared to be breathing, doctor

You do not have to resort to drugs, psychosis, or meditation to have an alternative experience of reality. The illusions shown here are based on the recent work of Professor Akiyoshi Kitaoka, and can seriously affect your universe as they dance, breathe, and rotate.

From the go-faster stripes on shoes to the cartoonist's just-been-there whizz lines, the illusion of motion is a constant challenge to artists and designers. Spokes on a wheel vanish as it spins faster, and blurred objects are often interpreted as moving. Computer and television screens need to be completely redrawn every twenty-fifth of a second to fool your brain into seeing a continuous moving image. Many simple organisms only see things when they change, and most people are highly stimulated by motion (e.g., driving a car). Some people get hooked on flux, others fear it, while Taoists and Buddhists recommend sitting by a waterfall and contemplating life as stillness in motion.

IT'S MAGIC

the highest and lowest forms of trickery

Sometimes things happen which seem impossible. When the writing on the wall appeared at Belshazzar's Feast, while some read it, and others either called for more or ran away in terror, at least a few must have wondered how it was done. Just as our senses can be fooled, so can our expectations of what is possible. The pictures shown here are all well-known effects that can seem magical if one does not know their secrets. Particularly entrancing to the mind are manifestations or disappearances, which tend to be explained away as having either psychological (hallucinatory), technological (trickery or alien), or spiritual (divine or psychic) causes.

The glass in the stage ghost illusion (*below*) is a great metaphor.

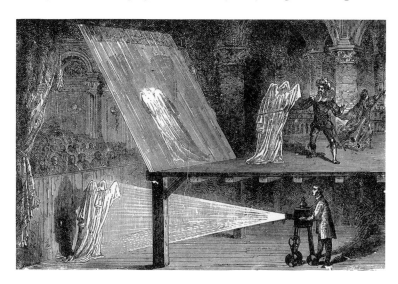

Above left: Scratching a tablecloth causes a coin to move from under a glass. Above right: Joseph Ferdinand Plateau's revolutionary Phenokistoscope, which produced the illusion of moving pictures. Below left: Alexander Graham Bell's new telephonic invention must have seemed like magic to many people. Below right: A Gyroscope magically defies gravity.

OTHER SENSES
seeing things differently

Next time you see a bee buzzing about a flower, stop to think that the bee is seeing a different flower than you are. Bees perceive ultraviolet light, and flowers use this fact to advertise themselves in higher frequencies (shorter wavelengths) than we can detect. The picture (*opposite top*) shows what the bee might be seeing.

Some people (1 in 20) are blessed with a strange condition called *synesthesia* where their auditory inputs, i.e., words and music, are translated into colours and shapes (*lower opposite*). They often have better memories and make better musicians than the rest of us.

Other people can clearly see the glowing auras (magnetic fields) of living things, sometimes with specific colours that give clues to their health. Some see a vertical line of glowing spinning wheels up the body (the chakras of Indian Tantra) or filigree lines and pinpricks of light (the meridians and nodal points of Chinese medicine).

We can hardly imagine what a bat really 'sees' with its ears, nor how the bumps on its back might have evolved to echo sensual music to a mate. In a way we really are as blind as bats ourselves.

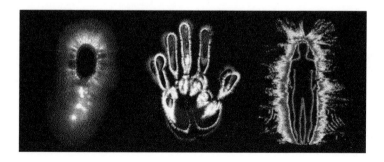

Above: The top row shows three species of flower as seen by human eyes, and below, the same flowers as seen by a bee in ultraviolet (photo: Bjørn Rørslett). Below: An artist's impression of the kind of overlay that is seen by someone who is synesthetic, as auditory signals are processed by the visual part of the brain to produce colours and shapes. Opposite: Kirlian (aura) photography.

Rainbows and Moonbows

you never see a rainbow from the side

A rainbow (or its rarer nocturnal sister, a moonbow) is a great analogue of precisely how little we see of the world. That thin ribbon of colored light is itself an accurate snapshot of the tiny slice of the electromagnetic spectrum that our senses can pick up in any detail. The rest of the spectrum (which is most of it) we are blind to, and today fill with radio, phone, and microwave internet signals, using digital white noise (whose only natural parallel is radioactive decay).

Most things we can see are not really there, atoms being almost entirely empty space, but rainbows and lunar halos (*lower opposite*) are particularly thought-provoking because they really aren't there at all. Or are they? Like the ladder of light you see across the ocean at sunset which always points just to you, rainbows are always centered, exactly facing each individual, in a different place in the world for each observer, a kind of inversion of normal perspective and a beautiful reminder of the relativistic nature of perception.

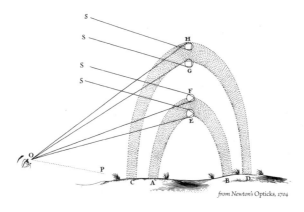

from Newton's Opticks, *1704*

Halos and Glories
windows into other worlds

The figure below shows a very rare atmospheric effect called a "lunar glory", caused by fine ice particles high in the atmosphere. Halos, glories, and rainbows are wonderful reminders that what we see is light, and light alone. Grass looks green but is in fact every colour but green, green being the one colour it reflects and does not absorb. The true nature of objects is hidden from us, the other side of the mirrors which reflect impressions into our eyes and minds.

Opposite we see the northern lights over Iceland, a visual clue to the extraordinary electromagnetic world of which we see such a tiny part and yet our thoughts are largely made of.

GETTING REAL
looking at the world in a new way

In *The Republic* the Greek philosopher Plato [428-347 BC] likens our lot to that of someone living in a cave, watching shadows on a wall, wondering what is casting them. It is incredible to think that the world we see is simply a product of our senses and the systems we use to make sense of them—the beautiful and extraordinary world out there is, for all non-practical purposes, still essentially a mystery. How do we really know we are not yukka plants on Venus dreaming all of this? Just because our senses are being tickled?

Perhaps this is why so many sages throughout the ages have referred to the spiritual journey as an "awakening", recommending exercises that constantly improve and refine all of our senses.

Anyway, I hope this little exploration has thrown some new light on these things, refreshed your perspective somewhat . . . See you!

BOOK V

Above: 6th century Byzantine mosaic, Ravenna, Italy, from Hessemer,
Arabische und Alt-Italienische Bau-Verzierungen, *1800. Opposite:*
Tattoo design from the Marqusas Islands. Overleaf: a sample of nature's infinite
symmetrical variety: Ernst Haekel's drawings of various species of diatoms.

SYMMETRY

The Ordering Principal

David Wade

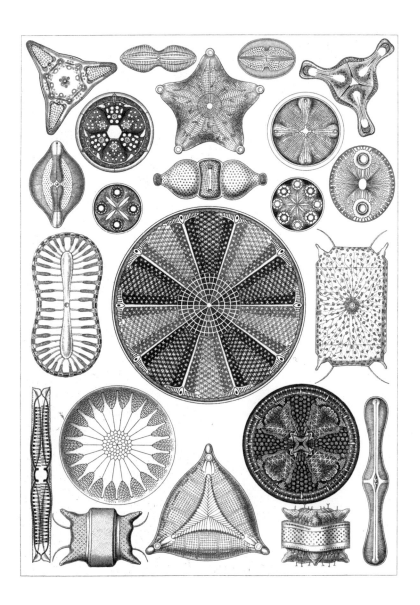

INTRODUCTION

Symmetry has a very wide appeal; it is of as much interest to mathematicians as it is to artists, and is as relevant to physics as it is to architecture. In fact, many other disciplines lay their own claims on the subject, each having their own ideas of what symmetry is, or should be. Clearly, whatever approach is taken, we are dealing here with a universal principle, although, in our day-to-day experience conspicuous symmetries are comparatively rare and most are far from obvious. So what is symmetry? Are there general terms for it? Can it, indeed, be clearly defined at all?

On investigation, it soon becomes clear that the whole field is hedged about with paradox. To begin with, any notion of symmetry is completely entangled with that of asymmetry; we can scarcely conceive of the former without invoking thoughts of the latter (as with the related concepts of order and disorder)—and there are other dualities. Symmetry precepts are always involved with categorization, with classification and observed regularities; in short, with limits. But in itself symmetry is unlimited; there is nowhere that its principles do not penetrate. In addition, symmetry principles are characterized by a quietude, a stillness that is somehow beyond the bustling world; yet, in one way or another, they are almost always involved with transformation, disturbance, or movement.

The more deeply one investigates this subject the more apparent it becomes that this is at the same time one of the most mundane and extensive areas of study, and that, in the final analysis, it remains one of the most mysterious.

ARRAYS

the regular disposition of elements

When it comes to understanding just what the common factors are among the many and various aspects of symmetry, the notions of *congruence* and *periodicity* take us a long way. Most symmetries present these aspects in one form or another, and the absence of one or the other usually leads to a reduction, or even a lack of symmetry.

For instance: two like objects, in no particular relation with each other, are merely similar (since although they may be congruent they are not arranged in any order) (*1, opposite*). The addition of a third object allows a degree of regularity to come into play, creating the basis of a recognizable pattern (*2*). So, in its simplest form, symmetry is expressed as a regularly repeating figure along a line (*below*), a series that may easily be extended into an *array* (*3*). Simple arrangements of this kind can in theory be indefinitely extended, but symmetry will be maintained just so long as both the repeating element and the spacing remain consistent.

We can recognize array symmetries in many natural formations, from the familiar rows of kernels in sweet corn (*4*), to the patterns of scales in fish and reptiles (*5*). And of course such regular arrangements feature in a great deal of human art and artefacts—as in the decorated shaman's cloak opposite (*6*). Naturally, there are often functional as well as aesthetic criteria operating in the formation of arrays, evident in the sort of patterns created by brickwork and roof-tiles (*7,8*).

1. *Mere similarity.*

2. *A pattern emerges with three elements.*

3. *Symmetrical arrays involve regular spacing. In essence, all symmetries are based on 'invariance' or 'self-coincidence'. In geometric symmetry, the imagined movement that is necessary to achieve this, whether it involves simple repetition, reflection, or rotation (see next page), is known as an isometry (see page 386).*

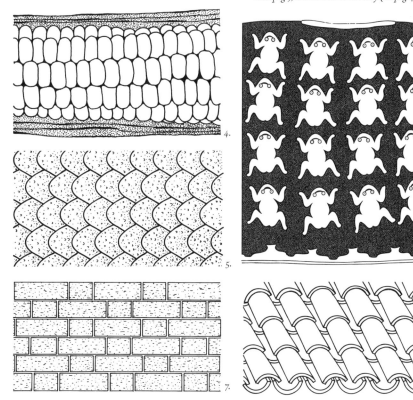

ROTATIONS AND REFLECTION
point symmetries

There are two further basic expressions of symmetry, *rotation* and *reflection*, and each of these relies on the notion of *congruence*, a general correspondence between each part of an element, however expressed (*below*). In simple rotational symmetry the component parts are laid at regular intervals around a central point (*1-4*).

Because the elements in these symmetries are simple unreversed replicas of each other, they are described as being *directly congruent*. In reflection symmetry, by contrast, the reversed elements are arranged about a mirror line, and so are *oppositely congruent* (*5,6*). Because the central point or line remains fixed in reflections and rotations, these are collectively known as *point symmetries*.

In its most basic form, rotational symmetry involves just two components arranged around a center. Ordinary playing cards are of this kind—any cut through the center of a card results in two identical halves. The triskelion symbol consists of three rotated parts; a swastika of four, and so on—with no upward limit to the number, other than the quantity of repeats that can be arranged around a given center.

Rotational and reflection symmetries can also be combined, in which case the lines of reflection intersect at a central point of rotation. Figures and objects of this kind are described as having *dihedral* symmetry (*7*).

 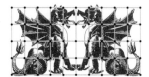 

1. The simplest form of rotation around a center, using just two elements

2. Playing-cards are probably the most familiar example of 2-rotation symmetry, demonstrating a self-coincidence of 180° (note that there is no reflection here).

3. Rotational symmetry may involve any number of elements

4. Triskelion, swastika, and window motifs using 3-, 4- and 5- rotational symmetry , with self-coincidences of 120°, 90° and 72° respectively.

5. Reflection about a line

6. Motifs with only reflection symmetry are among the most commonly found.

7. Dihedral symmetry

8. Motifs demonstrating dihedral symmetry, combining reflection and rotation.

GEOMETRIC SELF-SIMILARITY
gnomons and other self-similar figures

Symmetry is an invariable characteristic of both growth and form, whether in simple or complex, living or non-living, systems.

The *gnomon* demonstrates one of the simplest examples of geometrical growth (*see below*). The principle is this: when a gnomon is added to another figure, that figure is enlarged but retains its general shape—and this can be carried on indefinitely. This is essentially what happens in the elaborate forms created by shells and horns, where new growth is added to dead tissue.

Dilation symmetries also produce figures that are geometrically similar to an original. These derive from the enlargement (or reduction) of a form by way of lines radiating from a center. Dilation symmetries, which may extend from the infinitely small to the infinitely large, can use any angle from a center (*1*), or any regular division of the circle (*2*), or its entirety (*3*).

Dilation may also be linked to rotation, producing *continuous* symmetries that can give rise to equiangular spirals (*4*) (of which more later), or discontinuous symmetries (*5*), (in which case the increments are not necessarily a sub-multiple of a complete turn). Dilation symmetries also occur in three-dimensional space. As can be seen, spiral symmetries are intimately connected with the movements of rotation and dilation, and tend to emerge whenever these are combined.

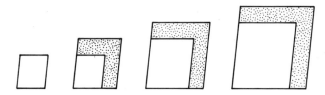

1. Dilation symmetries involve regular increase (or decrease)

2. Point-centered dilation

3. Dilation over 360°

4. Dilation combined with rotation

5. Discontinuous rotated dilation

6. Similarity symmetries arising from the regular arrangement of figures

RADIAL
centered symmetries

Radial symmetries are probably the most familiar of all regular arrangements. Being finite, they belong to the broad category of point-group symmetries—and they come in three distinct forms.

In two dimensions they are centered on a point in the plane, showing rotational symmetry, with any number of regular divisions of the circle; reflection is also frequently incorporated, creating dihedral symmetries (*1*). Many flowers show this arrangement, and of course centered, radial motifs appear in the decorative art of practically every culture.

In three dimensions, radial symmetries are either centered on a point in space, where each path fans out from the center to every outlying point (as in an explosion) (*2*); or they have a polar axis of rotation, typically cylindrical or conical (*3*). These last are the characteristic symmetries of plants.

The great majority of flowers have petal arrangements using a number taken from the Fibonacci series, i.e. 3, 5, 8, 13, 21 etc. (*more on this magical sequence on page 266*). The celebrated symmetry of snow-crystals, by contrast, is always six-pointed. As well as being a favoured symmetry of decorative motifs, planar-radial symmetry is also the most useful configuration for any device involving rotary motion—particularly the wheel in its various manifestations.

Radial symmetries of all kinds, being finite, belong to the category of point-group symmetries.

1. 2-D radial symmetry   2. 3-D radial symmetry   3. Radial symmetries around a polar axis

SECTIONS AND SKELETONS
internal symmetries of plants and animals

The great majority of plants express radial symmetry in one form or another. In fact the great divide between the kingdoms of plants and animals is reflected in their dominant symmetries. Because plants are usually fixed and nonmotile they tend to be radial, whereas the majority of animals move of their own volition and as a result are *bilateral,* or, more accurately, *dorsiventral (see page 258).*

The trunks and branches of trees usually indicate a radial arrangement in transverse cross-section, and the same is true of roots and vertical stems in general (*1*). Most regular (actinomorphic) flowers have a radial symmetry, as do many inflorescences (*2*). Placentation, too, is invariably arranged on a symmetrical plan (*below*). Mushrooms, mosses and the tubular leaves of rushes also adopt this symmetry.

Sessile animals, i.e. those which are attached and unable to move under their own power, usually have a plant-like, radial symmetry. The predominant number of these are marine creatures, such as sea-anemones and sea-urchins (*3*). Starfish and star corals are likewise center-structured. The jewel-like skeletons of the marine Protozoa (which include the Radiolaria and Foraminifera), which are found in such profusion in the seas that they account for up to 30% of ocean sediments, also tend to adopt radial symmetries in their body form (*4*).

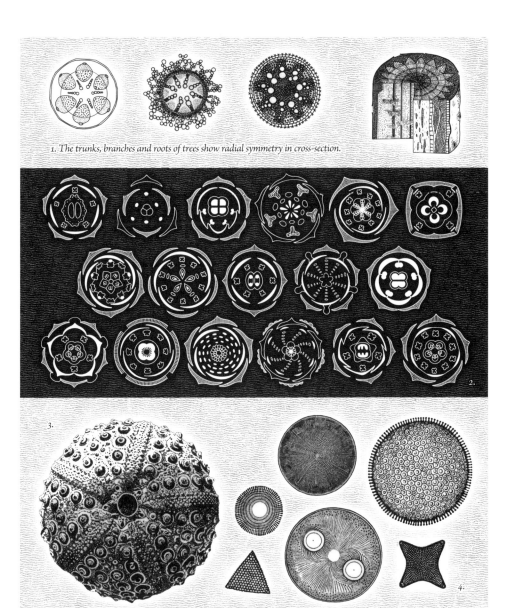

1. *The trunks, branches and roots of trees show radial symmetry in cross-section.*

SPHERICAL
the perfect three-dimensional symmetry

Just as the circle is the perfect figure in two dimensions, an ideal sphere is a perfect, radially symmetric, 3-D body. Both were known as such by the ancient Greeks, and were considered divine (the philosopher Xenophanes going so far as to replace the old pantheon of Gods with a single deity, which he assumed to be spherical). Pythagoras was the first to teach that the Earth itself was spherical in shape; more recent cosmologists have suggested that the entire expanding cosmos has the overall symmetry of a sphere. Interestingly, this shape appears at the very opposite extremes of scale—stars, planets, moons, the Oort cloud, and the globular clusters of galaxies are all spherical (1), and so are small water droplets. Each owe their symmetrical regularity to the fact that they are shaped by a single dominant force; the latter to surface tension, all of the former to gravity (which itself is spherically symmetric).

The action of surface tension is also responsible for the spherical shape of a host of microscopic creatures (2). These tend to be virtually fluid in composition and have to maintain an internal pressure that is in balance with that of their surrounding medium. In fact, most spherical creatures tend to be very small (where the distorting effects of gravity are minimized), and to live in water. The great majority of these have little or no motivity. In practical terms a sphere represents the smallest surface area for a given volume, which is why so many fruit (3) and eggs (4) are this shape. Since it minimizes surface area, and presents the same profile on every side, the sphere also offers a natural defense against predation. Hence the evolved response in those species which, whilst not spherical to begin with, roll themselves up into balls when attacked (5).

Symmetries in 3-D
spatial isometries

Just as the sphere is the three-dimensional equivalent of the perfect symmetry of the two-dimensional circle, the *transformations* of figures in space correspond with that of the regular division of the plane that we saw earlier, and similar isometric principles are involved (*1-6*).

If we look to the ways in which space can be symmetrically partitioned, the most elementary divisions follow from the regular plane-filling figures. So, just as the equilateral triangle, square, and hexagon fill two dimensions, the prisms based on these will completely fill space (*7*). When it comes to space-fillers that are regular in all directions the options are rather less obvious, but include the cube, the truncated octahedron (*5*), the cuboctahedral system (*8*) and the rhombic dodecahedron (*9*). The three spherical symmetrical systems (*10*) have a particular bearing on the regular solid figures.

Interestingly, among the huge variety of regular figures, nature consistently chooses one family above all others, namely, the pentagonal dodecahedra. These shapes, made up of hexagons and pentagons, are adopted by forms as diverse as the Fullerene molecule (*a*), soot-particles (*b*), radiolaria (*c*), and viruses (*d, below*). The intriguing aspect of these shapes, and perhaps the key to their usefulness in nature, is that while hexagons themselves cannot enclose space, any number can be enabled to do so with the addition of just twelve pentagons.

a. *b.* *c.* *d.*

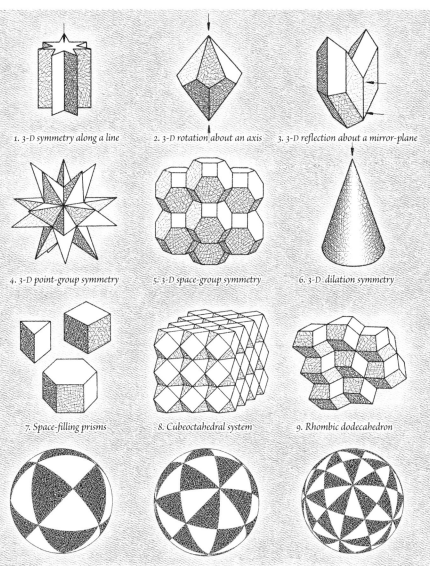

1. 3-D symmetry along a line   2. 3-D rotation about an axis   3. 3-D reflection about a mirror-plane

4. 3-D point-group symmetry   5. 3-D space-group symmetry   6. 3-D dilation symmetry

7. Space-filling prisms   8. Cubeoctahedral system   9. Rhombic dodecahedron

10. The three spherical systems of symmetry: tetrahedral, octahedral, and icosahedral.

STACKING AND PACKING
fruit, froth, foams, and other space-fillers

Finding the easiest and most efficient way of stacking a pile of oranges in a given area is one of those deceptively simple-sounding tasks that have far-reaching mathematical ramifications. The problem is easy enough to begin with. The obvious ways of packing spherical objects together are the triangular and square arrangements, (*1-3*); these configurations obviously relate to the regular division of the plane (*see page 387*). Having laid out the fruit in either of these patterns it is difficult to stack a second layer other than in the interstices formed by the first. They tend to fall, literally, into a pattern of minimum energy. There are three distinct cubic arrangements (*4, 5, 6*), but the face-centered assembly (*6*) has been shown to be the most efficient—although a final proof came only 400 years after Kepler first proposed it.

In many other circumstances, however, three-way junctions of 120° provide the most economical systems. Bee-cells, of course, are the classic example. They use the minimum amount of wax to create storage containers for their honey (*7*). Small groups of soap bubbles with free boundaries pull themselves into this efficient angular formation, known as the Plateau border (*8*).

When it comes to larger clusters of soap-bubbles, however, an entirely different magic angle is involved, namely 109.471°. In any froth or elastic foam (*9*) the interior surfaces tend to meet at this angle—which is exactly that formed by a line from the center to the corner of a tetrahedron (*10*). Interestingly, as a solid figure, the tetrahedron by itself will not completely fill space—although it will in combination with the octahedron.

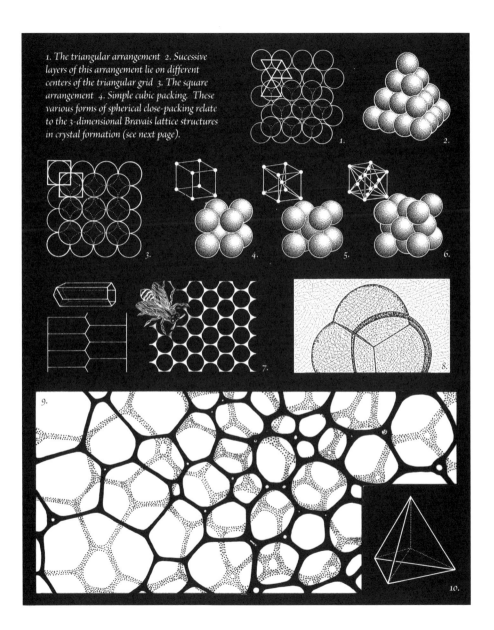

1. The triangular arrangement 2. Sucessive layers of this arrangement lie on different centers of the triangular grid 3. The square arrangement 4. Simple cubic packing. These various forms of spherical close-packing relate to the 3-dimensional Bravais lattice structures in crystal formation (see next page).

1.

2.

3.

4.

5.

6.

7.

8.

9.

10.

THE CRYSTALLINE WORLD
the stronghold of symmetrical order

Of all natural objects, well-formed crystals make the closest approximation to the mathematical purity of the regular solids (*shown at the bottom of page 387*), and they can indeed assume some of these shapes, although not all. However, the fascinating, pristine beauty of specimen crystals is simply an externalisation of an even more impressive internal structure—the crystalline state, with its constituent molecules lined up in tens, or even hundreds of millions, of obedient, identical molecules, is a realm of almost inconceivable orderliness.

Crystals of different substances adopt a wide range of different and characteristic forms, but their regularities are based on the unit-cell arrangements of one or other of just fourteen lattice structures (*below*). These Bravais lattices, the equivalent of 2-D graphs, enable the component molecules to repeat indefinitely in three different spatial directions, much like the 'repeat' of a wallpaper pattern.

The early scientific investigation of crystals was primarily concerned with classification, primarily in terms of the symmetries involved. By the mid-19th century crystals had been placed in thirty-two distinct classes, and by the end of that century all 230 possible space-groups had been listed by the Russian crystallographer Federov.

The discovery of X-ray diffraction in the early 20th century, however, completely transformed the science. Systematic analysis of the symmetrical patterns thrown onto a photographic plate by this method revealed for the first time the extraordinary internal world of crystals.

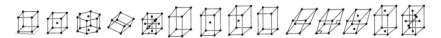

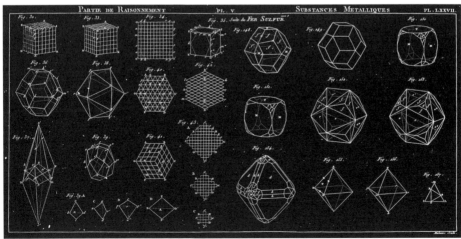

BASIC STUFF

symmetries at the heart of matter

Toward the end of the 19th century the pioneering physicist Pierre Curie stated what he felt to be a universal principle of physics, to the effect that symmetric causes will necessarily lead to equally symmetric effects. Now, as a general principle he was quite wrong, for symmetries are not always linked in the way that he implied. But his intuition of symmetric continuity is certainly true at the more basic levels of matter. The highly ordered world of the crystalline state, exposed to view by X-ray crystallography (1), is entirely determined by the underlying symmetries of the atomic and sub-atomic realms.

Mendeleev's Periodic Table, which placed the elements into a rational series, was one of the great milestones of 19th-century, classical physics. But early on in the 20th century it became clear that the properties of the elements were, in fact, reflecting regularities within the internal structures of their component atoms. As atomic theories developed further it became apparent that all chemical properties derived from the numbers of protons and electrons in their respective atomic structures, allowing them to group in orderly molecular arrangements (2).

By the 1960s it was realized that although the 'orbiting' electrons (3) were indeed fundamental particles, the protons and neutrons of the nucleus (4) were made up of yet smaller components—hadrons and leptons. The hadrons, in turn, are combinations of quarks which come together in the beautiful symmetries of the famous "8-fold way" (5).

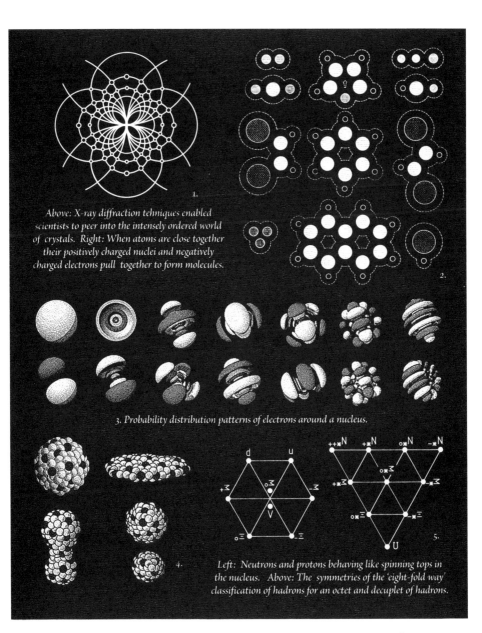

Above: X-ray diffraction tehniques enabled scientists to peer into the intensely ordered world of crystals. Right: When atoms are close together their positively charged nuclei and negatively charged electrons pull together to form molecules.

3. Probability distribution patterns of electrons around a nucleus.

Left: Neutrons and protons behaving like spinning tops in the nucleus. Above: The symmetries of the 'eight-fold way' classification of hadrons for an octet and decuplet of hadrons.

DORSIVENTRALITY
the symmetry of moving creatures

Animals, by definition, are multi-cellular, food-eating creatures, and practically all are capable of some form of motion; naturally, these attributes govern their general form. Whether an animal walks on the ground or burrows through it, whether it swims through water or flies through the air, its body will be made up of left and right sides that are roughly mirror versions of each other. Since they also have a front and a back (and usually a distinct top and bottom) they are not merely bilateral, but dorsiventral. This is the best arrangement to have if you need to move in a directed way (*see examples opposite*). It is not only animals that express this symmetry; forward-moving vehicles, such as automobiles, boats, airplanes etc, are, by necessity, symmetrically disposed along similar lines.

There are other characteristics of animal dorsiventrality that developed alongside the power of locomotion. A strong forward movement obviously requires a forward-placed vision to see where one is going, and a forward-placed mouth to feed efficiently. Fins and limbs, by contrast, are best placed laterally, in symmetrically balanced positions.

Although, for the reasons given above, dorsiventrality is the abiding symmetry of the animal kingdom, it is also fairly common in the plant world—typically in zygomorphic (irregular) flowers, in the great majority of leaf forms (*below*), and in many leaf arrangements.

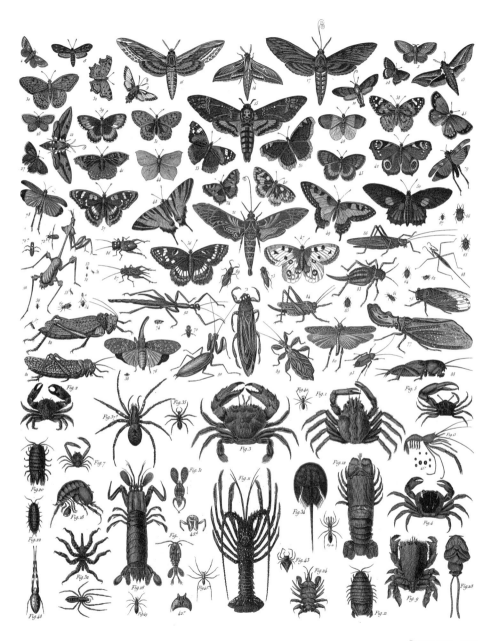

ENANTIOMORPHY
left- and right-handedness

Amongst other things, our dorsiventral body-form gives us a pair of hands that are similar in most respects, except that they are mirror-reversed. The same is true of our feet, of course, and of horns and butterfly wings and many other animal features (*1*). But the possibility for a figure, or an object, to exist in two distinct forms in this way is not limited to the mirror-symmetries adopted by living organisms. Any spiral, for instance, has to choose whether to go clockwise or anti-clockwise on the page (*2*), and similarly, all helices can appear in one or other of two different ways in three dimensions (*3*).

In fact the possibility of alternate forms applies to any object, animate or inanimate, that has a twist in its structure. Mollusk shells are found as both left-handed and right-handed types (some species opt for a particular handedness, in others the choice appears to be random) (*4*). There is a somewhat similar situation in the familiar twisting habits of vines and other climbing plants (the majority opt for right-handedness, but a substantial minority are lefties).

In chemistry this phenomenon is known as chirality—the most common mineral with this trait being quartz (*5*). Chirality is of particular importance in the field of organic chemistry, since many biological molecules are homochiral, that is to say, are of the same handedness, including amino acids (which are the components of proteins), and DNA (*6*). This, in effect, means that the entire chemical basis of life itself is chiral. At some early stage in the origins of life on Earth the earliest molecules to master the art of self-replication opted for a particular stereo-chemical profile, and in so doing determined the entire, right-handed, course of evolution.

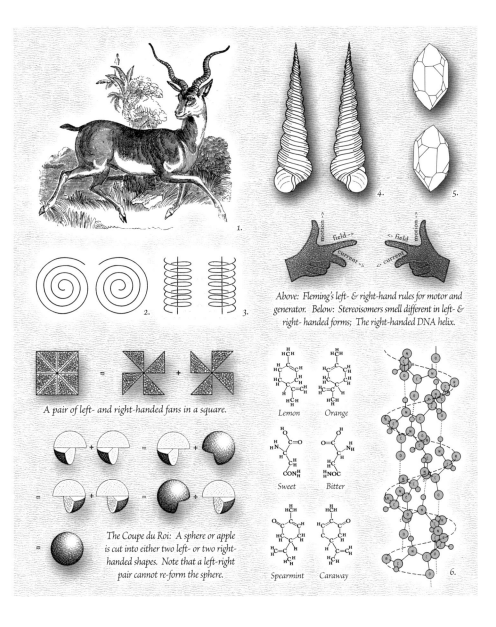

1.

4.

5.

2.

3.

Above: Fleming's left- & right-hand rules for motor and generator. Below: Stereoisomers smell different in left- & right-handed forms; The right-handed DNA helix.

A pair of left- and right-handed fans in a square.

Lemon *Orange*

Sweet *Bitter*

The Coupe du Roi: A sphere or apple is cut into either two left- or two right-handed shapes. Note that a left-right pair cannot re-form the sphere.

Spearmint *Caraway*

6.

CURVATURE AND FLOW
waves and vortices, parabola and ellipses

As we have considered symmetry thus far, the emphasis has been on the more static geometries of rotation, reflection, etc. With symmetries of curvature, many of which are implicated in motion and growth, these principles are extended to the dynamic (*1-3*).

The *conic sections* (*4*) were first investigated by Menaechmus in Plato's Academy in the 4th century BC, but it was not until the Renaissance that the importance of their role in physics began to be realized. In 1602 Galileo proved that the trajectory of a thrown object described a parabola. Not long after this Kepler discovered the elliptical nature of planetary motion. Later, it was realized that the hyperbolic curves could represent any relationship in which one quantity varied inversely to another (as in Boyle's Law). Discoveries of this kind epitomize the way in which a broader understanding of the symmetry principles inherent in mathematics began to uncover the hidden unity of nature.

Wave-forms also express symmetry, both in their length and period; a simple sine curve can be thought of as a projection on a plane of the path of a point moving round a circle at a uniform speed (*5*). In fact, circular motion is a component of any wave-like event. If this movement is regularly increased or diminished it produces a characteristic sine configuration.

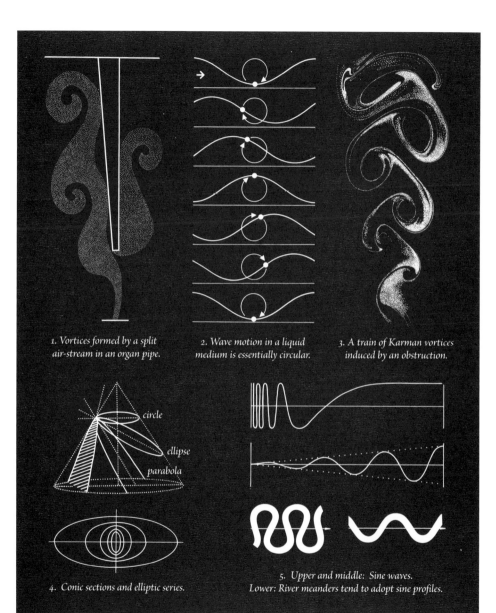

1. Vortices formed by a split air-stream in an organ pipe.

2. Wave motion in a liquid medium is essentially circular.

3. A train of Karman vortices induced by an obstruction.

circle

ellipse

parabola

4. Conic sections and elliptic series.

5. Upper and middle: Sine waves.
Lower: River meanders tend to adopt sine profiles.

SPIRALS AND HELICES
natures favourite structures

Of all the regular curves, *spirals* and *helices* are probably the most common. They are found throughout the natural world, in many forms, at every scale of existence—in spider-webs (*1*), galaxies (*2*) and particle tracks (*3*); in animal horns (*4*), sea-shells (*5*), plant structures, and DNA (*6*). It is clearly one of nature's favourite patterns.

In purely geometric terms, the common planar spirals are of three principle types (*below*): the Archimedean (*a*), the Logarithmic (*b*), and the Fermat (*c*). The Archimedean spiral is perhaps the simplest, consisting of a series of parallel, equidistant lines (as in old vinyl records). Logarithmic (or growth) spirals are the most intriguing and complex of all, particularly the 'golden' spiral (*8*) that is associated with the Fibonacci series (*see next page*). Logarithmic spirals in general have the property of self-similarity, i.e., of looking the same at every scale. In the Fermat (or parabolic) spiral, successive whorls enclose equal increments of area, which accounts for its appearance in phyllotaxis, the arrangements of leaves and florets on a stem (and in coffee-cups).

Helices are symmetrical about an axis, so always have a particular 'handedness' (*d*). Dilation symmetry can apply to helices, gradually increasing their width (*e*), and of course they may be expressed in any number of strands, in the way that ropes are laid (*f*).

a.   *b.*   *c.*   *d.*   *e.*   *f.*

7. *An evolute spiral.*

8. *The 'golden' logarithmic spiral.*

FABULOUS FIBONACCI

golden angles and a golden number

Around the end of the 12th century a young Italian customs officer became intrigued by (and gave his name to) a number series that has fascinated mathematicians ever since. Nicknamed "Fibonacci", Leonardo of Pisa had discovered the cumulative progression where each number is the sum of the preceding two, i.e., 1, 1, 2, 3, 5, 8, 13, 21, 34 etc. He also recognized that this series has some very special mathematical properties. The Fibonacci numbers are frequently involved in plant growth patterns, notably in petal and seed arrangements. Flower petals are almost invariably fibonaccian in number; fir-cones use series of 3 and 5 (or 5 and 8) intertwined spirals; pineapples have 8 rows of scales winding one way, 13 the other way—and so on. The series is also found in phyllotaxy, the configurations of leaves and branches in plants.

The Fibonacci series is focussed on the "golden number", Φ, or *phi*— as they get higher the ratio between successive numbers gets closer and closer to 1.618. There is a related quality too in the format of successive primordia in phyllotaxy which use the 'golden' angle of 137.5° ($360°/Φ^2$). This arrangement provides the most efficient use of space in the succession of branches, leaves and flowers. Fibonacci patterns are not restricted to organic formations; they have been observed in many aspects of the physical world, from nanoparticles to black holes.

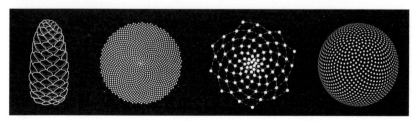

1. *Phyllotaxis, order 13:8 in a cactus.* 2. *Order 8:5, 8 leaves forming in 5 anticlockwise turns, with every 8th leaf above another* 3. *Another example of 8:5 phyllotaxis.* 4. *A rare case of Lucas phyllotaxis, order 11:7 (see page 312).* 5. *A sunflower head demonstrates 89:55 Fibonacci phyllotaxis on a Fermat spiral. Count the spirals each way.*

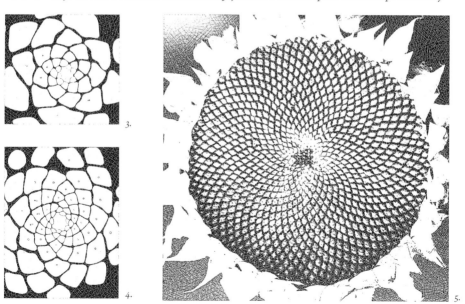

BRANCHING SYSTEMS
patterns of distribution

Branched networks can be thought of as having a real existence, like those of trees, rivers, etc, or simply as mental concepts that exist independently of any physical representation. In the latter case, fairly complex systems can be generated from quite simple rules (*lower opp.*).

One of the more fascinating aspects of branching is that similar habits can be expressed in entirely different settings; there are, for instance, branching hierarchies in lightning strikes that closely resemble those in river systems. There may even be a close correspondence between formations that disperse and those that concentrate (*below*). In either case, functioning branching systems involve the efficient distribution of energy in one form or another—they are the simplest way to connect every part of a given area using the shortest overall distance (or least work).

The hidden symmetries operating within branching formations concern the rates and ratios of *bifurcation*. In a simple progression, for instance, three streamlets may feed into a stream, three streams into each tributary, and finally, three tributaries into a river. This sort of progression is, in fact, a common pattern, found not only in rivers and plants, but in animal vascular systems. Although the rules that determine branching in nature tend to be more involved than this, nevertheless, relatively simple algorithms may create highly complex forms.

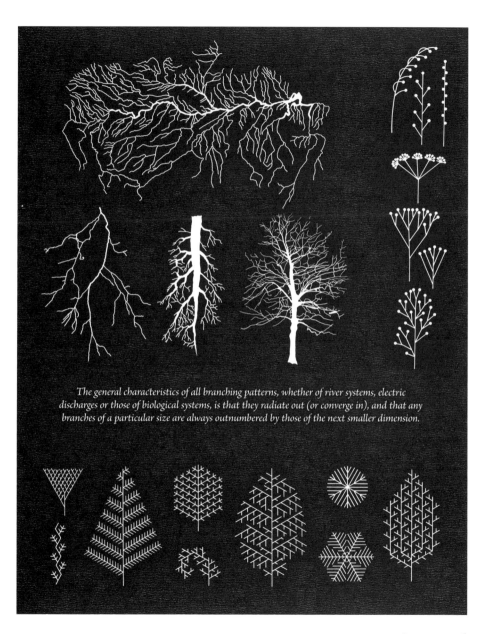

The general characteristics of all branching patterns, whether of river systems, electric discharges or those of biological systems, is that they radiate out (or converge in), and that any branches of a particular size are always outnumbered by those of the next smaller dimension.

Fascinating Fractals

self-consistency to the nth degree

There are many natural phenomena, perhaps the greater part, about which the term "symmetrical" seems to have little relevance. The amorphous shapes of clouds, the rugged contours of mountains, the turbulence of streams, the patchiness of lichen, etc, especially taken together, create a distinct impression of confused irregularity. But there are consistencies in all of these things, the uncovering of which has greatly extended the notion of self-similarity, and of symmetry itself.

Many natural formations, even though they may appear highly complex and irregular, possess a recognizable statistical self-similarity. This means that they look the same across a range of different scales, and the degree of this *fractality* can be accurately measured. A converse application of this notion is that highly complex phenomena may have a hidden order—that relatively simple formulae can create highly involved figures. The renowned Mandelbrot set (*background, opposite*) is probably the best known and most complex example of this effect.

In fact, many organic structures exhibit the *fractal* properties of self-similarity; animal circulatory systems, for instance. The branching, systems of blood vessels, which repeat on an ever-reducing scale, allow the most efficient circulation of blood to every part of the body.

In mathematics many kinds of fractals are unlimited by scale and can, in theory, go on to infinity, but this is seldom the case in the real world, especially in living creatures where the rule is "fitness for purpose". Blood-vessels do not reduce indefinitely, any more than the whorls-within-whorls of the fractal cauliflower extend to infinity. Nature uses fractal geometry where it is advantageous.

Sierpinski gasket *Koch snowflake* *Sierpinski carpet/cube* *Sierpinski hexagon*

Fractals are linked to enormous advances in computer science and Chaos Theory, but their geometry has a history of its own. The above forms, dating from the early 20th century, were originally seen as mathematical curiosities that demonstrated the mingling of finite spaces and infinite boundaries.

PENROSE TILINGS & QUASICRYSTALS
surprising five-fold symmetries

In the mid-1980s the world of crystallography was taken aback by the announcement of an entirely new kind of material, midway between the crystalline and amorphous states. What was particularly surprising about this new state of matter was that it appeared to be based on a 5-fold symmetry, apparently violating the basic laws of crystallography. Until this time the conventional understanding was that only 2-, 3-, 4- and 6-fold symmetries could create the lattice structure on which crystals were formed. The new material, Shechtmanite (*3*) (named after its discoverer), soon became classified as a *quasicrystal*, and other examples of these materials (which, on the scale of solids, lie somewhere between crystals proper and glass) gradually appeared.

High-magnification microscopic images and X-ray diffraction patterns of quasicrystalline structures reveal unusual dodecahedral symmetries, and the appearance of the 'golden' φ ratio (*below*). Interestingly, the loose symmetries on which they are based had been prefigured by the Oxford mathematician Roger Penrose in the early 70s. Penrose had produced a pair of non-periodic tilings, based on approximate pentagonal symmetry (*4,5,6*). As with quasicrystals, these patterns have elements of a long-range order despite their 5-fold symmetry—and they can fill the plane in an infinite number of ways!

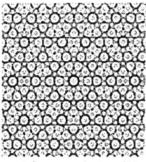

1. A flow pattern showing 5-fold symmetry.

2. An unusual 5-fold Islamic decorative mosaic.

3. A microphoto of Schechtmanite, showing its 5-fold structure.

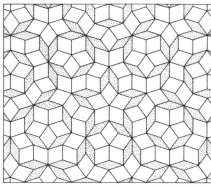

4. Penrose tiling no. 1, using two golden diamonds.

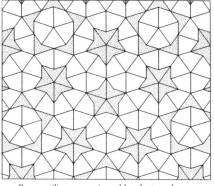

5. Penrose tiling no.2, using golden darts and arrows.

6. Pentagons alone cannot fill a plane; Penrose tiles can.

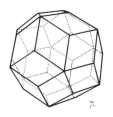

7. The rhombic triacontahedron, the 3-D analogue of a Penrose tiling, building block of a quasicrystal.

8. Schechtmanite 'snowflakes' form when an aluminium/ manganese alloy is cooled rapidly.

7.

8.

ASYMMETRY

the paradox of inconstancy

Where does symmetry end and asymmetry begin? Take a closer look at the circular Roman mosaic shown opposite the title page of this *Symmetry* section of this book (*page 234*). Is it symmetrical or not? There is an obvious overall symmetry, but a closer examination reveals that there are different designs in each of the roundels, and as many in each of their borders. So perhaps this composition is best characterized as having a somewhat disturbed symmetry—it exemplifies the paradox mentioned in the Introduction, namely, that the notion of symmetry is essentially inextricable from that of asymmetry.

One of the most important discoveries in recent science is that the notion of 'broken' symmetry has deep cosmological implications (*more of this on page 282*), but it is clear that a great many things in the world are like this. The fact is that wherever one looks there are many kinds, as well as degrees, of deviation from symmetry. The human body, for example, is bilateral (or dorsiventral) in its general form and some internal organs, like the lungs and kidneys follow this symmetry, but others, such as the alimentary canal, heart and liver do not. And even the overall symmetry is only approximate. Most of us have a dominant hand and eye, and there are subtle differences in the respective left and right sides of faces.

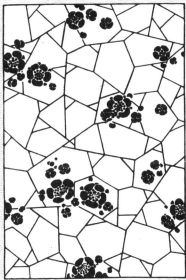

Opposite page: In living organisms the reasons for deviations from bi-lateralism tend to derive from evolutionary fitness. Where a mirror-symmetry is appropriate or necessary it is retained, where it isn't, it may be modified or abandoned. Many species opt for lop-sidedness, but we can be sure that the Crossbill, Fiddler crab and Begonia leaf had very good reasons to adopt their respective asymmetries.

This page: In art and design there can be various motives for deliberately introducing asymmetries. These include religious or superstitions, or simply the impulse to create a certain dynamic tension (particularly noticeable in Japanese art). Ironically, whatever the reasons behind the use of deliberate asymmetries, there is a tacit acknowledgement of the notion of symmetry itself. So asymmetry in art is usually a reactive response, on some level or other, to this basic ordering principle.

Self-Organising Symmetries
regularities in non-linear systems

There are many natural patterns that present more subtle regularities than the highly ordered symmetries of crystals. Some of these are generated by quite simple rules, others by a complex of factors; many result from some form or other of self-organization. These *'Li'* (*opposite, and see pages 388-391*) express a certain universality, their symmetries tend to be thematic and fluid rather than rigid and static. The simple ripple patterns on a sea-shore, for instance, are created by a multiplicity of contributory factors, including tides, currents and winds—not to mention the more general effects of gravity and warmth from the sun. All of these are drawn into a self-organising, self-limiting order whose charm lies precisely in the fact that it is repetitive, yet infinitely variable.

Rivers are also self-organising. Whether they are a gentle stream or a broad torrent they tend to follow similar meandering paths. There is an invariant quality in these loops and bends that conform to well-defined mathematical parameters. Similar constraints govern the hierarchical patterns of river-drainage. Rivers shape the terrain that they flow through, and are in turn shaped by it, but there are many subtle factors that limit and influence their form.

'Scale-invariant' symmetries also appear in fracture patterns of the kind found in mud cracks and ceramic crackle-glaze. Formations of this sort usually appear as a result of stresses induced by shrinkage. There are variations in the modes of cracking in different materials and in different conditions, but all are characterized by an overall consistency, and many have scaling properties. They are formed, and limited, by the release of stress, so they are progressive and self-organising—and of course they tend to be fractalline in nature.

Symmetries in Chaos
regularities in highly complex systems

Invariance equates with symmetry, so, on the face of it, turbulence, which is the very image of a totally disturbed system, would appear to be an unlikely candidate for symmetries of any kind. The physics of turbulent systems is still not completely understood, but the recognition of the role of *strange attractors* in the process has brought new insights and a new mathematical instrument to bear on such complex systems.

The cryptic geometry of strange attractors was part of the new non-linear maths of *Chaos theories* (the revolution in which fractals first appeared). It involves the concept of viewing dynamical systems as occupying geometrical space, the coordinates of which are derived from the systems variables. In linear systems the geometry within this phase space is simple, a point or a regular curve; in non-linear systems it involves far more complex shapes, the *strange attractors*. One of the most famous of these is the Lorenz attractor (*1,2*), which forms the basis of chaotic models of weather prediction (including Ice-Ages). Another classic example is the *dripping tap experiment* (*3*) where beautiful regular forms are found within apparent randomness.

As we have seen, Fractal geometry is intrinsic to many aspects of Chaos theory—and fractals are, predictably, firmly associated with attractors. In fact all strange attractors are fractal, as is *Feigenbaum mapping*, which is a sort of master attractor. The *Feigenbaum number* which lies at the heart of this mapping, predicts the complex, period-doubling values across a whole range of non-linear phenomena, including turbulence (*4*). The Feigenbaum value is recursive, and appears whenever there is repeated period doubling. It is, in short, a universal constant like *pi* or *phi*, and has a similar symmetrical potency.

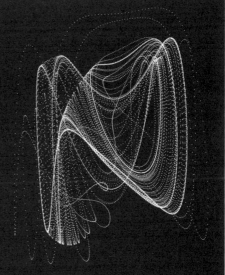

1. The Lorenz attractor displays two symmetrical states, between which it occasionally flips.

2. A weaker Lorenz attractor produces a more complex zone of probabilities.

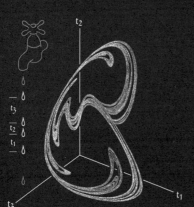

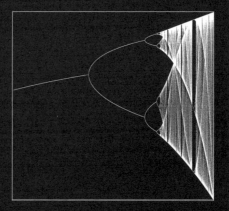

3. The times between successive drips from a tap, plotted as x, y, and z, form a strange attractor in 3-dimensional phase space.

4. A dynamical system bifurcation diagram, demonstrating the presence of the fractal Feigenbaum constant.

SYMMETRY IN PHYSICS
invariance and the laws of nature

Since the amount of energy in a closed system is invariant, the law of conservation of energy is now seen as a symmetry law. In fact, there is a real sense in which the history of physics (at least in the modern period) might be characterized as a successive uncovering of such universal conservation principles. The great discoveries of Galileo and Newton concerning gravity, for instance, were essentially the recognition of physical laws that deeply affect the material world, and yet are in some sense independent of it. Newton's Law, in postulating a symmetrical force acting on all objects, discovered the invariant quality of gravity— that it is the same everywhere in the universe. By extending these laws to a moving or accelerating observer, Einstein added further symmetries, the basis of his theory of General Relativity.

Gravity is now recognized as just one of four fundamental forces underlying all natural phenomena. In one of the greatest intellectual achievements of the 20th century the mathematician Emmy Noether established the connection between these dynamic forces and the abstract notion of symmetry. Since the laws of physics apply equally throughout ordinary space, they may be regarded as possessing translational symmetry, which is a consequence of (or equivalent to) the law of the Conservation of Momentum. Physical laws do not change over time either, which means that they are symmetric under translations in time, leading to a *conservation law*, in this case, the Conservation of Energy. In physics, there is now an absolute connection between symmetry and the laws of nature, so that physicists consciously search for *invariance* in their quest for new conservation laws.

Reality, it seems, is threaded through with concealed symmetries.

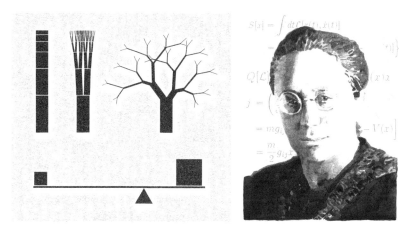

Top left: Hidden symmetries: Leonardo Da Vinci's conjecture that the total cross-sectional area of a tree remains the same at all branching levels, and a balance illustrating force = mass × distance.
Top right: Emmy Noether and her 1915 theorem: "For every continuous symmetry of the laws of physics, there must exist a conservation law. For every conservation law, there must exist a continuous symmetry."
Below: The refraction or bending of light in different media is most simply understood in terms of Noether's Theorem by realising that a photon always takes the quickest path available from source to destination.

Symmetry in Art
constraint and creative potentiality

The artistic impulse appears to be a universal human response, but its aims, methods, and roles within societies are as diverse as the cultural settings themselves. Art can have a magical or religious purpose, and may be representational or decorative—but whatever its aims or functions, it often expresses a style which ties it to a particular time and place. Where symmetries of any kind are present in art they will be intimately involved with such a style, since symmetry, in art as elsewhere, is an organising principle. Humans seem to be symmetry-conscious creatures, pattern-seekers by nature, so symmetry principles are never entirely absent as a consideration in art generally. The role of ratio, proportion and symbolism in the Fine Arts and architecture is examined later (*page 286*), but broadly speaking, it is in the decorative arts where symmetrical arrangements are most in evidence.

The arts of most tribal people use the basic symmetry functions of reflection and rotation. Bilateral arrangements in particular are an effective way of organising a composition, a method widely used in both 'primitive' and advanced societies. Dihedral symmetries are also widespread, finding their ultimate expression in the fine rose windows of Gothic cathedrals (*10*). There are, however, great cultural variations in the role of symmetry in art. In some it plays a small part, while others thoroughly explore its possibilities. Interestingly, this fascination (or the lack of it), applies across a whole range of societies, from tribal to those more advanced—right up to the present. Naturally, those artistic traditions whose taste inclined toward symmetry have always tended to develop a richer vocabulary in this respect, and have explored a greater range of decorative possibilities.

1. Pueblo pottery

2. Celtic strainer

3. Inca plate

4. Islamic motif

5. Seljuk mosaic

6. Romanesque device

7. Persian ceramic

8. Box; Nth. Pacific coast

9. Detail of Ainu coat

10. Examples of Gothic rose windows

A PASSION FOR PATTERN
the perennial appeal of repeating designs

Pattern arises almost of itself from any repeated operation (such as knitting, weaving, brickwork, tilework, etc.), and patterning has often become an integral part of a culture's stylistic conventions. In fact, although most cultures have used pattern as part of their decorative repertoire, some, at different periods and in different parts of the world, seem to have become fixated on patterning as a mode of artistic expression. The complex varieties of Islamic pattern are well-known, but there are equally strong traditions in the Celtic world, in Mesoamerica, and in Byzantium, Japan and Indonesia. Even those of us from cultures that are not so pattern-obsessed are perfectly capable of appreciating repeated ornament. It has a certain universality.

Regular patterning always involves a measuring of the space to be decorated. Because of this, the artist, knowingly or otherwise, engages with the rules governing the symmetry-groups of plane division (*see appendix page 386-387*). In practice, these limitations are not so much a constraint on design as a further opportunity to introduce variety.

Interestingly, at least two artistic traditions—those of Ancient Egypt and Islam—came fairly close to using all 17 classes of planar patterns. The unconscious but systematic exploration of symmetry groups in this way seems to blur the distinction between the artistic activity of pattern creation and that of science, whose entire enterprise can be characterized as pattern detection.

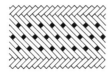   

SYMMETRIA
sublime proportions

The Renaissance saw a revival of interest in classical notions of symmetry. Vitruvius' Roman idea of symmetry as a harmonious arrangement of parts actually derived from older Greek views of a fundamental order and harmony within the universe, dating back to the philosophy of Pythagoras and his followers, for whom geometry (in particular the geometry of ratios and proportion) was the key to a deeper understanding of the cosmos. The idea of a harmonious correspondence between the parts of a system and the whole is a compelling one—and there is a great deal of evidence that certain special proportions were employed in ancient architecture, both in the European and other traditions. This usage was continued to some extent in those cultures that inherited the classical tradition—in the Islamic world, and in Gothic cathedrals for instance, as well as in the Renaissance revival.

In his seminal work *De Architectura*, Vitruvius made the definitive statement on these principles—"Symmetry results from proportion; proportion is the commensuration of the various constituent parts with the whole" (*see too page 300*). Under the influence of these ideas, the Renaissance architect Alberti introduced a Pythagorean system of ratios into architecture, relating these concepts to dimensions of the human body—an idea that was enthusiastically taken up by the artists Albrecht Dürer and Leonardo Da Vinci, among others.

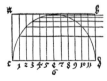  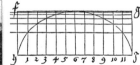

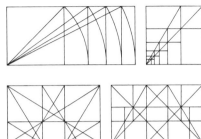

1. Modular series of proportionate rectangles can be generated from various ratios, including √2, √3, and phi.

2. Many ancient cultures used systems of harmonious proportion in their architecture.

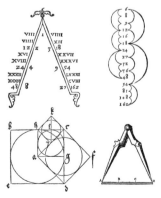

FORMALISM

symmetry symbolizing stability

Symmetry is frequently involved in places and occasions that seek to project formality, concepts of the status quo and, by extension, social order and constitutional rule. This is the underlying reason for the symmetries in the architecture of palaces, governmental buildings and places of worship. Ceremonial displays, formal gardens and formal dancing are also based on regular arrangements for similar reasons. Symmetry is used here to symbolize qualities of endurance and stability—which of course any established order would wish to identify with (and which its followers would wish to imitate). The tacit intention of formalism then, in any sphere, is an alignment with some or other perceived notion of order.

In any formal scheme of this kind individualism tends to be submerged within the greater pattern. The so-called Ancient Mature civilizations, (such as those of Pharaonic Egypt, Mesopotamia and Meso-America) in which all behavior was highly prescribed, provide the most extreme examples of formalised societies. The massive monuments that they left offer the most compelling evidence of their rigid world views. The awesome symmetries of pyramids, ziggurats and the like were not only the link between heaven and earth, but were models of the intensely hierarchical societies that produced them. Above all, their impressive, symmetrical monuments symbolized enduring stability.

These ancient civilizations declined under the impact of more dynamic societies, but their use of symmetry as a metaphor for official order and decorum persisted. Ritual and ceremony still have an important role in political life, and symmetry is still an important part of the whole symbolism of legitimacy.

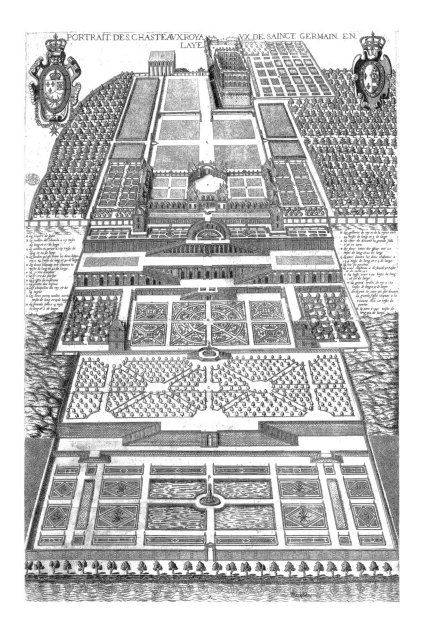

EXPERIENTIAL SYMMETRIES
percepts and precepts

It is clear that symmetry is an all-encompassing principle. We have seen that it is involved in natural structures in countless ways, and that symmetry concepts have become an essential tool for a deeper understanding of the physical world. It is also apparent that symmetry has an aesthetic dimension, and that it contributes to that most elusive of concepts, Beauty. What is rather less tangible is the part that this ordering principle plays in our ordinary experience of life as social beings—needless to say, it has an important role here too. To begin with, symmetry is an essential component of the basic social norms of reciprocity. We expect fair dealings in social exchanges, and this basic sense of fairness is as natural to humans as it apparently is to our cousins, the higher primates. By extension, any system of justice is bound to reflect these notions of proportionality; this is symbolized by the image of the balance-scale, that most graphic representation of symmetry.

Notions of proportionality and reciprocity also make an essential contribution to systems of religious belief. Most religions hold that our actions in our present lives determine our fate in the hereafter, to an exact degree. Heavens often have inverted equivalents in the form of Hells. However, not all religious injunctions are so oppressive. Perhaps the most elegant of all religious precepts comes in the form of the *Golden Rule*, which was promulgated by many great spiritual leaders, including Confucius, Jesus Christ and Hillel (it is also found in The *Mahabharata* and Leviticus, and recommended by the Stoic philosophers). The Rule recommends that we treat others as we ourselves would wish to be treated, an ethical stance that is hard to improve upon—and one that expresses a beautiful symmetry.

Above: A kaleidoscope turns a random group into a beautiful object.

Below: Matter and antimatter, an electron and a positron.

Above: The jostling action of quanta assume an overall symmetrical distribution.

Below: Symmetry in a coffee cup.

BOOK VI

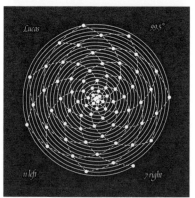

The two types of spiral phyllotaxis found in plants on Earth:
Fibonacci (1, 1, 2, 3, 5, 8, 13, 21...) and Lucas (2, 1, 3, 4, 7, 11, 18, 29...).

THE GOLDEN
SECTION
NATURE'S GREATEST SECRET

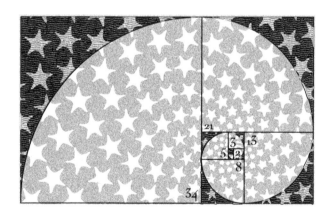

Scott Olsen

INTRODUCTION

Nature holds a great mystery, zealously guarded by her custodians from those who would profane or abuse the wisdom. Periodically, portions of this tradition are quietly revealed to those of humanity who have attuned their eyes to see and ears to hear. The primary requirements are openness, sensitivity, enthusiasm, and an earnestness to understand the deeper meaning of nature's marvels exhibited to us daily. Many of us tend to walk through life half asleep, at times numbed, if not actually deadened to the exquisite order that surrounds us. But a trail of clues has been preserved.

The secretive tradition centers on a study of number, harmony, geometry, and cosmology that stretches back through the mists of time into the Egyptian, Babylonian, Indian and Chinese cultures. It is evident in the layout and relationships of the stone circles and underground chambers of ancient Europe, as well as in Neolithic stones discovered in Britain, fashioned in the form of the five regular solids. There are further clues in Maya and other Mesoamerican artifacts and buildings, and across the ocean the Gothic masons embedded it in their cathedral designs.

The great Pythagorean philosopher, Plato, in his writings and oral teachings, hinted, though enigmatically, that there was a golden key unifying these mysteries.

Here is my promise to you: if you are willing to proceed step by step through this compact little study, it will be well nigh impossible not to grasp by the end a satisfying and stunning glimpse, if not deeply provocative insight, into Nature's Greatest Secret.

THE MYSTERY OF PHI
the golden thread of perennial wisdom

The history of the golden section is difficult to unravel. Despite its use in ancient Egypt and the Pythagorean tradition, the first definition we have comes from Euclid [325-265 BC], who defines it as the division of a line in extreme and mean ratio. The earliest known treatise on the subject is *Divina Proportione* by Luca Pacioli [1445-1517], the monk drunk on beauty, and illustrated by Leonardo Da Vinci, who according to tradition coined the term *sectio aurea*, or "golden section". However, the first published use of the phrase occurs in Martin Ohm's 1835 *Pure Elementary Mathematics*.

There are many names for this mysterious section. It is variously called a golden or divine ratio, mean, proportion, number, section or cut. In mathematical notation it goes by the symbol τ, "*tau*", meaning "the cut", or more commonly Φ or φ, "*phi*", the first letter of the name of the Greek sculptor Phidias, who used it in the Parthenon.

So what is this enigmatic cut, and why is there so much fascination about it? One of the eternal questions asked by philosophers concerns how the One becomes Many. What is the nature of separation, or division? Is there a way in which parts can retain a meaningful relationship to the whole?

Posing this question in allegorical terms, Plato [427-347 BC] in *The Republic* asks the reader to "take a line and divide it unevenly". Under a Pythagorean oath of silence not to reveal the secrets of the mysteries, Plato posed questions in hopes of provoking an insightful response. So why does he use a line, rather than numbers? And why does he ask us to divide it unevenly?

To answer Plato, we first must understand ratio and proportion.

RATIO, MEANS & PROPORTION
continuous geometric proportion

Ratio (*logos*) is the relation of one number to another, for instance 4:8 ("4 is to 8"). However, proportion (*analogia*) is a repeating ratio that typically involves four terms, so 4:8 :: 5:10 ("4 is to 8 is as 5 is to 10"). The Pythagoreans called this a four-termed discontinuous proportion. The invariant ratio here is 1:2, repeated in both 4:8 and 5:10. An inverted ratio reverses the terms, so 8:4 is the inverse of 4:8, the invariant ratio now 2:1.

Standing between the two-termed ratio and the four-termed proportion is the three-termed mean in which the middle term is in the same ratio to the first as the last is to it.

The geometric mean between two numbers is equal to the square root of their product. Thus, the geometric mean of, 1 and 9 is $\sqrt{(1 \times 9)}$ = 3. This geometric mean relationship is written as 1:3:9, or, inverted, as 9:3:1. It can also be written more fully as a continuous geometric proportion where these two ratios repeat the same invariant ratio of 1:3. Thus, 1:3 :: 3:9. The 3 is the geometric mean held in common by both ratios, binding, or interlacing them together in what the Pythagoreans called a three-termed continuous geometric proportion.

Plato holds continuous geometric proportion to be the most profound cosmic bond. In his *Timaeus* the world soul binds together, into one harmonic resonance, the intelligible world of forms (including pure mathematics) above, and the visible world of material objects below, through the 1, 2, 4, 8 and 1, 3, 9, 27 series. This results in the extended continuous geometric proportions, 1:2 :: 2:4 :: 4:8, and 1:3 :: 3:9 :: 9:27 (*see opposite*).

Ratio: between two numbers *a* and *b*

Ratio between *a* and *b* $a : b$ or a/b
Inverse ratio $b : a$ or b/a

Means: *b*, between *a* and *c*

Arithmetic Mean *b* of *a* and *c* $b = \dfrac{a + c}{2}$

Harmonic Mean *b* of *a* and *c* $b = \dfrac{2ac}{a + c}$

Geometric Mean *b* of *a* and *c* $b = \sqrt{ac}$

Proportion: between two ratios

Discontinuous (4 termed)   Continuous (3 termed)
$a : b :: c : d$ $a : b :: b : c \implies a : b : c$
  e.g., $4 : 8 :: 5 : 10$ note *b* is the geometric
  has invariant ratio $1 : 2$ mean of *a* and *c*

Plato's World Soul:
Extended continuous geometric proportion

$1 : 2 :: 2 : 4 :: 4 : 8$ $1 : 3 :: 3 : 9 :: 9 : 27$
  invar. ratio $1 : 2$ invar. ratio $1 : 3$
   or $1/2$ or $1/3$

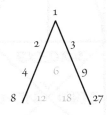

Lambda diagram

PLATO'S DIVIDED LINE
knowing precisely where to cut

So, returning to our puzzle, why does Plato ask us to make an uneven cut? An even cut would result in a whole : segment ratio of 2:1, and the ratio of the two equal segments would be 1:1. These ratios are not equal and so no proportion is present! There is only one way to form a proportion from a simple ratio, and that is through the golden section. Plato wants you to discover a special ratio such that *the whole to the longer equals the longer to the shorter*. He knows this would result in his favorite bond of nature, a continuous geometric proportion. The inverse also applies, *the shorter to the longer equals the longer to the whole*.

And why a line, rather than simply numbers? Plato realized the answer is an irrational number that can be geometrically derived in a line, but cannot be expressed as a simple fraction.

Solving this problem mathematically, and assuming the mean (longer segment) is 1, we find the greater golden value of 1.6180339... (for the whole), and the lesser golden value 0.6180339... (for the shorter). We term these Φ "fye" the Greater and ϕ "fee" the Lesser respectively. Notice that both their product and their difference is Unity. Furthermore, the square of the Greater is 2.6180339, or $\Phi+1$. Notice also that each is the other's reciprocal, so that ϕ is $1/\Phi$.

Throughout the following pages we will generally speak of the Greater as Φ, the mean as Unity (1), and the Lesser as $1/\Phi$.

Notice (*below left to right*) that Unity can act as the Greater (whole), Mean (longer segment) or as the Lesser (short segment).

PHI ON THE PLANE
pentagrams and golden rectangles

Moving from the one-dimensional line onto the two-dimensional plane, the golden section soon appears Starting with a square, an arc centered on the midpoint of its base swung down from an upper corner easily produces a large golden rectangle (*below left*). Importantly, the small rectangle which we have added to the square is *also* a golden rectangle. Continuing this technique creates a pair of these smaller golden rectangles (*opposite top left*). Conversely, removing a square from a golden rectangle leaves a smaller golden rectangle, and this process can be continued indefinitely to produce a golden spiral (*opposite lower right*).

The golden section, which as we have seen unifies parts and whole like no other proportion, is intimately involved with the natural geometry of the pentagram (*opposite lower left*), the very emblem of life. Every point of intersection creates lengths which are in golden relationships to one another. An arm of a pentagram contains the key to another golden section spiral as a continuous series of increasing or shrinking golden triangles (*opposite top right*).

The golden cut of a line may be achieved by building a double square on the line and following the diagram (*below right*).

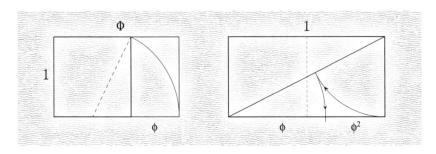

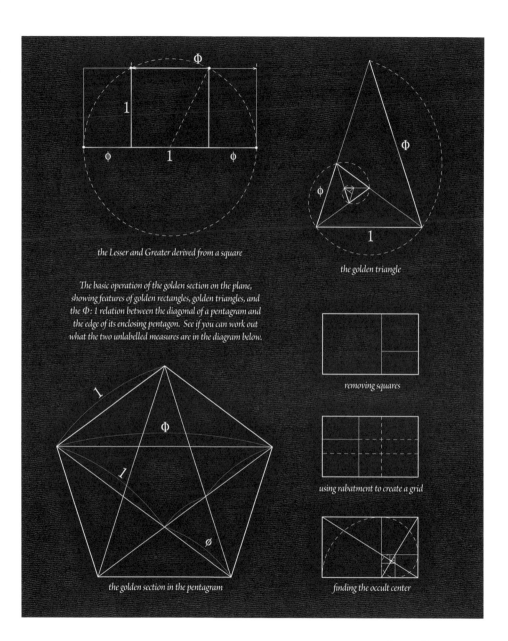

the Lesser and Greater derived from a square

the golden triangle

The basic operation of the golden section on the plane, showing features of golden rectangles, golden triangles, and the Φ: 1 relation between the diagonal of a pentagram and the edge of its enclosing pentagon. See if you can work out what the two unlabelled measures are in the diagram below.

removing squares

using rabatment to create a grid

the golden section in the pentagram

finding the occult center

THE FIBONACCI SEQUENCE
stepping stones to gold

Nature widely expresses the golden section through a very simple series of whole numbers. The astounding Fibonacci number series: 0, 1, 1, 2, 3, 5, 8, 13, 21, 34, 55, 89, 144, 233, 377... is both additive, as each number is the sum of the previous two, and multiplicative, as each number approximates the previous number multiplied by the golden section. The ratio becomes more accurate as the numbers increase. Inversely, any number divided by its smaller neighbor approximates Φ, alternating as more or less than Φ, forever closing in on the divine limit (*opposite lower right*). Each Fibonacci number is the approximate geometric mean of its two adjacent numbers.

Although officially recognized later, the series appears to have been known to the ancient Egyptians and their Greek students. Ultimately Edouard Lucas in the 19th century named the series after Leonardo of Pisa [c. 1170-1250], also known as Fibonacci (son of the bull), who made the series famous through his solution of a problem regarding the breeding of rabbits over a year's time (*right*).

Fibonacci numbers occur in the family trees of bees, stock market patterns, hurricane clouds, self-organizing DNA nucleotides, and in chemistry as with the uranium oxide compounds U_2O_5, U_3O_8, U_5O_{13}, U_8O_{21}, and $U_{13}O_{34}$ intermediate between UO_2 & UO_3.

A turtle has 13 horn plates on its shell, 5 centered, 8 on the edges, 5 paw pins, and 34 backbone segments. There are 144 vertebrae in a Gabon snake, a hyena has 34 teeth, and a dolphin 233. Many spiders have 5 pairs of extremities, 5 parts to each extremity, and a belly divided into 8 segments carried by its 8 legs.

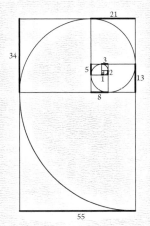

The Fibonacci Golden Spiral

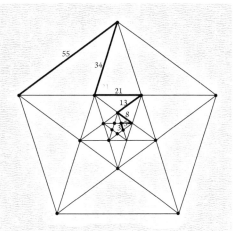

Fibonacci numbers approximate pentagram lengths

0 + 1 = 1	1/1 = 1	1/1 = 1
1 + 1 = 2	2/1 = 2	1/2 = 0.5
1 + 2 = 3	3/2 = 1.5	2/3 = 0.6666
2 + 3 = 5	5/3 = 1.6666	3/5 = 0.6
3 + 5 = 8	8/5 = 1.6	5/8 = 0.625
5 + 8 = 13	13/8 = 1.625	8/13 = 0.6154
8 + 13 = 21	21/13 = 1.6154	13/21 = 0.6190
13 + 21 = 34	34/21 = 1.6190	21/34 = 0.6176
21 + 34 = 55	55/34 = 1.6176	34/55 = 0.6182
34 + 55 = 89	89/55 = 1.6182	55/89 = 0.6180
55 + 89 = 144	144/89 = 1.6180	89/144 = 0.6181

Each term is the sum of the previous two

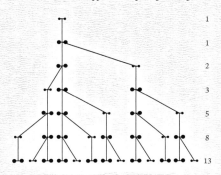

Numbers of breeding pairs of rabbits

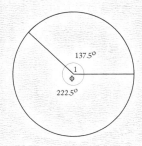

The golden angle, $360°/\Phi^2$

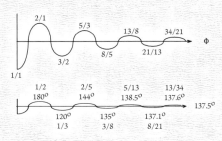

Fibonacci ratios converge on the golden ratio

PHYLLOTAXIS PATTERNS
leaves on a stem

Emerging as a science in the 19th century, phyllotaxis has been extended to the spiral patterns of seeds in a sunflower head, petals in the daisy, scales of pine cones, cacti areoles, and other patterns exhibited in plants. In the 15th century Da Vinci [1452-1519] observed that the spacing of leaves was often spiral in arrangement. Kepler [1571-1630] later noted the majority of wild flowers are pentagonal, and that Fibonacci numbers occur in leaf arrangement.

Appropriately, in 1754 Charles Bonnet coined the name *phyllotaxis* from the Greek *phullon* "leaf" and *taxis* "arrangement". In 1830, Schimper developed the concept of the divergence angle of what he called the "genetic" spiral, noticing the presence of simple Fibonacci numbers. In 1837, the Bravais brothers discovered the crystal lattice and the ideal divergence angle of phyllotaxis: $137.5° = 360°/\Phi^2$.

The diagram by Church (*top row opposite*) shows the main features of spiral phyllotaxis. As the seed head expands, new primordia are formed at angles of 137.5°. In the seventh item we can see the Archimedean spiral which connects the growth. The diagrams below (*after Stewart*) show primordia plotted at angles of 137.3°, 137.5° and 137.6°. Only the precise angle produces a perfect packing.

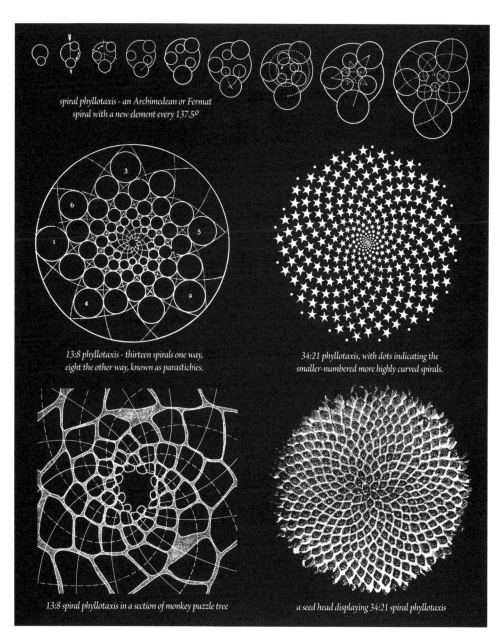

spiral phyllotaxis - an Archimedean or Fermat spiral with a new element every 137.5°

13:8 phyllotaxis - thirteen spirals one way, eight the other way, known as parastichies.

34:21 phyllotaxis, with dots indicating the smaller-numbered more highly curved spirals.

13:8 spiral phyllotaxis in a section of monkey puzzle tree

a seed head displaying 34:21 spiral phyllotaxis

ORDER BEHIND DIVERSITY
she loves me, she loves me not

Despite its seemingly endless variety and diversity, nature employs only three basic ways to arrange leaves along a stem: *disticious*, like *corn*, *decussate* or *whorled*, such as mint, and the most common, spiral phyllotaxis (for about 80% of the 250,000 different species of higher plants), where the divergence (rotation) angle between leaves has only a few values, these being close Fibonacci approximations to the golden angle, 137.5°. This pattern aids photosynthesis, each leaf receiving maximum sunlight and rain, efficiently spirals moisture to roots, and gives best exposure for insect pollination.

Opposing spirals of seeds in a sunflower generally appear as adjacent Fibonacci numbers, typically, 55:34 (1.6176) or 89:55 (1.6181). Scales of pinecones are typically 5:3 (1.6666). or 8:5 (1.6). Artichokes likewise display 8 spirals one way, 5 the other. Pineapples have three spirals, often 8, 13 and 21 each (*below*), where 21:13:8 approximates $\Phi : 1 : 1/\Phi$, with 21:13 (1.6153), 13:8 (1.625), and 21:8 (2.625), aspiring toward Φ^2, or $\Phi + 1$. Similarly, the pussy willow branch spirals 5 times with 13 buds appearing.

Next time you are out in the park, woods, countryside, or along a trail, take a moment to examine the petals on a daisy, count the spirals on a pinecone, or note the buds on a pussy willow.

8 gradual   *5 gradual*   *13 medium*   *8 steep*   *21 steep*

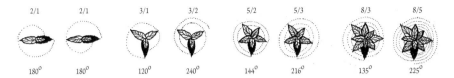

|2/1|2/1|3/1|3/2|5/2|5/3|8/3|8/5|
|180°|180°|120°|240°|144°|216°|135°|225°|

Simple phyllotaxis deriving from Fibonacci numbers - in each case a:b, a leaves are produced in b turns, meaning that the leaf divergence angle is (b/a)360°. As a and b increase, the divergence angles approach 137.5° and 222.5°.

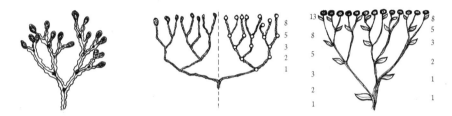

A frond of brown alga (left), with a schematic (center) showing the number of bifurcations exhibiting Fibonacci numbers. Sneezewort (right) also displays Fibonacci numbers in the count of its stems and leaves as it grows.

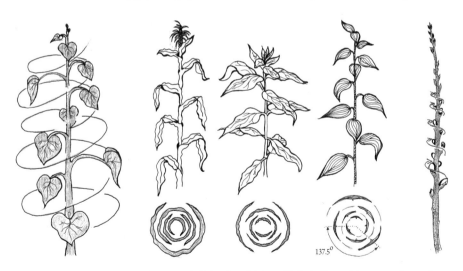

The three phyllotactic patterns, disticious, whorled, and spiral (after Ball), flanked by two Fibonacci spiral examples. The plant on the left displays 8 leaves in 5 turns, the pussy willow on the right produces 13 buds in exactly 5 turns.

Lucas Number Magic

integers perfectly formed from irrationals

In addition to the Fibonacci numbers, nature occasionally uses another series, named after Edouard Lucas. Lucas numbers (2, 1, 3, 4, 7, 11, 18, 29, 47, 76, 123, 199....) are similar to Fibonacci numbers in that they are additive (each new number is the sum of the previous two numbers), and multiplicative (each new number approximates the previous number multiplied by the modular Φ). In fact any additive series will converge on the golden ratio, the Fibonacci and Lucas series just do it the quickest. Note that the first four integers (*the basis of the Tetraktys*) are all Lucas numbers.

What is fascinating about the Lucas numbers is that they are formed by alternately adding and subtracting the golden powers of Φ and its reciprocal $1/\Phi$, the two irrational parts either zipping together or peeling apart to form the integers (*opposite top*). These are not approximations, but absolutely exact! This extraordinary feature may be extended to the construction of Fibonacci numbers (*lower opposite*). Incredibly, it turns out that all integers can be constructed out of golden section powers, providing us with a tantalizing new way of constructing mathematics: integers are secretly hiding their component golden powers.

Together with Fibonaccis, Lucas numbers (though more rare) are sometimes found in the phyllotactic patterns of sunflowers (at times as much as 1 in 10 in some species), and in certain cedars, sequoias, balsam trees, and other species. In general, the Lucas divergence angle of $99.5° = 360°/(1 + \Phi^2)$ occurs in 1.5% of observed phyllotactic plant patterns, as compared to 92% for the Fibonacci driven divergence angle (*see page 294*).

Lucas no.			
0	$2 = \Phi + 1/\Phi^2$	=	1.61803398 ... + 0.38196601 ...
1	$1 = \Phi - 1/\Phi$	=	1.61803398 ... - 0.61803398 ...
2	$3 = \Phi^2 + 1/\Phi^2$	=	2.61803398 ... + 0.38196601 ...
3	$4 = \Phi^3 - 1/\Phi^3$	=	4.23606797... - 0.23606797...
4	$7 = \Phi^4 + 1/\Phi^4$	=	6.85410196 ... + 0.14589803 ...
5	$11 = \Phi^5 - 1/\Phi^5$	=	11.09016994 ... - 0.09016994 ...
6	$18 = \Phi^6 + 1/\Phi^6$	=	17.94427191 ... + 0.05572808 ...
7	$29 = \Phi^7 - 1/\Phi^7$	=	29.03444185 ... - 0.03444185 ...
8	$47 = \Phi^8 + 1/\Phi^8$	=	46.97871376 ... + 0.02128623 ...
9	$76 = \Phi^9 - 1/\Phi^9$	=	76.01315561 ... - 0.01315561 ...
10	$123 = \Phi^{10} + 1/\Phi^{10}$	=	122.9918693 ... + 0.0081306 ...
11	$199 = \Phi^{11} - 1/\Phi^{11}$	=	199.00502499 ... - 0.00502499 ...

The Lucas Series: Even-termed members are formed by the addition of the greater and lesser powers of the golden section, odd-termed members by subtraction. Notice how the decimals in the odd terms are perfectly sliced off.

	7	
	=	
G^4	+	L^4
6		0
.		.
8		1
5		4
4		5
1		8
0		9
1		8
9		0

The number 7 is formed by zipping together the fourth powers of Φ and 1/Φ. Notice how the decimals sum to 9.

Fib. no.				
2a	$1 = \frac{\Phi^2 + 0}{\Phi^2} = \Phi^0 + 0/\Phi^2$	=	G^0	= 1
3	$2 = \frac{\Phi^3 + 1}{\Phi^2} = \Phi^1 + 1/\Phi^2$	=	$G^1 + L^2$	= 1.61803398... + 0.38196601...
4	$3 = \frac{\Phi^4 + 1}{\Phi^2} = \Phi^2 + 1/\Phi^2$	=	$G^2 + L^2$	= 2.61803398... + 0.38196601...
5	$5 = \frac{\Phi^5 + 2}{\Phi^2} = \Phi^3 + 2/\Phi^2$	=	$G^3 + 2\,L^2$	= 4.23606797... + 0.76393202...
6	$8 = \frac{\Phi^6 + 3}{\Phi^2} = \Phi^4 + 3/\Phi^2$	=	$G^4 + 3\,L^2$	= 6.85410196 ... + 1.14589803...
7	$13 = \frac{\Phi^7 + 5}{\Phi^2} = \Phi^5 + 5/\Phi^2$	=	$G^5 + 5\,L^2$	= 11.09016994... + 1.90983005...
8	$21 = \frac{\Phi^8 + 8}{\Phi^2} = \Phi^6 + 8/\Phi^2$	=	$G^6 + 8\,L^2$	= 17.94427191... + 3.05572808...

Like the Lucas series, Fibonacci numbers can be expressed in terms of powers of the golden section. Notice the Fibonacci numbers reappearing in the equations - these can be further collapsed into golden power terms by repeatedly using the same technique.

ALL CREATURES
the divine symphony of life

Nature exhibits an array of beautiful and wondrous forms. Plants, trees, insects, fish, dogs, cats, horses, and peacocks all display a poetic interplay between symmetry and asymmetry. Golden relations are often displayed through golden rectangles (*see beetles and fish opposite, after Doczi*), and their subsequent sectioning into component squares and smaller golden rectangles. This perpetuates the ratios of the original whole into its self-similar parts, reflecting the Φ:1:1/Φ proportional symmetry that we call the divine proportion. As Schwaller de Lubicz stated in *The Temple of Man*: "The impulse of all movement and all form is given by Φ."

The prevalence of natural pentagonal forms may result from the symphony of golden relationships in the pentagon and pentagram (*below and center row opposite, from Colman*). Many marine animals, like starfish, exhibit 5-fold form. Sometimes, as in a passion flower, the form is decagonal, one pentagon superimposed upon another.

Even the building blocks for life, ammonia (NH_3), methane (CH_4), and water (H_2O) all have internal bond angles which approximate the internal 108° angle of a pentagon.

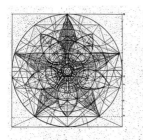 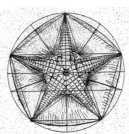 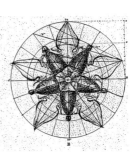

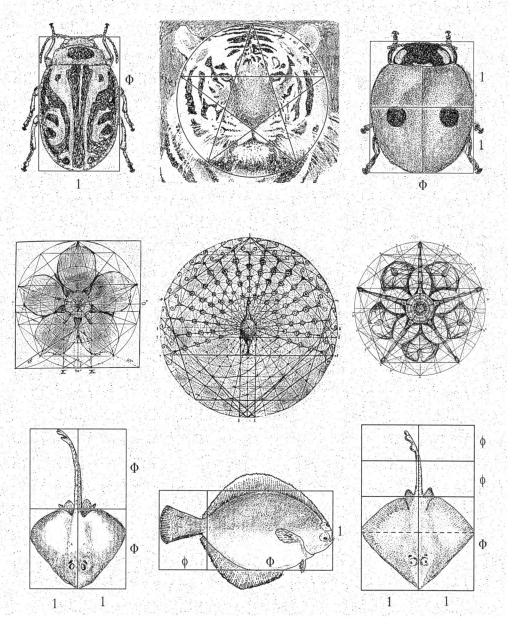

PHI IN THE HUMAN BODY

in the image of the divine

For over twenty years my students have been subjected to in-class measurements where their height relative to the location of their navel is determined. The purpose is to see whether the navel actually divides the body in the golden section, as some suggest the ancient *Canon of Polyclitus* purported. Over the years there have been a few who have exhibited what appears to be a perfect golden cut. However, in performing the calculations, the majority fit very closely into whole number Fibonacci approximations, particularly, the 5:3 range, and occasionally 8:5.

The golden ratio manifests throughout the human body. The three bones of each of your fingers are in golden relationship, and the wrist divides the hand and forearm at the golden section. Fibonacci numbers appear in your teeth, which sum to 13 in each quarter of your mouth over a lifetime, divided into a childhood 5 and an adult 8. The journey from child to adult also contains another surprise: a baby's navel (representing its past) is at its midpoint, and its genitals occur at the golden point, but when fully grown these reverse, as an adult's midpoint is at the genitals (the future) with the navel approximating the golden section (*opposite lower left*).

In Da Vinci's drawing of a head (*opposite top right*) a golden rectangle frames the face, and positions the eyes, nose, and mouth.

Below we see Dürer's drawings of less-than-golden faces.

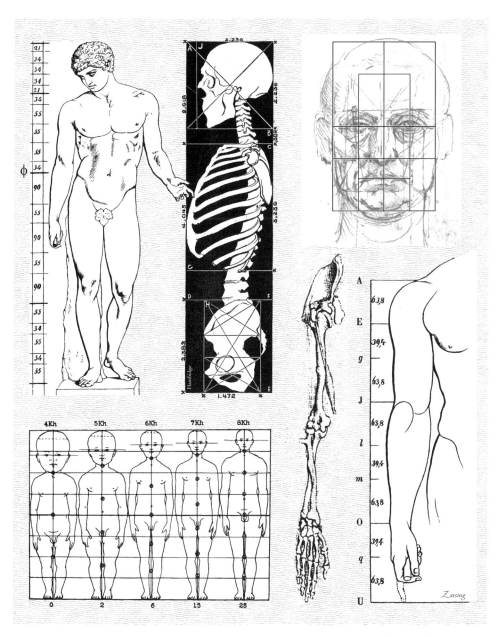

GROWTH & DIMINUTION
through the looking glass

Nature pulses with cycles and rhythms of increase and decrease. Heraclitus, a Presocratic influence on Plato, noted: "The way up and the way down are one and the same." Observe the waxing and waning of the moon, the circle of the year, the interplay of day and night, the breath of the tides, the systole and diastole of the beat of the heart, and the expansion and contraction of the lungs. The explosive growth of a star is often followed by implosion, and the negative entropy in the ordered organization of life is balanced by the positive entropy of disorder and death.

In chaos theory, the golden section governs the chaos border, where order passes into and emerges out of disorder. Demanding simplicity and economy, nature appears to require an accretion and diminution process that is simultaneously additive and multiplicative, subtractive and divisional. This demand is satisfied perfectly only by the golden section powers, and in practice by Fibonacci and Lucas approximations.

In the table (*opposite top*), notice how we can move upward in growth by both addition and multiplication, and move down, diminishing, by subtraction and division. The fulcrum is Unity, acting as the geometric mean in golden relationship to both the increase of the deficient Lesser and the decrease of the excessive Greater.

Think of an oak tree. It shoots up as fast as it can from an acorn, only to slow, mature and fractalize its space toward a limit, becoming a new relative unity, what Aristotle called an entelechy, the form it grows into. Like Alice in Wonderland, nature simultaneously grows and diminishes to relative limits.

n	Greater	Mean	Lesser
7	Φ^7	Φ^6	Φ^5
6	Φ^6	Φ^5	Φ^4
5	Φ^5	Φ^4	Φ^3
4	Φ^4	Φ^3	Φ^2
3	Φ^3	Φ^2	Φ
2	Φ^2	Φ	1
1	Φ	1	$1/\Phi$
0	1	$1/\Phi$	$1/\Phi^2$
-1	$1/\Phi$	$1/\Phi^2$	$1/\Phi^3$
-2	$1/\Phi^2$	$1/\Phi^3$	$1/\Phi^4$
-3	$1/\Phi^3$	$1/\Phi^4$	$1/\Phi^5$
-4	$1/\Phi^4$	$1/\Phi^5$	$1/\Phi^6$
-5	$1/\Phi^5$	$1/\Phi^6$	$1/\Phi^7$
-6	$1/\Phi^6$	$1/\Phi^7$	$1/\Phi^8$
-7	$1/\Phi^7$	$1/\Phi^8$	$1/\Phi^9$

growth - the way up ->

diminution - the way down ->

The Golden Series shown opposite displays the unique simultaneous additive and multipicative qualities of the Golden Section.

Multiplication:
$$G_{n+1} = G_n \times \Phi$$
Addition:
$$G_{n+1} = G_n + M_n = G_n + G_{n-1}$$

Division:
$$G_{n-1} = G_n / \Phi$$
Subtraction:
$$G_{n-1} = M_n = G_n - L_n = G_n - G_{n-2}$$

These equations may be extended for Lesser and Mean values.

Each term is simultaneously the sum of the preceding two and the product of the previous term multiplied by Φ.
So $\Phi^4 = \Phi^2 + \Phi^3 = \Phi^2 \times \Phi^2 = \Phi^3 \times \Phi$

No other number behaves likes this, fusing addition and multiplication.

G	M	L
144	89	55
89	55	34
55	34	21
34	21	13
21	13	8
13	8	5
8	5	3
5	3	2
3	2	1
2	1	1
1	1	0

FIBONACCI

G	M	L
322	199	123
199	123	76
123	76	47
76	47	29
47	29	18
29	18	11
18	11	7
11	7	4
7	4	3
4	3	1
3	1	2

LUCAS

The Fibonacci approximate geometric mean is corrected alternately by +1 or -1 under the square root. So 3 is the approximate geometric mean of 2 and 5, as $\sqrt{[(2 \times 5)-1]} = \sqrt{9}$, and 5 is the approximate geometric mean of 3 and 8, $= \sqrt{[(3 \times 8)+1]} = \sqrt{25}$.

The Lucas approximate geometric mean is corrected alternately by +5 or -5 under the square root. So 4 is the approximate geometric mean of 3 and 7, $= \sqrt{[(3 \times 7)-5]} = \sqrt{16}$, and 7 is the approximate geometric mean of 4 and 11, $= \sqrt{[(4 \times 11)+5]} = \sqrt{49}$.

Exponentials and Spirals

an extended family of wonderful curves

In nature, gnomonic growth occurs through simple accretion. It produces the beautiful logarithmic spiral growth we see in mollusks, which constantly add new material at the open end of their shells. Importantly, the shell grows in size, increasing in length and width, without varying its proportions. This accretive process, also used by crystals, is the simplest law of growth.

The golden spiral, derived from Fibonacci numbers, and from the arm of a pentagram (*below*), is a member of the family of logarithmic spirals. These are also called growth spirals, equiangular spirals, and sometimes *spira mirabilis*, "wonderful spiral". When a spiral is logarithmic the curve appears the same at every scale, and any line drawn from the center meets any part of the spiral at exactly the same angle for that spiral. Zoom in on a logarithmic spiral and you will discover another spiral waiting for you. They are to be contrasted with Archimedean spirals, which have equal-spaced coils, like a coiled snake or hose.

Nature uses numerous different logarithmic spirals in leaf and shell shapes, cacti and seed-head phyllotaxis, whirlpools and galaxies. Many can be approximated using a family of golden spirals derived from equal divisions of a circle (*see opposite, after Coates & Colman*).

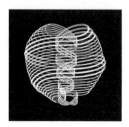 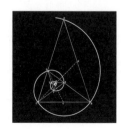 

GOLDEN SYMMETRY
proportion from asymmetry

Nature presents us with a wonderful holographic portrait, where the smaller portions mirror the whole (cosmos) itself. Recognizing that structural self-similarity connects, or binds, what he called the hidden "implicate order" to the outer "explicate order", physicist David Bohm remarked: "The essential feature of quantum interconnectedness is that the whole universe is enfolded in everything, and that each thing is enfolded in the whole."

As we have seen, this marriage of the whole and its parts is elegantly accomplished via proportional symmetry, and in particular it is most efficiently produced by the golden section. This simple cut appears to be the driving impulse of nature itself, fractalizing with self-similarity into all the parts, and driving the growth process through spiraling golden angles and Fibonacci numbers.

It is the asymmetric push, the dynamic energy of the golden ratio manifesting as life, form and consciousness that provides the impetus to the rhythmic swing, the initial push of the pendulum.

The theme is explored in John Michell's painting, *The Pattern* (*opposite*). Concerning Intelligible symmetry, Michell writes:

> *"Socrates called it the 'heavenly pattern', which anyone can discover,*
> *and once they have found it they can establish it in themselves."*

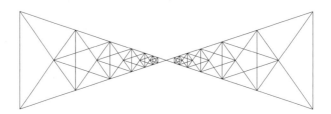

Someone must have hit the right note, because everything suddenly began falling into place.

Phi in Human Culture
sympathetic magic—as above, so below

A careful comparative study of cultures, their art, architecture, religion, mythology and philosophy, often reveals that, like phyllotaxis, the multiplicity and diversity of styles and types are underlain by strikingly simple universal principles. Plato maintained that the goal of aesthetics is not simply to copy nature, but rather to peer deeply into her, penetrating her tapestry to understand and employ the sacred ratios and proportions at work in her beautifully simple but divine order.

Concerning this, Plotinus [205-270] wrote:

> *"The wise men of old, who made temples and statues in the wish that the gods should be present to them, looking to the nature of the All, had in mind that the nature of soul is easy to attract, but that if someone were to construct something sympathetic to it and able to receive a part of it, it would of all things receive soul most easily. That which is sympathetic to it is what imitates it in some way like a mirror able to catch the reflection of the form."*

The designers of Beijing's early 15th century Forbidden City (*opposite*) used three equal and adjacent golden rectangles to frame their project, two of which enclose the moat. See if you can locate them. They then used the principle of *rabatment* (*see page 402*) to site and proportion further elements. In rabatment, squares are sectioned off inside golden rectangles to produce smaller golden rectangles, producing further guide lines (*see also the Tablet of Shamash, page 299*).

In the twelve pages which follow we examine in further detail some of the ways in which humanity has attempted to manifest, or craft, the divine forms of nature into the human environment.

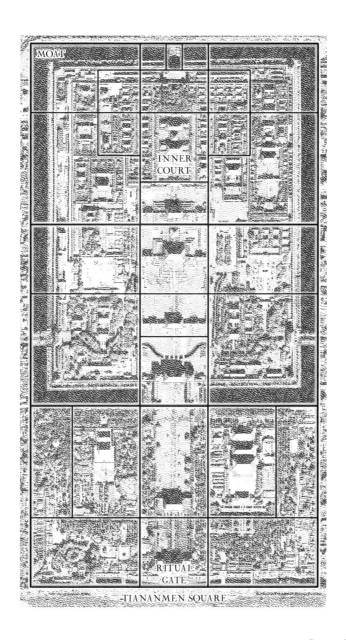

MOAT

INNER COURT

RITUAL GATE

TIANANMEN SQUARE

ANCIENT OF DAYS
tombs, temples, and pyramids

Like many ancient high cultures, the ancient Egyptians employed a sophisticated canon of number, measure and harmonic proportions in their magnificent monumental pyramids, temples and artwork. The simple ratios and grids they employed included the √2 diagonal of a square, the √3 bisection of an equilateral triangle, and the √5-based golden section, which appears both as golden ratio Fibonacci rectangles and in its pure pentagonal form. Fibonacci golden section approximations are suggested in the analyses of Hakoris chapel (8:5) and the Dendera Zodiac (5:3) (*opposite*). Moses built the Ark of the Covenant to a plan of 5:3 (2.5 × 1.5 cubits). Also note the pentagonal analyses apparent in the plan of the Osirian and the stunning statue of Menkaure (pharoanic builder of the smaller of the three Giza pyramids). The famous mask of Tutankhamen lends itself to a similar analysis.

Golden proportions and their Fibonacci approximations are found in Olmec sculpture (De La Fuente) and Maya temple and art panel ruins in Palenque (C. Powell). A 5:3 mandala (*below center*) regularly appears in Mesoamerican sculpture, architecture and codices (*below: Izapa Stela 89, & Olmec Monument 52, from Norman*).

Next time you are in the museum see what you can discover.

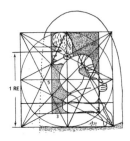 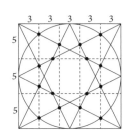 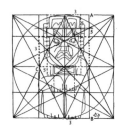

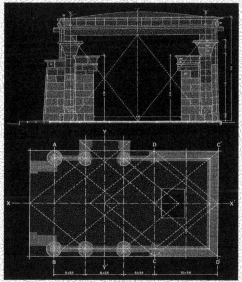

8:5 triangles in the chapel of Hakoris at Karnak (after Lauffray)

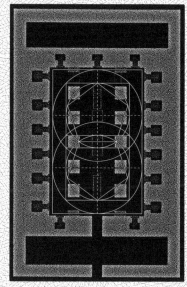

Lawlor's pentagonal analysis of the Osirian

a 5:3 mandala underlying the Dendera Zodiac (after Harding)

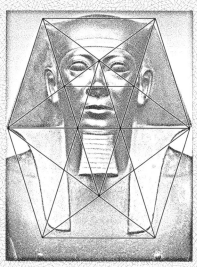

pentagonal geometry in a bust of Menkaure

MY CUP RUNNETH OVER
half full or half empty

After careful study of Egyptian and Greek art, and what he called the architecture of plants, shells, man, and the five regular solids, Jay Hambidge developed a theory of dynamic symmetry, in which the same principle of self-similar growth of areas was found displayed throughout nature's living "form rhythms". He maintained that the dynamism was to be discovered in incommensurable lines that were commensurable in square, i.e., in area. Thus the ratios of $\sqrt{2}$, $\sqrt{3}$ and $\sqrt{5}$ became central to his work, with a special place for the whirling squares established in spiral rotation in the continued reduction of the golden rectangle.

Hambidge's geometrical analyses of various items of Greek pottery are shown below and opposite and his full set of designer rectangles is shown later (*see appendix, page 404*). It has been claimed that Hambidge had a rectangle for everything, and that potters would have struggled to meet his exacting standards, but this is not to detract from his sincerity or his scholarly credentials.

There are certain lessons that may be drawn here—students of this subject may experience excessive enthusiasm over all things golden or, conversely, suffer complete skepticism and ossification.

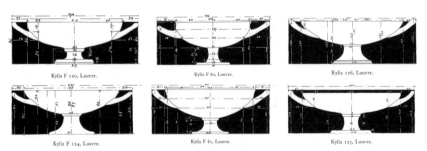

Kylix F 120, Louvre. Kylix F 80, Louvre. Kylix 126, Louvre.

Kylix F 124, Louvre. Kylix F 81, Louvre. Kylix 125, Louvre.

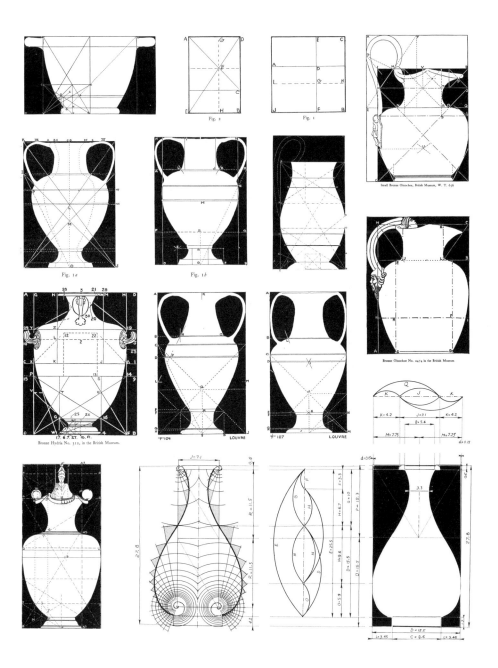

Fig. 2

Fig. 1

Small Bronze Oinochoe, British Museum, W. T. 656

Fig. 1 *a*

Fig. 1 *b*

Bronze Oinochoe No. 2474 in the British Museum

17. 6. 7. 27. 16. R.
Bronze Hydria No. 312, in the British Museum.

"F"104   LOUVRE

"F" 107   LOUVRE

K = 4.2   J = 7.1   K = 4.2
B = 5.4
M = 7.75   M = 7.75
d = 0.15

A SACRED TRADITION
old wine in new bottles

The philosophical and sacred number traditions of the Greeks and Romans were carefully carried into the new Christian religion as Jesus replaced Apollo and Hermes as the divine intermediary. The early tradition of the church placed emphasis upon the presence of Christ within, and the discovery of the Kingdom of Heaven in its divine proportion here on earth, in nature itself. Clement of Alexandria recognized Christianity as the "New Song", the sacred wine of the Logos occupying a new vessel.

Concerning the Logos (ratio or word), at the start of St. John's Gospel, 1:1, we read: "In the beginning was the Logos, and the Logos was with God and the Logos was God." The only ratio that is simultaneously one and with one is the golden section.

Scripture with its symbolical and allegorical meaning can only be fully understood through a study of sacred number. By the science of gematria, the name Jesus ΙΗΣΟΥΣ sums to 888, Christ ΧΡΙΣΤΟΣ is 1480, and the two together 2368. These three names are in the golden proportion 3:5:8, with Christ the golden mean.

In Roman and Christian architecture the golden section was again used alongside integer ratios, and geometric diagonals √2, √3, and √5. Some examples are shown (*opposite and below*).

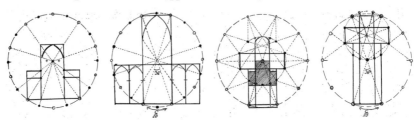

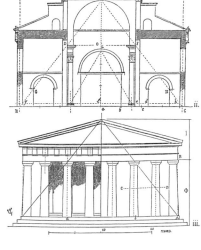

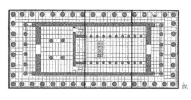

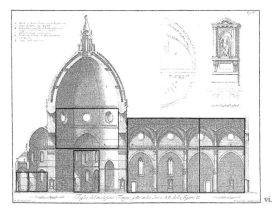

Clockwise from above: i) Portal relief over the south door of Chartres Cathedral displaying hidden pentagonal geometry (after Schneider). ii) Equilateral and 'Egyptian' 8:5 triangles in the Basilica of Constantine (Viollet-le-Duc). iii) 8:5 triangle defining the Parthenon (Viollet-le-Duc). iv) The plan of the Parthenon is a √5 rectangle, i.e., a square and two golden rectangles. v) Corinthian column capital displaying hidden pentagonal symmetry (after Palladio). vi) Duomo, Florence, designed by Brunelleschi, showing golden rectangle relationships.

Opposite page: Moessel's decagonal analyses of the plans of Gothic churches and cathedrals embodying numerous golden proportions.

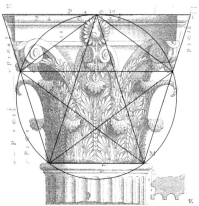

Phi in Painting
further Da Vinci secrets

By carefully linking the ratios and proportions of a work of art, ensuring that the parts reflect and synchronize with the whole, a painter can create an aesthetic, dynamic, living embodiment of the harmonic and symmetrical principles lying behind nature itself.

Like the groundplan of the Parthenon (*previous page*), Leonardo Da Vinci's painting of *The Annunciation* (*below*) employs a √5 framing rectangle (*below*). Using rabatment this is divided into one large square, and two golden rectangles which have both been further divided into a small square and a small golden rectangle. The device defines the main areas of the painting. In fact, in all the examples shown here the horizon is at the golden section of their height.

It is also not uncommon for artists to frame their pictures in 3:2, or 5:3 rectangles, simple Fibonacci approximations. Salvador Dali's *Sacrament of the Last Supper* is a good example of the use of 5:3.

We can clearly see the aesthetic quality rendered by the combined asymmetry and proportional symmetry of the golden section.

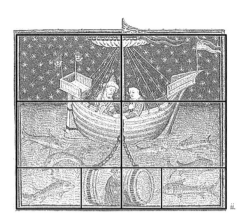

Clockwise from top left: i) The Virgin of the Rocks, by
Leonardo Da Vinci. ii) Alexander being lowered in a barrel,
from The Alexander Romance (after Schneider). iii) The
Beach, by Vincent Van Gogh. iv) The Birth of Venus, by
Sandro Botticelli v) The Baptism of Jesus, by Jean Colombe.

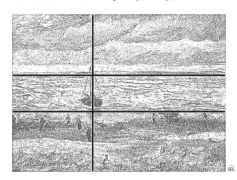

MELODY & HARMONY
in search of the lost chord

Harmonics (number in time) was one of four disciplines studied in the Pythagorean Quadrivium, together with Arithmetic (pure number), Geometry (number in space), and Spherics (number in space and time). The golden section is a theme common to all. In the Platonic tradition, the intention was to lift the soul out of the realm of mere opinion (*doxa*), by attunement with the ratios and proportions contained in the harmonies and rhythms of music. This allows the soul to pass into the Intelligible realm of knowledge (*episteme*), moving through the realm of mathematical reasoning (*dianoia*) up into direct intuition (*noesis*) of the world of pure Forms, the ratios themselves.

The structure of both rhythm and harmony is based upon ratio. The most simple and pleasing musical intervals, the octave (2:1) and the fifth (3:2), are the first Fibonacci approximations to the golden section. The series continues with the major and minor sixths (5:3 and 8:5). The scale itself holds the next step (13:8), for astonishingly, if we include the octave, musicians play eight notes in a scale, taken from thirteen chromatic notes. Finally, simple major and minor chords consist of the 1st, 3rd, 5th and 8th notes of the scale.

The golden section has been used by composers from Dufay (*opposite top after Sandresky*) to Bach, Bartok, and Sibelius, as a way of structuring a work of music. Russian musicologist Sabaneev discovered in 1925 that the golden section particularly appears in compositions by Beethoven (97% of works), Haydn (97%), Arensky (95%), Chopin (92%, including almost all of his *Etudes*), Schubert (91%), Mozart (91%), and Scriabin (90%).

the vocal prelude of Dufay's Vasilissa, ergo gaude, composed around 1420

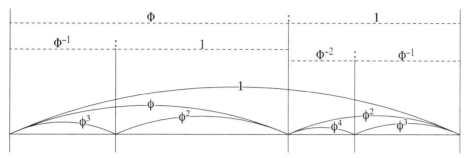

the structure of the whole Vasilissa is based on the golden section

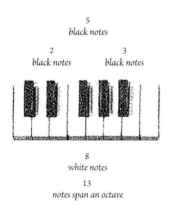

5
black notes

2
black notes

3
black notes

8
white notes

13
notes span an octave

Fibonacci numbers appear in the modern scale and in pure harmonic intervals like the octave (2:1), the fifth (3:2), and the major and minor sixths (5:3) and (8:5).

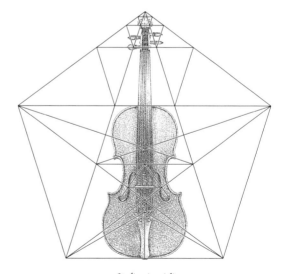

a Stadivarius violin

ALL THAT GLISTERS

is not gold

Today we consistently find ourselves reaching for that plastic card in our wallets and handbags. Most credit cards measure 86mm by 54mm, almost exactly an 8:5 rectangle and one of the most common Fibonacci approximations to the golden rectangle.

Because of its aesthetic qualities, embodied in its unique ability to relate the parts to whole, golden ratios are used in the design of many modern household items, from coffeepots, cassette tapes, playing cards, pens, radios, books, bicycles, computer screens and smartphones, to tables, chairs, windows and doorways. It even comes into literature, in the page layout of medieval manuscripts (*opposite lower right*) and as the small winged *Golden Snitch* in the Harry Potter stories.

Other important rectangles also find their way into our daily lives. The continuous geometric proportion most perfectly expressed in the golden series is mimicked in the International Standard Paper Size, which employs the continuous geometric proportion of $2:\sqrt{2}::\sqrt{2}:1$. Whereas removing a square from a golden rectangle produces another golden rectangle, folding a $\sqrt{2}$ rectangle in half produces two smaller $\sqrt{2}$ rectangles. Thus folding a sheet of A3 $(2:\sqrt{2})$ in half, gives you two sheets of A4 (each $\sqrt{2}:1$).

Golden dividers are a useful tool to have lying around the house (*above the calculator opposite*). They can be made at any size, and opened to produce the golden section in any object that you are curious about. They are relatively easy to construct: simply mark three equal rods with the golden section, drilling holes in two of them at the mark and cutting the third. Observe the example shown, fasten in four places, and sharpen the tips to complete.

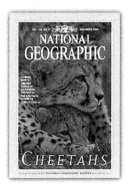

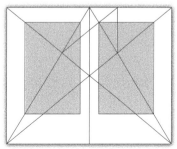

THE GOLDEN CHALICE

a marriage of roots

Plato said learning is remembrance. The teacher acts as a midwife, and by close communion with the student, passes a spark (of resonance) lighting a flame, resulting in the birth of the innate idea. Contemplation of a drawing assists this process.

The construction shown below demonstrates how √3 is derivable as the hypotenuse of a right-angled triangle with Φ and 1/Φ as legs. The Golden Chalice (*v., opposite*) combines this √3 revelation along with √2 derived from √Φ and 1/Φ as legs. Critchlow's Kairos drawing (*vi., opposite*) derives a pentagram (with its Φ and 1/Φ) from a circle and a √3 equlilateral triangle. All these results are exact!

Critchlow, concerned about the qualitative, ethical aspects of sacred geometry, writes:

> *"We are born into a world which appears as an indefinite dyad, a duality, a 'myself' and 'others', until such time as we reach a maturity which can be called 'relationship'. This reveals itself as the unity that is the true case and we can realize it through the 'golden mean' of people's relationship with all others, including the environment. In the Kairos diagram, the golden mean is linking the trinitarian equilateral triangle to the life-emblem of the five-pointed star."*

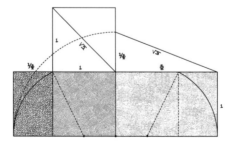

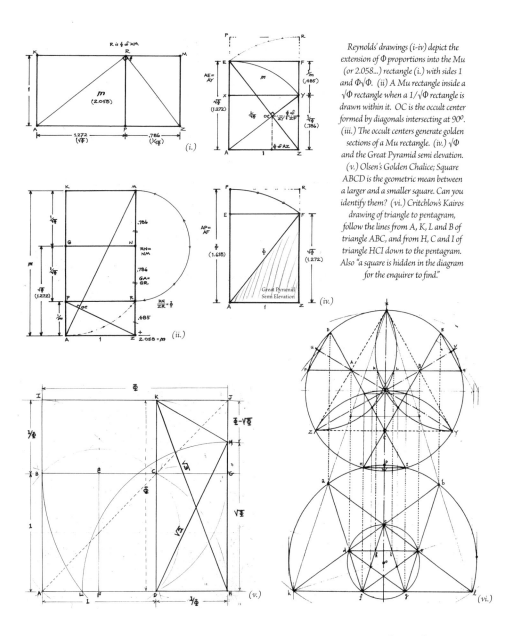

Reynolds' drawings (i-iv) depict the extension of Φ proportions into the Mu (or 2.058...) rectangle (i.) with sides 1 and Φ√Φ. (ii.) A Mu rectangle inside a √Φ rectangle when a 1/√Φ rectangle is drawn within it. OC is the occult center formed by diagonals intersecting at 90°. (iii.) The occult centers generate golden sections of a Mu rectangle. (iv.) √Φ and the Great Pyramid semi elevation. (v.) Olsen's Golden Chalice; Square ABCD is the geometric mean between a larger and a smaller square. Can you identify them? (vi.) Critchlow's Kairos drawing of triangle to pentagram, follow the lines from A, K, L and B of triangle ABC, and from H, C and I of triangle HCI down to the pentagram. Also "a square is hidden in the diagram for the enquirer to find."

Golden Polyhedra

water, ether, and the cosmos

The Golden Section plays a fundamental role in the structure of 3-D space, especially in the icosahedron and its dual, the dodecahedron (*opposite bottom right*), created from the centers of the icosahedron's faces. A rectangle drawn inside an icosahedron has edges in the ratio Φ:1 (or 1:ϕ) (*see below left and inside a cube opposite top*). The rectangles inside a dodecahedron are Φ^2:1 (or 1:ϕ^2) (*inside a cube lower opposite*). Nested inside an octahedron, the icosahedron cuts its edges in the ratio Φ:1 (*below center*). The exquisite early drawings by Kepler, DaVinci (*opposite*) and Jamnitzer [1508-1585] (*page 296*) show their fascination with the Φ and root relationships in the 5 Platonic and 13 Archimedean polyhedra.

Continuing this theme is the truncated icosahedron (*opposite upper right*), known to us today as the structure of C_{60}, or the common soccer ball; the rectangle in this solid has edges in the ratio 3Φ:1. The icosidodecahedron (*opposite top left*) has a radius:edge of Φ:1 and the rhombic triacontrahedron (*opposite lower left*) is made of thirty Φ:1 diamonds.

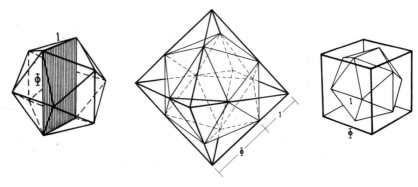

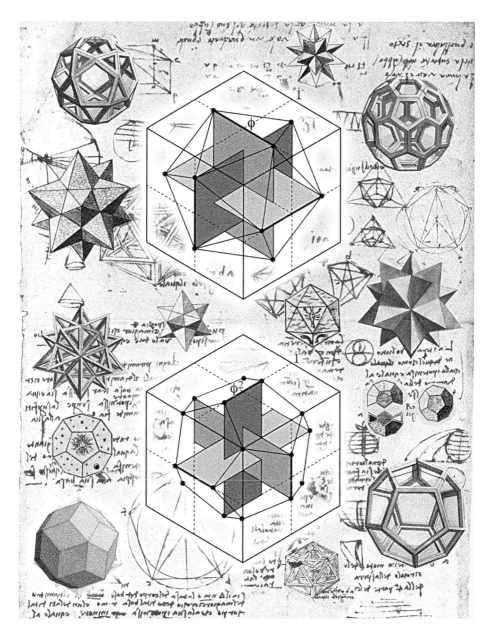

φ

φ²

PHI IN THE SKY

Aphrodite's golden kiss

Not only the microcosm and mesocosm display a liking for the divine proportion. Golden ratios abound in the solar system, and, strangely, seem to occur particularly frequently around Earth. For example, both the relative physical sizes *and* the relative mean orbits of Earth and Mercury may be given by Φ^2:1, or a simple pentagram, to an accuracy of 99% (*opposite top left*).

Nothing, however, compares to the extraordinary relationship between Earth and our nearest planet, Venus which draws a beautiful fivefold rosette around us every eight years. Eight Earth years is also thirteen Venusian years, the Fibonacci numbers 13:8:5 here appearing to connect space and time. Furthermore, Venus' perigee and apogee (her furthest and closest distances to Earth) are defined as Φ^4:1 to an accuracy of 99.99%, shown opposite as two nested pentagrams (*lower opposite, after Martineau*).

The two largest planets, Jupiter and Saturn, also produce a perfect golden ratio from Earth. Line them all up toward the Sun and a year later Earth is back where she started. Saturn will not have moved far and 12.85 days later Earth is again exactly between Saturn and the Sun. 20.79 days later Earth is found between the Sun and Jupiter. These synodic measures exist in space and time and relate as 1:Φ to 99.99% accuracy (*after Heath*).

Moving yet further into the macrocosm, irrespective of whether or not they become reconstrued as dark energy stars, Paul Davies discovered that rotating black holes flip from a negative to a positive specific heat when the ratio of the square of the mass to the square of the spin parameter (rotation speed) equals Φ.

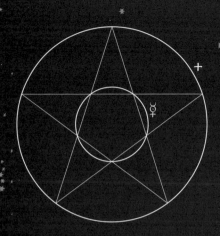

Two circles formed by a pentagram show the mean orbits of Earth and Mercury in the ratio $\Phi^2 : 1$. The sizes of the two planets are in the same ratio!

A technique for drawing the mean orbits of Earth and Venus. The two planets orbit the Sun at average distances in the ratio $(1 + 1/\Phi^2) : 1$.

The beautiful **fivefold** rosette pattern of comings and goings that Venus makes around Earth every **eight** years (or **thirteen** Venusian years).

Venus' furthest and closest distances from Earth, when she is in front of and behind the Sun, are precisely in the ratio $\Phi^4 : 1$.

RESONANCE & CONSCIOUSNESS
buddhas, shamans, and microtubules

Consciousness is one of the great mysteries of humanity. Like life itself (*symbolized opposite center in the five-fold flower by Pablo Amaringo*), it may result from a resonance between the Divine (whole) and nature (the parts) exquisitely tuned by the amazing fractal properties of the golden ratio, allowing for more inclusive states of awareness.

Penrose, the inventor of pentagonal tilings (*background opposite and below*), and Hameroff have provocatively suggested that consciousness may emerge through the quantum mechanics of microtubules. It is possible then that consciousness could reside in the geometry itself, in the golden ratios of DNA, microtubules, and clathrins (*opposite, by Gregory*). Microtubules, the structural and motile basis of cells, are composed of 13 tubulin, and exhibit 8:5 phyllotaxis. Clathrins, located at the tips of microtubules, are truncated icosahedra, abuzz with golden ratios. Perhaps they are the geometric jewels seen near the mouths of serpents by shamans in deep sacramental states of consciousness. Even DNA exhibits a Φ resonance. Each twist fits in a rectangle measuring in the Fibonacci ratio of 34:21 angstroms, and the cross-section through the molecule is decagonal.

Buddha said "The body is an eye." In a state of Φ-induced quantum coherence, one may experience samadhi, cosmic conscious identification with the awareness of the Universe Itself.

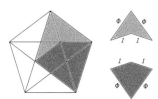 

side view of a microtubule

looking into a microtubule

a double pentagon quintuplo flower

the ten-fold rosette cross-section of DNA

the soccer ball structure of a clathrin

THE PHILOSOPHER'S STONE
new vision and insight—a promise kept

We have come a long way, from a divided line to the essence of consciousness. The stated intention was to provide you with new vision and insight through examination of nature's greatest secret, the golden section, the most simple but profound asymmetric cut. Perpetuated throughout the cosmos at all levels, it marries endless variety with ordered proportional symmetry, unifying parts and whole from the large down to the little and back up again in a eurythmic symphony of form.

Together, on this journey, we just may have discovered the Pearl of Great Price, the precious Stone that transmutes base knowledge into golden wisdom. Next time you pick up a starfish, brush your teeth, admire a painting, see a pinecone, kick a soccer ball, gaze at the evening star, pick a flower, listen to some music, or even use your credit card, stop and think for a moment. You are a whole made up of lesser parts, and you are part of a greater whole.

This is nature's greatest secret. The golden section is interwoven into the very fabric of our existence, providing us with the means to resonate, to attune with successively broader stages of self-identity and unfoldment upon the path of return to the One.

It is humanity's duty to reconnect and resonate with this deep code of nature, beautifying our world and our relationships with eurythmic forms and golden standards of excellence. As nature does effortlessly, our duty is nothing less than to transmute our world, transforming it into the heavenly state of beauty and symbiotic peace that it was always intended to be.

APPENDICES & INDEX

ANCIENT EUROPEAN ROCK ART

Much early European art was produced in the Upper Paleolithic era, with exquisite figurative cave paintings of animals appearing in what is now France and Spain between 35,000 BC and 10,000 BC (*not shown in this book*). A later tradition of geometric and abstract petroglyphs (rock carvings) in passage graves reached its artistic peak in Brittany, France (*e.g. Gavrinis, right*) and Ireland (*e.g. Newgrange and Loughcrew, facing page*) around 3500 BC.

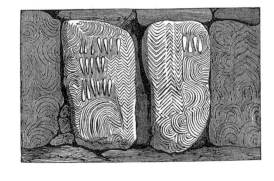

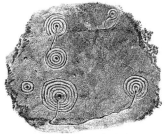

Loughcrew, Co. Meath, Ireland

Old Bewick, Northumberland, England

Gavrinis passage tomb, Brittany, France

Loughcrew passage tomb, Co. Meath, Ireland

Loughcrew, Co. Meath, Ireland

Kerbstone 1, Newgrange, Co. Meath, Ireland

Coverstone of a cist, Coilsfield, Ayrshire, Scotland

Kerbstone 52, Newgrange, Co. Meath, Ireland

Kerbstone 18, Newgrange, Co. Meath, Ireland

Chamber roof slab, near Sess Kilgreen, Co. Tyrone, Ireland

Loughcrew passage tomb, Co. Meath, Ireland

351

Ancient British Rock Art

The plates on these and the previous two pages are from many sources, but are collected together in *Ancient British Rock Art*, by Chris Mansell (Wooden Books 2007). Mostly produced in the Neolithic period between 4000 BC and 1500 BC, they clearly show the Neolithic fascination with simple formal elements.

This was a long-lived and widespread Western European art movement, with 'cup and ring' markings, such as the ones shown here, being carved in stone simultaneously in Northumberland (England) and Galicia (Spain). The artistry peaked in Britain and Brittany in the passage grave art shown on the previous page, much as the European-wide tradition of Celtic art would likewise peak in England and Ireland thousands of years later.

Almost nothing is known about these markings. Some are thought to refer to astronomical cycles, but for the majority, their meaning remains a mystery.

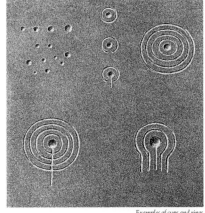

Examples of cups and rings

Achnabreck, Argyllshire, Scotland

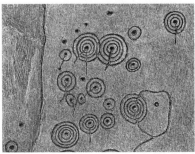

Carnbaan, Argyllshire, Scotland

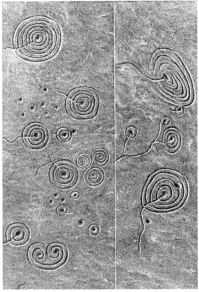

Achnabreck, Argyllshire, Scotland

Old Bewick, Northumberland, England

Ballymenach, Argylleshire, Scotland

Carlowrie, Yorkshire, England

Rosshire, Scotland

Rothiemay, Moray, Scotland

Cargill , Perthshire, Scotland

353

MAZES AND LABYRINTHS

The legendary builder of the first labyrinth is Daedalus, who constructed one for King Minos of Crete to contain the minotaur, and a large number of later Roman mosaic labyrinths show Theseus battling a minotaur at their center. However, it is impossible to get lost in a classical labyrinth—you just follow the path to get to the center. Another puzzle is that examples of the seven-coil form have been found in India dated to 2500 BC and in Native American cultures dated to 1000 BC. A dense complex of over a dozen stone labyrinths on Bolshoi Zayatsky Island, Russia, has also been dated to 1000 BC. A notable revival of labyrinth-building occurred in medieval Europe when they were placed in cathedrals. Then, from the 18th century, *mazes* began to be built, in which one could get lost.

The classical seven-coil labyrinth is intimately connected with the classical Greek spiral meander border (*see 1-5, right, to understand why*). Take two units of spiral meander (*1*) and stretch and pull the left side to make an eighth segment of a circle (*2*). Continue pulling around to make a quarter of a circle (*3*), then half a circle (*4*), and then all the way around (*5*) to complete a seven-coil labyrinth. Taking three units of meander would likewise make an eleven-coil labyrinth.

An alternative way to construct the seven-coil form is shown below. Starting with a cross-shaped seed, you then join loose ends over the top to complete the pattern. This works perfectly with a stick on sandy beaches.

Adapted from *Mazes and Labyrinths in Great Britain*, by John Martineau (Wooden Books, 2005).

Temple Cowley, UK (destroyed 1852)

Troy Town boulder maze, Scilly Isles, UK

Turf labyrinth, Rockcliffe Marsh, UK (vanished)

Watts Memorial Chapel, UK

Design in Harley manuscript, British Museum

17th century manuscript, British Museum

Hedge labyrinth, Cawdor Castle, Nairnshire, UK

Watts Memorial Chapel, Surry, UK

Turf labyrinth, Kingsland, Shropshire, UK (vanished)

Turf labyrinth, Hilton, Cambridgeshire, UK

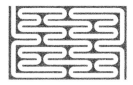

The diagram above expands into the 'Chartres' 11-coil medieval labyrinth (left, and Kingsland, above right) in the same manner as shown on the facing page. The maze to the right dates to the 1820s and was the first to use 'islands' to make it unsolvable using the 'hand-on-wall' trick.

Earl of Stanhope's maze, Chevening, Kent, UK

355

BRAIDS, KNOTS, AND PLAITS

Some of the earliest constructed objects, e.g. fishing nets and baskets, require entwining and fastening skills. Tools needing some kind of knot to function properly date to at least 300,000 BC.

More complex items came later. European Neanderthals (c. 90,000 BC) had knowledge of such techniques, and 30,000-year-old flax fibre for linen fabrication has been found at the Dzudzuana cave in the foothills of the Caucasus.

The plaits, braids and knots on these pages demonstrate a wonderful marriage of utility and form. Their decorative and symbolic use often comes to rival then surpass mere functionality; e.g. the ornate braided slings of the prehistoric Andean/Incan cultures, and the wonderfully refined knotwork of the Celts (*see pages 366–7*).

Transforming fibre into thread involves spinning, where short lengths of fibre (animal hairs or vegetable fibres), are drawn and twisted to make a continuous thread. From 10,000 BC threads were spun on wooden dropspindles, spinning wheels then appearing around the 11th century.

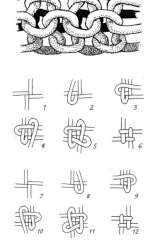

5-strand plait. 3 to Right , 2 to Left; outside right over 2 to inside left, outside left over 2 to inside right.

5-strand plait. 3 to Left, 2 to Right; outside left over 1, under 1 to inside right, outside right over 1, under 1 to inside left.

8-strand plait; arranged 3/1/3/1; under, over, under from the left, treating the 3 as 1.

4-strand plait. 2 to Left, 2 to Right; outside left behind 2 then over to inside left, outside right behind 2 to inside right.

Card loom 16 strands, 4 colours; move A to x, move D to y, repeat with pair 2 and its opp. pair, repeat with each following pair, turning c.clockwise.

4-strand plait tying white knot, then black knot, etc, with the knots in same direction each time, creates spiral.

Twined braid chevron, multiple colours, 16 strands, twine over pairs to center using outer 2 from left and right.

Now repeat for 2nd row, pull tight, repeat; you can twine rows clockwise then counterclockwise.

Diagonal striped braid.

Left: Find some lengths of thread and follow the steps shown to make your own decorative tassels.

Note: Images on this, and the following three pages, are from *Weaving, Methods, Patterns & Traditions of an Ancient Art* by Christina Martin (Wooden Books, 2005).

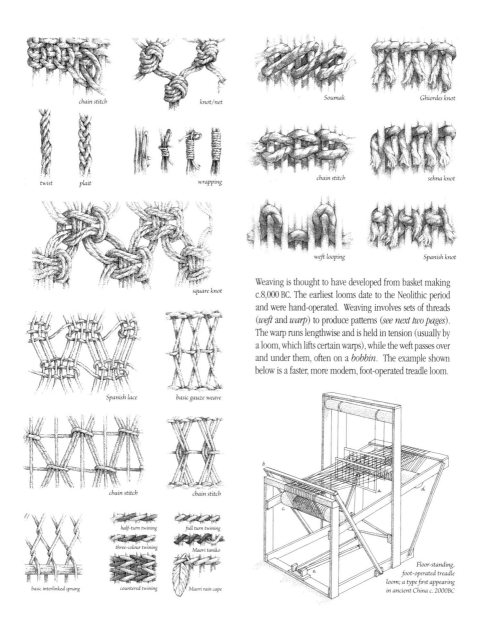

chain stitch

knot/net

twist

plait

wrapping

square knot

Spanish lace

basic gauze weave

chain stitch

chain stitch

basic interlinked sprang

half-turn twining

three-colour twining

countered twining

full turn twining

Maori taniko

Maori rain cape

Soumak

Ghiordes knot

chain stitch

sehna knot

weft looping

Spanish knot

Weaving is thought to have developed from basket making c.8,000 BC. The earliest looms date to the Neolithic period and were hand-operated. Weaving involves sets of threads (*weft* and *warp*) to produce patterns (*see next two pages*). The warp runs lengthwise and is held in tension (usually by a loom, which lifts certain warps), while the weft passes over and under them, often on a *bobbin*. The example shown below is a faster, more modern, foot-operated treadle loom.

Floor-standing, foot-operated treadle loom; a type first appearing in ancient China c. 2000BC

357

WEAVES

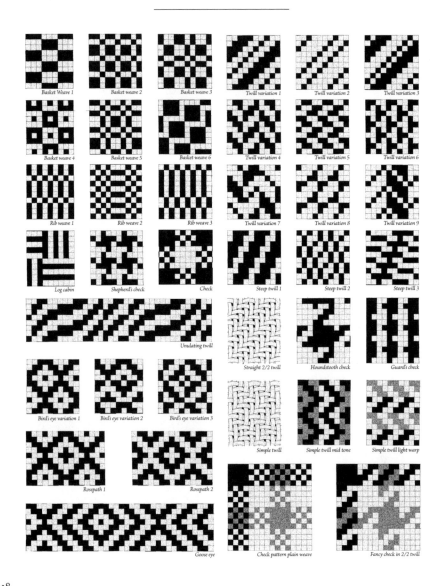

Basket Weave 1

Basket weave 2

Basket weave 3

Twill variation 1

Twill variation 2

Twill variation 3

Basket weave 4

Basket weave 5

Basket weave 6

Twill variation 4

Twill variation 5

Twill variation 6

Rib weave 1

Rib weave 2

Rib weave 3

Twill variation 7

Twill variation 8

Twill variation 9

Log cabin

Shepherd's check

Check

Steep twill 1

Steep twill 2

Steep twill 3

Unulating twill

Straight 2/2 twill

Houndstooth check

Guard's check

Bird's eye variation 1

Bird's eye variation 2

Bird's eye variation 3

Simple twill

Simple twill mid tone

Simple twill light warp

Rosepath 1

Rosepath 2

Goose eye

Check pattern plain weave

Fancy check in 2/2 twill

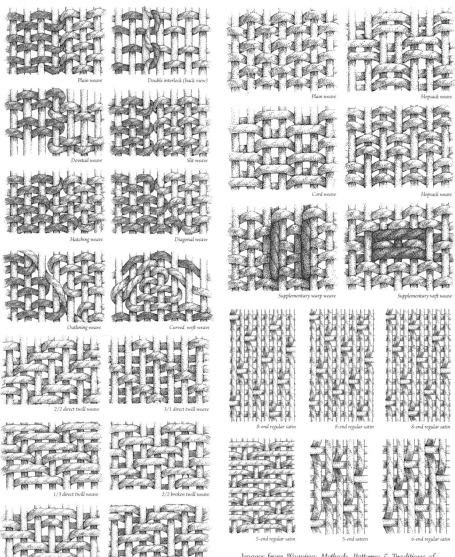

Plain weave

Double interlock (back view)

Dovetail weave

Slit weave

Hatching weave

Diagonal weave

Outlining weave

Curved weft weave

2/2 direct twill weave

3/1 direct twill weave

1/3 direct twill weave

2/2 broken twill weave

Chevron (herringbone) weave

2/2 reverse weave

Plain weave

Hopsack weave

Cord weave

Hopsack weave

Supplementary warp weave

Supplementary weft weave

8-end regular satin

8-end regular satin

8-end regular satin

5-end regular satin

5-end sateen

6-end regular satin

Images from *Weaving: Methods, Patterns & Traditions of an Ancient Art* by Christina Martin (Wooden Books, 2005).

359

USEFUL GRIDS FOR CELTIC ART

Left: Emerging spontaneously from natural processes, the living grids of winter tree branches are one of our earliest experiences of a being within a matrix of lines. *Right*: Nets haul life from the depths, they gather and enfold. Creative thinkers use the net of the mind to catch creatures of the imagination with as much stealth and purpose as any hunter.

Below: Ochre carvings 100,000 years old from Blombos cave in South Africa. Here, at the dawn of humanity, grids were the earliest and first expression. The emergence of such useful primary shapes of rhomb and triangle from the simplest of marks must have been an act of magic and a mind-expanding breakthrough for early hominids.

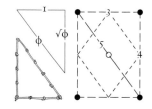

Above: Ancient peoples revered the 3-4-5 triangle as the building block of the universe (3, 4, and 5 are the first true integers, with the perfect number 6 as the area). The Egyptians made a 'mystical substitution', seeing 3 & 5 as terms of the Fibonacci sequence (1, 1, 2, 3, 5, 8, 13, 21 ...); they knew that within this series 3 and 5 related as 1 and ϕ, with 4 taking the role of $\sqrt{\phi}$.

Left: Symbolic and practical 3-4-5 triangles. A Druid's Girdle of 12 knots (still the most useful device for builders to set right angles by). Celtic artists often used subgrids based on rhombs, like 1×3/4 (i.e. 3×4 rectangles, with diagonal 5). George Bain called these "Pictish proportions". Also common are 80° and 100° rhombs, based on the 9-sided enneagon (*e.g. see page 11*).

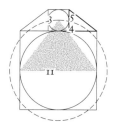

Above: The 3:11 relative dimensions of the Moon and the Earth, *and* the profile of the Great Pyramid can be constructed from this diagram drawn from a 3-4-5 triangle (after J. Michell). Two 3-4-5s also make the profile of Kephren's pyramid. The alchemical writer Jacob Boehme saw the rhomb as divinity reflected in man. Perhaps diamonds really *are* forever.

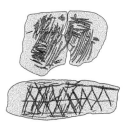

Right: The 6-fold compass-drawn flower familiar to all schoolchildren is made of seven circles and produces the first grid to emerge from the use of a compass of fixed radius. Used by every culture on Earth, it is the primary diagram of sacred geometry and quickly lays out 3-, 4-, 6-, and 12-fold symmetries, as well as 1:√3 proportions.

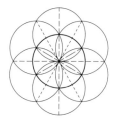

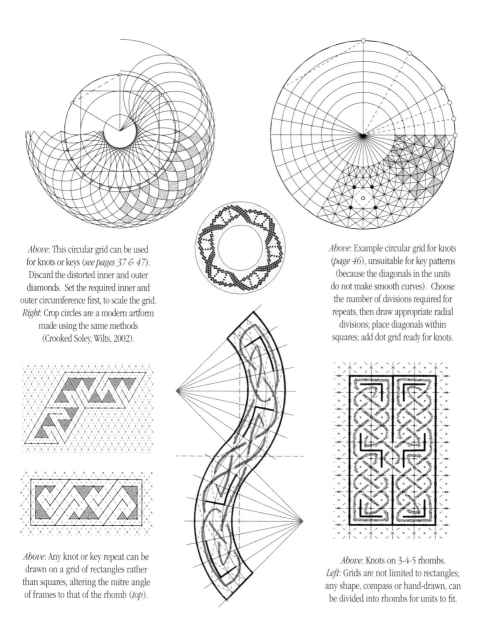

Above: This circular grid can be used for knots or keys (*see pages 37 & 47*). Discard the distorted inner and outer diamonds. Set the required inner and outer circumference first, to scale the grid.
Right: Crop circles are a modern artform made using the same methods (Crooked Soley, Wilts, 2002).

Above: Example circular grid for knots (*page 46*), unsuitable for key patterns (because the diagonals in the units do not make smooth curves). Choose the number of divisions required for repeats, then draw appropriate radial divisions; place diagonals within squares; add dot grid ready for knots.

Above: Any knot or key repeat can be drawn on a grid of rectangles rather than squares, altering the mitre angle of frames to that of the rhomb (*top*).

Above: Knots on 3-4-5 rhombs.
Left: Grids are not limited to rectangles; any shape, compass or hand-drawn, can be divided into rhombs for units to fit.

CELTIC SPIRALS

Left: The spiral is ubiquitous. Found at all scales from galactic arms to molecular bonds, it can be seen as a physical expression of the archetypal circle in motion, a circle with an oscillating center. Perfect circles are rare in nature and only really seen in connection with light phenomena, e.g. rainbows, or the perception of light by the circular lenses of our eyes.

Above: Carved tetrahedral granite ball (*Scotland, 2000 BC*). Hundreds of these small geometrical carvings have been found. Keith Critchlow has identified symmetries of all five Platonic solids, executed more than a 1,000 years before Plato. Concentration of finds at important sites suggests their use as teaching aids at Neolithic universities.

Right: At the tips of our tool-wielding fingers, we all carry our own unique spirals; human life is sustained by the spiral muscle of the heart; hair growth spirals from the crowns of our heads. Celtic arts are packed with spiral forms. *Right & opposite top center*: Triskele-based spiral and leaf forms from 4th-century BC grave goods found at Waldalgesheim in Germany.

Below: Ferns start their year as curled spiral shoots. Nature seems to find spirals excellent solutions for incremental growth. Shells are built by industrious polyps using the simple scaling principle of gnomonic growth, where each expansion is identical to the previous stage, only proportionally increased in size (also common in ancient architecture).

Above: Spirals are synonymous with the flow patterns seen in the curls of waves, ripples, whirlpools, and water spouts. Unbounded flow responds spirally to forces acting upon it, both in water and in plasma (clouds of charged electrons, the first form of matter in the universe, see also page 364). Perhaps flowing forces also shape spiral growth in living bodies.

Above: Spirals born from straight lines. Vortex rings shown by oil-based ink floating on the surface of water. A single 'cut' through the surface of the water creates a wake of ripples that stabilize into 'mushroom' shapes almost identical to those found in Celtic art. Analogous forms can be found in flowers, animal and insect horns, and the shape of the womb.

Above: Single bird's-head spiral from the *Book of Kells*. Part of the final spiral arc is erased to make space for a trumpet-petal join (dotted line).

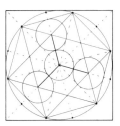

Above: A 12-fold division of a circle aligns a hexagon to the diagonal axes of a square, giving the 'tilt' found in many Celtic roundels (e.g. page 5).

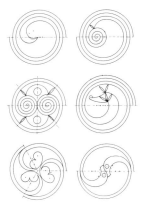

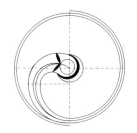

Below: A four-fold close-packing grid of circles sets the spacing for vertical and horizontal 'mushrooms' joined with four-armed spirals (after Bain).

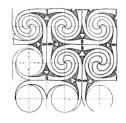

Below: The hexagonal close-packing grid used to design pages 25 (medium circles) & 27 (small shaded circles and large circles which touch them).

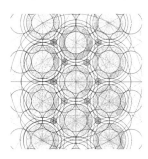

Left: Duck-head adapted to double spiral (*see page 17, top*). Above: Double spiral horse-head. Draw thin spiral path and quarter central area.

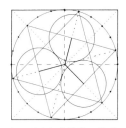

Above: A circle divided into 24 gives another 'tilt' between the diagonals of a square and 3-fold axes. *Below, left & right*: Single, double, and triple spirals.

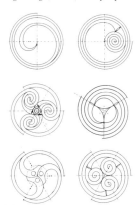

CELTIC KEYS

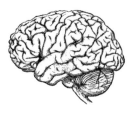

Right: In the art of the Shipobo people, the artistic process is only one step removed from visionary trance. They adorn their clothes, homes, and skin with key-like forms seen after drinking potent plant entheogen which helps them both *see* and *hear* shapes which are "engraved on their consciousness", and later remembered by humming (the shapes) whilst drawing.

1, 2, 5
1, 2, 3, 7
1, 2, 3, 4, 9
1, 2, 3, 4, 5, 11
1, 2, 3, 4, 5, 6, 13
1, 2, 3, 4, 5, 6, 7, 15

Above & right: Counting 'S'-curves: x, 2, $x+2$, 4, 6, $x+6$, 8, $x+8$ ... (x is length of first unit). Reverse to draw the other end of the 'S' (e.g. 1-2-5-*2-1*).

Below: Greek meanders. Found by the Celts in Coptic prayer books and turned 45° to make keys (*pages 28–31*).

Left: The closest natural analogue to key patterns are the crevices (*sulci*) and ridges (*gyri*) of the brain's folds. Folding processes are also fundamental to embryo development, forming the digestive tract and organs. Similar pattens are also made by beetles and corals. There are few ways to squeeze space so effectively as folding.

Right: The back-to-back mirrored 'S'-curves which make this key are similar to the 1-2-3-7-3-2-1 'S's of the top left panel on page 31, but use a different count for the path: 2-2-4-8-4-2-2 (*see below*). Notice how the white line is made of continuous 'Y' shapes when the path is thickened, and look out for inverted versions where black 'Y' shapes can hide the pattern's structure.

2, 2, 6
2, 2, 4, 8
2, 2, 4, 4, 10
2, 2, 4, 4, 6, 12
2, 2, 4, 4, 6, 6, 14
2, 2, 4, 4, 6, 6, 8, 16

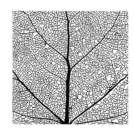

Above: Cellular compartments within leaves look very like keys. Square spirals are excellent solutions for space division, essential in plants for maximum distribution of photosynthetic cells, ensuring leafy light-drinking organs receive maximum exposure. Again we see human imagination mimicking nature's imagination, both finding the same equitable answers.

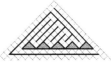

Above: These triangular repeats demonstrate how increasing the dimensions of a unit creates extra branches in the 'foot' shapes, and increases the number of folds. This can be developed further, making more and more intestinal turns.

Above: Keys laid on a circular grid of radially-arranged 'V'-shaped units. Ends of outer units align to the center of the circle. Keys can be hard to fit on such grids, so unusual solutions may be needed (*e.g. the dovetail-shaped wedges, above*).

Above: Regular key pattern drawn with freehand curves instead of lines.

Below left and right: Keys based on rotated single spirals joined in vertical columns. Apart from the top and bottom rows, all columns contain the same spiral. Edge triangles are filled without continuing the key device.

Above: The eight permutations of a single spiral on a diagonal grid.

Left: Key patterns from the *Book of Durrow* f.1v (*see page 53*) laid out using regularly spaced squares.

Above: A circle distorts a key of 2-2-4-4-6-12-6-4-4-2-2 'S'-shapes on a regular grid. Concentric circles and a degree of flexibility and careful judgment by eye are used to help adjust edges so that they merge with the rectangular center.

CELTIC KNOTS

Left: As means to join, build, and bind, knots have served us from the earliest times, tying themselves to our languages, symbols, and metaphors. In marriage we "tie the knot", at some wedding ceremonies literally so. We find ourselves tied up with tasks, tied to contracts, bound by our word, and roped into tying up loose ends.

Above: Knots were once cutting-edge technology, different forms serving different functions (weaving, crochet, and knitting all involve specialized types of knots). Sailors and climbers trust their lives to their knots. Knots have also been used as mnemonics by knotters of handkerchiefs and the Inca, who developed a language of knots for record-keeping called quipu (above).

Below: Knot topology, a branch of math devoted to the properties of knots, is used to study polymer bonds and chirality (handedness). Theorists have suggested that knot theory may help fashion logic gates for topological quantum computers. Knots can only exist in three-dimensional space; when modeled in any other number of spatial dimensions they come undone.

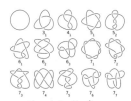

The *periodic table of knots*

Artists of the ancient world sought not to imitate nature, but rather to imitate her in her mode of operation. Celtic patterns are the ideal example of stylized thinking as natural philosophy. Knots have a particular effect on respiration. A measured breath is essential to drawing smooth curving paths, slowing the heartbeat. Practice shapes both the artist and the art.

Above, right to left: DNA's double helix, both knot and spiral, pushes life to the tolerance of the laws of physics. Like a line, it *is* itself *and* describes itself; The healing Caduceus of Mercury, god of thresholds, thieves, and knowledge; Birkeland currents, cables of plasma seen at every scale in the universe, whose patterns appear around planets, stars, and galaxies (in the infrared spectrum).

Above: Serpent knot from St. Patrick's bellshrine (Ireland, 12th century).

Above: Muscles knot our bones and tendons together, making motion possible. Here *seratus anterior* muscles weave around the rib cage providing strength and flexibility similar in structure to a basket. Pattern is woven through us on so many levels. From quark to galaxy, butterfly to sea shell, we are patterns within patterns within patterns.

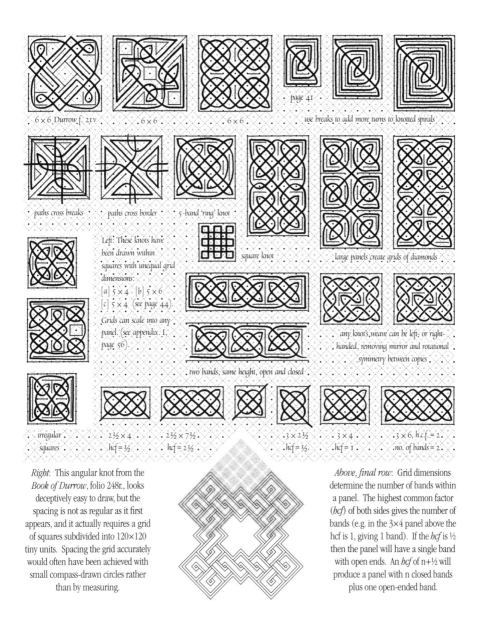

6 × 6 Durrow f. 21v · · · · 6 × 6 · · · · 6 × 6 · · · · use breaks to add more turns to knotted spirals

page 41

paths cross breaks · · · paths cross border · · · 5-band 'ring' knot · · · large panels create grids of diamonds

Left: These knots have
been drawn within
squares with unequal grid
dimensions:
[a] 5 × 4 · [b] 5 × 6
[c] 5 × 4 (see page 44).
Grids can scale into any
panel. (see appendix. I,
page 56).

square knot

any knot's weave can be left- or right-
handed, removing mirror and rotational
symmetry between copies

two bands, same height, open and closed

irregular	2½ × 4	2½ × 7½	3 × 2½	3 × 4	3 × 6, h.c.f. = 2.
squares	hcf = ½	hcf = 2½	hcf = ½	hcf = 1	no. of bands = 2.

Right: This angular knot from the
Book of Durrow, folio 248r., looks
deceptively easy to draw, but the
spacing is not as regular as it first
appears, and it actually requires a grid
of squares subdivided into 120×120
tiny units. Spacing the grid accurately
would often have been achieved with
small compass-drawn circles rather
than by measuring.

Above, final row: Grid dimensions
determine the number of bands within
a panel. The highest common factor
(*hcf*) of both sides gives the number of
bands (e.g. in the 3×4 panel above the
hcf is 1, giving 1 band). If the *hcf* is ½
then the panel will have a single band
with open ends. An *hcf* of n+½ will
produce a panel with n closed bands
plus one open-ended band.

CELTIC MANUSCRIPT GRIDS

2 : φ
Lindisfarne, folio 2v.

2 : √3+1
Kells, f. 7v & 32v.

3 : √5
Lindisfarne, f. 26v.

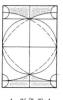

1 : 2(√5-2)+1
Macdurnen, f. 115v.

3 : 2
Mulling, f. 35v.

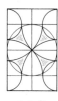

1 : 3-√2
Mulling, f. 81v

The Ionian Lambdoma (*right*) shows the relation between powers of two and three (musical octaves and perfect fifths). It also contains harmonic means (e.g. 6-8-12), arithmetic means (e.g. 6-9-12), and geometric means (e.g. 64-72-81).

1	2	4	8	16	32	64
	3	6	12	24	48	96
		9	18	36	72	144
			27	54	108	216
				81	162	324
					243	486
						729

Left: *The Harburg Gospels* folio 126*v*, when the width of the panel is taken as 128 units (2^6) the corresponding height will be 162 units (3^4). If 128 is seen as an octave, then distances within the panel correspond to musical notes: a=F, $2a$=F♯, b=A, $2c$=B♭ are just a few of the musical ratios used. Again, we see the Celts embedding numerical insight into their arts, making a visual synthesis of music via the hidden treasure of numerical harmonics.

Right: Illuminator's tools: ground pigments bound with egg white or gum arabic, a brush compass, and quartz lens (with small feet for tool access beneath). Some lenses focus ambient light upon the center of magnification.

Below: Timeline of Celtic art in context.

100,000 BC	5,000 BC	3,000 BC	700 BC	56 BC	500–800	900
earliest grids	Carnac, France	Stonehenge	Greeks and Celts	Romans invade Britain	Celtic Christian art	Islamic illumination

368

CERAMICS AND GLASS

CLAY is a plastic (shapeable) substance formed by the gradual erosion of minerals such as feldspar to give minute particles of *hydrated silicates* mixed with water and other compounds. The discovery around 10,000 BC that clay heated to high temperatures changes to become hardwearing and strong is one of the turning points in mankind's story. Fired in a kiln at temperatures between 800°C and 1200°C, clay remains slightly porous and is known as *earthenware*. Firing at higher temperatures causes the clay to partially vitrify, producing *stoneware*. Porcelain is a fine white body fired to vitrification to become translucent. *Pyrometric cones*, which melt at different degrees of heat absorbtion, are often used to measure firing cycles and digital thermometers are also popular. It is also possible to judge kiln temperature by the colour of the glowing ceramic (the temperature of metals can also be estimated from this list).

Lowest visible red to dark red	470-650°C
Dark red to cherry red	650-750°C
Cherry red to bright cherry red	750-800°C
Bright cherry red to orange	800-900°C
Orange to yellow	900-1100°C
Yellow to light yellow	1100-1300°C

Clay objects can be formed by hand and with simple tools, by turning on a potter's wheel or by pouring *slip* (a mixture of clay and water) into a mould. Once formed the clay is allowed to dry, after which it is known as *greenware* and is very brittle. It can be fired unglazed in a 'biscuit firing', and then fired a second time with an application of glaze, or it can be fired in one cycle with or without an application of dry glaze.

GLAZE when fired, melts to form a hard glassy coating. It allows earthenware vessels to hold liquids. Mixed from finely ground ingedients it can be applied by dusting onto the clay object, or by mixing with water to be painted, poured on, or dipped into. Glazes are a specialized type of glass combining silica, alumina to increase viscosity when melted, and a flux to lower the melting point. Lead ♄ glazes use lead ♄ oxide as a flux. Soda ash, potash or other alkaline fluxes make alkaline glazes which often form crazing patterns of fine cracks as they cool. Opacifiers, such as tin ♃ oxide, are also used. Coloring materials can be mixed with the glaze itself, painted on the clay body before glazing (underglaze) or on top of the glaze (overglaze). Examples include; iron ♂ oxide for ambers and browns, copper ♀ oxide for greens and turquoises, cobalt oxide for blues, and manganese dioxide for lilac, purple and brown.

GLASS is a strong, hard wearing, inert, biologically inactive, and of course transparent material. It is made primarily from silica (*silicon dioxide*), the most abundant mineral on Earth. Normal solids have regular molecular structures, however, many materials if cooled quickly assume a non-crystalline solid structure - a glass in the general sense. Silica is one of the few materials that forms a glass at normal cooling rates. Pure silica has a melting point of 1723°C. To reduce this melting point to about 1000°C soda ash or potash is added, and lime is added to counter the solubility that soda ash or potash cause in the glass. The mix is then heated in a kiln at about 1100°C until fused. Other ingredients sometimes used are lead ♄, which imparts more brilliance, and boron that improves the thermal properties useful for labware.

Glass normally has a green tinge from iron ♂ impurities, but an entire rainbow of colours can be made using different metals. Metallic gold ☉ in small concentrations produces a ruby glass. Silver ☽ compounds produce colours from orange-red to yellow. Adding more iron makes a stronger green. Copper ♀ oxide produces a turquoise colour, while metallic copper produces a very dark opaque red. Cobalt makes blue glass. Manganese can be added for an amethyst colour. Tin ♃ oxide together with antimony and arsenic oxides makes opaque white glass.

Glass was first manufactured around 2500 BC. The Ancient Egyptians made small jars and bottles by winding continuously heated glass threads around a bag of sand on a rod. Glass blowing was discovered in the first millennium BC and enabled the quick production of large leakproof vessels. Glassblowing uses three furnaces - one for the molten glass, a second for reheating the piece being worked on as necessary, and a third for annealing, i.e., cooling the glass slowly enough to avoid cracking and reduce stresses. As well as the blowpipe, tools used in glassblowing include shaping blocks, an iron rod known as a *ponty*, flat paddles, tweezers, and various shears. Intricate glassware ideal for an alchemical lab can be formed by heating, manipulating, and joining preformed rods, tubes and simple blown vessels using alcohol lamps, or nowadays propane or oxygen flames.

ARTISTS' PIGMENTS

PIGMENTS must be insoluble and reasonably light-fast. They are prepared for use by grinding finely into a paste with a little water using a glass muller on a glass surface (if coarse, grind in a pestle and mortar first). For oil paint use oil instead of water.

☉ **GOLD** hammered very thinly to make gold leaf can be applied to most surfaces. It can be made from leaf into a paint with gum arabic or gelatine, often called shell gold.

☽ **SILVER** like gold can be applied as leaf or made into a paint but it tarnishes in time with exposure to air.

♀ **COPPER** ores malachite (green) and azurite (blue) make good pigments, however the finer they are ground the paler their colour. Pouring together strong solutions of blue vitriol (*copper sulphate*) and soda ash (*sodium carbonate*) precipitates an artificial malachite. Verdigris is *copper acetate*, soluble in water or alcohol for use, it can also be dissolved in resin in which case it will turn brown in air if not varnished. It can be grown as a crust on copper strips suspended in a mason jar with vinegar at the bottom, left in a warm place. The oldest known artificial pigment is Egyptian blue, a *copper silicate*. By dry weight: mix 10 parts limestone (whiting) with 11 parts malachite and 24 parts quartz. Grind thoroughly to homogenize. Add a flux of soda ash or potash, heat to around 900°C then keep at 800°C for at least 10 hours. Cool and grind for pigment.

♂ **IRON**. Red ochre, yellow ochre, raw sienna and raw umber are all *iron oxides*, the latter two are also well known in 'burnt' forms made by calcining the raw. Natural green earth pigments contain *iron silicate*. Manmade *iron oxides* are also useful pigments ranging from yellows to reds to browns.

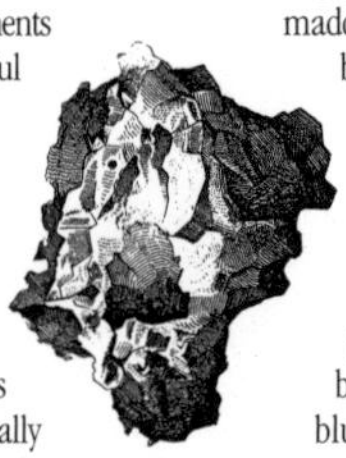

☿ **QUICKSILVER** in its red ore cinnabar, *mercuric sulphide*, makes a fine pigment. Vermilion is artificial cinnabar made by mixing together molten sulphur and quicksilver to form black *mercuric sulphide*. Heated in a suitable closed earthenware vessel this sublimates to form red *mercuric sulphide*, chemically the same compound, but transformed in colour. Quicksilver is highly toxic; do not try at home.

♄ **LEAD** pigments are toxic. Minium is *lead oxide*, a bright reddish orange, made by prolonged high temperature heating of lead in air. **WHITE LEAD** is *lead carbonate*. Place lead strips in earthenware jars with a little wine vinegar and digest somewhere warm. After some months a crust of white lead should have formed.

♃ **TIN**. Now rarely used, lead-tin yellow (*lead stannate*) ranges from a light lemon yellow to a more pinkish colour. Mix 3 parts minium thoroughly with 1 part tin oxide. Pass through a very fine mesh to help homogenize the mix. Heat slowly to 600°C, keep at this tempertaure for 2 hours, heat further, and keep at 800°C for another hour. Cool slowly.

COBALT is the key ingredient in smalt, a blue glass powder. Heat quartz and a potash flux with enough *cobalt oxide* to make an opaque blue glass to 1150°C to fuse. Remove while hot and plunge into cold water to break up before grinding into pigment. Cobalt blue, discovered in 1802, is *cobalt aluminate*. Grind 1 part *cobalt chloride* and 5 parts *aluminium chloride* and heat for 5 minutes in a test tube over a strong gas flame. **ANTIMONY** is used in Naples yellow, an artificial *lead antimonate* that dates back to Ancient Egypt, made by calcining a lead compound with an antimony compound. **ULTRAMARINE** is prepared from mineral lapis lazuli. Sprinkle finely ground lapis lazuli with linseed oil. Make a paste from equal parts of carnauba wax, pine resin and colophony. Add one sixteenth part linseed oil, one quarter part turpentine and the same of mastic. Mix 4 parts of this paste with 1 of the lapis lazuli and digest for a month. Knead the mixture in warm water until the blue particles separate and settle. Ultramarine was first synthesized in 1828.

LAKE pigments are made from organic sources such as madder (red), unripe buckthorn berries (yellow), ripe buckthorn berries (green) and cochineal beetles (carmen). Mix a saturated solution of potash and grind and mash the source matter in it until no more colour comes out. Mix 6 spoons of alum with half a pint of warm water for each pint of colored potash solution. Pour in the alum solution to precipitate pigment. Insoluble **INDIGO** powder can be used as a pigment. The Maya made a fine artificial blue by heating a mix of indigo and *palygorskite clay*. 200°C for about 5 hours is suitable.

BONE BLACK. Boil animal bones (chicken bones are good) until fat free. Wrap tightly in aluminium foil and heat the package in a strong gas flame for an hour. Cool, unwrap and grind for pigment. **LAMP BLACK** is carbon gathered by placing a metal surface over a lamp flame. Not suited for painting its fineness makes it ideal for ink.

ARTISTS' MEDIA

PAINT is a mixture of pigment and a binder. **GUM ARABIC** is a popular water based binder, used to make **WATERCOLORS**, or, with an opacifier such as chalk added, **GOUACHE**. Crush pieces of gum arabic to a fine powder, add twice their volume of hot water, stir to dissolve. To reduce brittleness add a small amount of candy sugar. Mix 1 part gum arabic soultion with 2 parts pigment paste in water (all parts are by volume).

EGG TEMPERA is a very long lasting medium. Gently separate the white from the yolk then roll the yolk from palm to palm until dry. Hold the yolk membrane downward and pinch to release the liquid into a vessel while holding the membrane. Mix this yolk with equal parts of water or white wine vinegar, for use with pigment paste. **GLAIR** is made with egg white and is ideal for delicate illumination work on parchment. Beat egg white until the foam is dry. The liquid at the bottom of the vessel is glair.

SIZE is any coating that fills or coats a surface to protect and prepare it for the next layer. **RABBIT SKIN GLUE**, a specific type of animal glue, is an excellent size and can also be used as a quick drying medium mixed directly with water based pigment paste. Soak 1 part rabbit skin glue in 18 parts water until swollen, then heat gently (without boiling) in a double boiler until dissolved. **CASEIN**, derived from milk, is a size that can also be used as a quick drying tough paint medium. Sift 2 parts powdered casein into 8 parts water and remove lumps by stirring. Add 1 part *ammonium carbonate* and allow to stand for half an hour, then add 8 parts of water. **STARCH** is another size: stir 1 part starch powder into 3 parts cold water to form a paste then slowly stir into 3 parts boiling water. When the solution starts to clear remove it from the heat. To use, dilute with water. **FISH GLUE**, extracted from fish by heating the skin or bones in water, is a good size for use on parchment.

OIL PAINT is surprisingly easy to make. Follow the instructions opposite for grinding pigment, using **LINSEED OIL**, **WALNUT OIL**, or **POPPY OIL**, and it is ready for use. If the pigments are already finely ground one can work them into paint with oil simply using a palette knife. Oil paints do not dry but harden through chemical reaction, giving oil painters time to work and rework their paintings. Ochres speed the oil's 'drying', charcoal black slows it down. The craft

of oil painting rests on mastering the use of the many resins and spirits available. The following recipes are just a taste of the possibilities. Utmost care must be taken using volatile and flammable materials.

VARNISHES protect oil paintings, even if a glossy finish is not desired it is still best to apply one (after the painting has completely dried), and then use a wax finish. **GLAZES**, often very similar to varnishes, are used to thin paint to apply a veil of colour while keeping it strong enough to adhere. The traditional rule is to paint 'fat over lean', each successive layer having less pigment and more oils and resins. **DAMAR RESIN** comes in pale yellow lumps. Mixing equal parts in **PURE GUM SPIRITS OF TURPENTINE** (hereafter just 'turpentine') and agitating daily until the resin is dissolved makes a good varnish that doubles as a glaze. **MASTIC** makes a good varnish mixed and heated with twice its volume of turpentine. For a thin high gloss varnish mix 1 part **VENICE TURPENTINE** or **CANADA BALSAM** with 2 of turpentine. A good sweet smelling varnish for sized and sealed wood is 3 parts venice turpentine and 1 part **OIL OF SPIKE LAVENDER** warmed together to blend. **AMBER** varnishes are hard and versatile, serving as painting media, final varnishes, or as fixatives when thinned. Nowadays they are made with **COPAL** as a substitute: crush 1 part of the copal resin to powder and bottle with 4 parts benzene until nearly dissolved, then mix with 3 parts turpentine and heat gently to fully dissolve. If this warm solution is left unsealed the benzene will evaporate to leave a copal and turpentine varnish. Add 1 part beeswax to 3 parts of this for a good wax to reduce gloss on a varnished painting. **FIXATIVES**, used to fix pigment in place, are essential to the preservation of drawings in charcoal, chalk and pastel. Mix 1 part **SHELLAC** with 50 parts methyl alcohol. To use place the picture on the floor and blow the fixative vapor just above it to give an even coat.

ENCAUSTIC uses beeswax as a medium. Carefully heat 1 part beeswax and 3 parts turpentine until the wax has melted, then stir while cooling. Grind pigments thoroughly into the wax before applying with a brush or palette knife. Another recipe uses equal parts of soft elemi resin, beeswax, oil of spike lavender and turpentine. **FRESCO** is the specialized technique of painting directly on lime plaster. Mix lime-proof pigments to paste with water and paint directly onto fresh plaster.

USEFUL RECIPES

CHARCOAL is produced by heating wood in the absence of the oxygen in air. It can also be made from bone. Charcoal burns hotter and cleaner than wood and is useful in smelting and forging for these reasons. Wood charcoal is mosty carbon and has been made since prehistory. Conical piles of wood were made with openings at the bottom and a central shaft for limited air flow, the pile was covered with turf or wet clay, and the firing started at the bottom of the shaft. Any suitably closed container of dry wood placed in a hot enough fire will produce charcoal with a little experimentation. It is important to allow just enough gap for gases to escape the container without allowing the free flow of air that would reduce the wood to ash. Twigs of vine or willow charcoal are popular for drawing. To produce small quantities follow the instructions for making bone black on page 370 replacing the bones with stripped twigs.

ANIMAL GLUE is made by simmering animal hides (rabbits work well), tendons and hooves in water until they have broken down to give a thick glue which can be strained off. Take care not to heat too quickly or the mixture will burn and darken. The glue can be dried out to store. Mix with hot water 1:1 by volume to use. Glue made this way has been used for millennia and is good for carpentry – hide glue joints are repairable and reversible. Hide glue is kept liquid for working in a double boiler.

LEATHER is made by **TANNING** animal skins to keep them pliant even after they have become wet and dried out again. First scrape off all the fat and meat from the flesh side, then rub a strong solution of potash or lime into the fur side and leave for a couple of days until the fur becomes loose. Scrape the fur side with a sharp knife until clean. Traditionally the next stage is *bating*, an unassuming term for rubbing carnivore dung (usually dog) into the skin to break down its elasticity with enzyme reactions. Once the hide is no longer springy and lays flat the dung is washed out thoroughly. *Tannins* are leached from crushed oak bark in water, into which the skin is immersed for three days. After this the skin can be stretched

out to dry and is ready. Skins can also be tanned with brains, each animal has just enough for its own hide. Clean the skin as above. Cook the brains in a small amount of water, squashing them with your hands to mix well. When the soup is as hot as you can still work with rub it into the flesh side then the fur side using your hands. Leave it for about seven hours then immerse the hide in water overnight. The water must then be worked out of the skin using a wooden wedge and a rounded stick. These tools help keep the skin stretched and loose while it dries. Smoking over a fire once dry helps prevent it stiffening again if it gets wet.

PARCHMENT, or **VELLUM**, is an animal skin treated with slaked lime and dried while stretched to produce a smooth surface for writing and painting upon. A summary of a 12th C. recipe is as follows: Stand goat skins in water for a day and a night, remove and wash thoroughly. Prepare a bath of milk of lime and immerse the skins, folding them on the flesh side, for a week (two in winter), agitating twice or thrice a day. Remove the skins and take off the hair. Make a fresh milk of lime bath, replace the skins and agitate daily for a week. Remove them and wash thoroughly. Soak in clean water for two days, then remove and tie the skin to a circular frame with cords. Dry, then shave the skin with a sharp knife and leave two days in the sun. Moisten and scour the flesh side with pummice powder. After two days repeat and fully smooth the flesh side with pummice powder while wet. Tighten the cords to flatten. Once dry the sheets are ready.

PAPER can be made with no chemical intervention, in which case the soaked, boiled, beaten and shredded plant fibers become a *mechanical pulp*. However, using an alkali breaks down the *lignin* from the *cellulose* fibers to give better results in a *chemical pulp*. Boil plant stems in an alkali such as slaked lime until the white fibers are left floating in a brown alkaline soup. Strain this pulp, soak in clean water, strain again and resoak. This pulp can be sieved through a mold of wire mesh on a wooden frame to make sheets of paper (*see illustration, left, showing use of frames and rag cotton pulping equipment to rear*).

GYPSUM is a common mineral. Calcined at around 150°C most of its chemically bound water is driven off to produce **PLASTER**. Mixing dry plaster powder with water reforms gypsum, firstly as a paste then expanding and hardening into a solid. A good preparation should be evenly mixed. **GESSO** is a thick, creamy primer for rigid surfaces. Sieve finely ground chalk or gypsum into rabbit skin glue (*see facing page*), using roughly equal volumes of glue and powder. After a few minutes stir gently and apply multiple even coats, allowing each to dry. Keep the gesso warm and add a little water to further thin each coat and reduce the risk of cracking. Sand and polish when finished to give an excellent surface for painting and gilding.

INK made from **IRON GALL** is light-fast and burns into the page. Oak galls are swellings on oak trees caused by insect attack. Use the following by weight; 4 parts oakgalls, 1 part green vitriol (*iron sulphate*), 1 part gum arabic, 30 parts water. Grind the oakgalls finely and soak in half the water. Dissolve the green vitriol and gum arabic in the rest of the water, then mix both liquids. The instant black colour will deepen if left for a month or two with occasional stirring. Excess iron salts will make an ink that turns brown at the edges while excess oakgall makes a weak black. **SEPIA** from Mediterranean cuttlefish and other such molluscs, is very long lasting with rich dark brown tones, but it is not light-fast. **INDIAN INK**, or sometimes **CHINESE INK**, is a *colloidol suspension* of carbon in water. Finely ground charcoal added to a thin gum arabic solution will make a simple Indian ink. The gum arabic binder also helps keep the carbon in suspension. Red Chinese ink replaces carbon with vermilion.

SOAP is made by *saponification*, the reaction between alkalis and animal or vegetable fats. Soaps made with caustic potash are liquid, while caustic soda makes soaps that are solid. The most popular fats used are lard, goat suet, beef tallow, olive oil and palm oil. A cold process with solid caustic soda or caustic potash allows an accurate approach at home. The following parts by weight can be used for 10 parts solid caustic soda, or 14 parts caustic potash, dissolved in 20 parts hot water; 72 parts beef tallow OR 73 parts lard OR 75 parts olive oil OR 71 parts palm oil. Gently melt the fat, if solid. The two liquids

are best mixed at around 40°C, mixing too warm or at uneven tempertures are common errors. Pour the fat then the caustic soda into a suitable vessel and stir or shake vigorously. Mixed well the two liquids should not separate, if they do they must be reshaken or stirred. After a week the soap can be tested to see if it produces suds. Test for excess alkalinity with indicator paper.

MORTAR was first used in ancient Egypt, as a mixture of gypsum and sand. Cement mortar is 1 part Portland cement, anything from 3 to 6 parts of sand depending on the strength needed (less sand is stronger), and water. Adding a coarse aggregate to this mix makes **CONCRETE**. Lime mortar is made by mixing 1 part quicklime and 2 parts fine sand with water. The quicklime, slaked in the mixture, hardens into limestone when exposed to air.

LIME or **QUICKLIME** is calcium oxide prepared by heating limestone to around 900°C. Add lime to plenty of water to produce alkaline calcium hydroxide or **SLAKED LIME** and much heat. **MILK OF LIME** is a cooled suspension of fine slaked lime in water.

DYES need to be fixed to a fabric's fibers so that they do not wash out. This often requires a **MORDANT**, the most popular being *alum* which mordants tea (rose), beetroot (gold), red onions (orange), madder (red), elderberries (lilac) and others. Mix a quarter of your fabric's weight of alum in enough water for the fabric. Wet the fabric in warm water then immerse in the mordant and heat for one hour stirring occasionally. Cool overnight. Boil your dyestuff in water for half an hour then add enough water to immerse the fabric. Heat for one hour or until the fabric's colour is as you want it (it will lighten after rinsing and drying). Cool the fabric, rinse and dry. For a stronger colour use more dyestuff, not more mordant. Indigo, or woad, require no mordant. Collect urine in a bottle or vat and stand it uncapped (or with a little exposure to air) in the sun until it has fermented. The strong smell of ammonia tells us it is ready. Add one teaspoon of very finely ground indigo per litre of urine. Stand in the sun for another day and you should have a pale green solution. Wash your fabric or wool with soap, rinse out the soap thoroughly, and place in the solution. Keep it submerged for 10 minutes then remove and squeeze out excess liquid. The fabric or yarn will turn blue in the air.

ONE- & TWO-PIECE ISLAMIC PATTERNS

The patterns below are all made of only one or two different shapes and are constructed on either a square grid or a triangular grid. They can all be drawn relatively easily on squared graph paper or isometric paper, or alternatively only require one or two stencils, making them ideal for use in the classroom. Some vertices in the square patterns lie midway between grid intersections. The two curved patterns use the compasses to trace arcs centered on, and passing through, points on their grids. The coloring schemes can vary from those shown.

An Infinite Puzzle Set

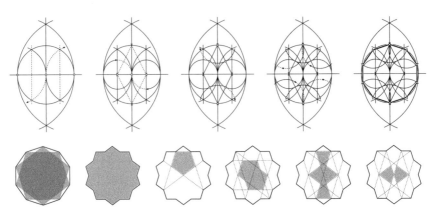

The *Umm al-Girih* is the starting point for a whole range of patterns. An excellent way to explore these patterns is to make a puzzle set of pieces. Follow the diagrams above to construct a regular decagon – a radius of about 2'' is a suitable size for the first circle – and then derive each shape from this decagon; star, pentagon, 'merged' double pentagon, 'bottle', and 'kite'. Make a stencil for each shape from stiff card or thin plastic and cut out as many pieces as needed from colored card or paper to complete a puzzle set. The possibilities with such a set are limited

only by the number of pieces cut, especially if one starts to explore colour schemes or aperiodic and self-similar repeat structures. To complete the patterns below, plus those on page 95, cut out the numbers of pieces shown. In order to leave a neat rectangular outline half and quarter shapes need to be cut as detailed. Counting, and maybe even making, the number of pieces needed for the pattern opposite, from the I'timad al-Daula Mausoleum in Agra, India, is left to the enthusiastic reader, or perhaps a classroom full of students.

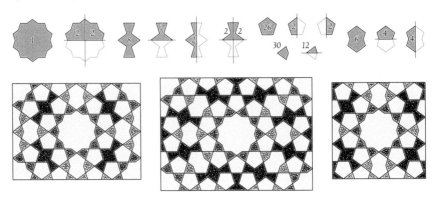

USEFUL SUBGRIDS

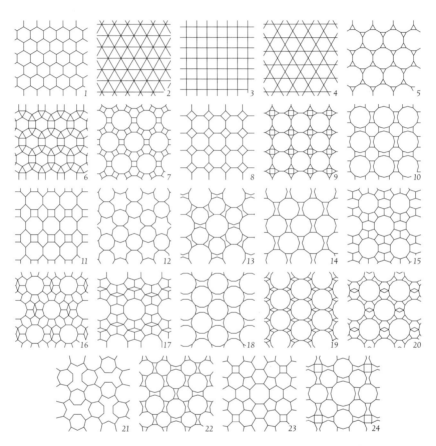

Most patterns on the *Islamic Design* pages rest on relatively simple polygonal subgrids. Those used are shown here with the pages on which they occur: 1. p.63-5 - 2. dual of 1. - 3. p.69, p.85 (*middle left*), p.86 - 4. p.92, p.93 - 5. p.76, p.79 (*top row*), p.81 (*top right*), p.83 (*top center and top right*) - 6. p.67, p. 79 (*third row*) - 7. p.77, p.83 (*bottom left*) - 8. p.69 (*alternative for 3.*), p.85 (*top right and bottom right*), p.86, p.70, p.71 (*top row*) - 9.

p.79 (*second row and bottom*), p.81 (*top left*) - 10. p.85 (*bottom left*), p.104 - 11. p.71 (*second row left*) - 12. p.83 (*bottom middle*) - 13. p.60 - 14. p.75 (*bottom right*), p.94, p.95 (*top*), p.96, p.98, p.99 (*all patterns*) - 15. p.75 (*bottom right*), p.94, p.95 (*top*), p.96, p.98, p.99 (*all patterns, alternative for 14.*) - 16. p.95 (*bottom*) - 17. p.58 - 18. p.100 (*left*) - 19. p.100 (*right*) - 20. p.101 - 21. p.102 - 22. p.103 - 23. p.105 (*top*) - 24. p.105 (*bottom*).

SQUARE KUFIC

Of all the ornamental styles developed from early Kufic script *Square Kufic*, set rigorously on a square grid, is the most obviously geometric. Alphabetic writing encodes the sounds of speech and thus conveys words, sentences, new information, and, above all, meaning to the reader. Square Kufic presents a curious inversion of this function as it remains well nigh illegible to a great many Arabic readers, its purely graphic twists, turns, simplifications, and compromises to letterform leaving them lost. It is easiest to

decipher when the word or phrase written is already well known to the viewer, thus rather than conveying new information, or preserving a text accurately for posterity, Square Kufic acts primarily as a talismanic invocation of sacred words and phrases already familiar. Simple words or phrases are often arranged in rotating repetitions (*top row*), longer passages (*middle row*) are arranged spiraling round from the outside, often starting at the bottom right corner (*bottom row*).

Praise be to God

Muhammad

Ali

Allah - Muhammad - Ali

Surat al-Ikhlās - chapter 112 of the Quran

Surat al-Fātiha - first chapter of the Quran

5

4

3

2

1

BRAIDED BORDERS

Gilded interlaced borders are frequently found in the Islamic arts of the book. They are used to frame central geometric panels in frontispieces, section, and chapter titles throughout a work and, on occasion, whole pages of text, particularly in illuminated Qurans. One technique that is commonly used is to construct these braided borders on a simple grid of dots, often colored blue and red. The following selected examples are provided as an introduction and brief reference to such designs for aspiring illuminators.

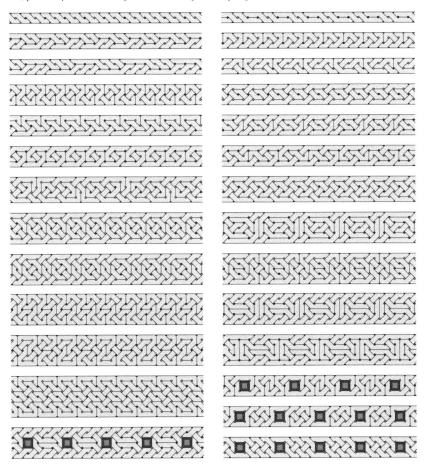

Calyx Elements

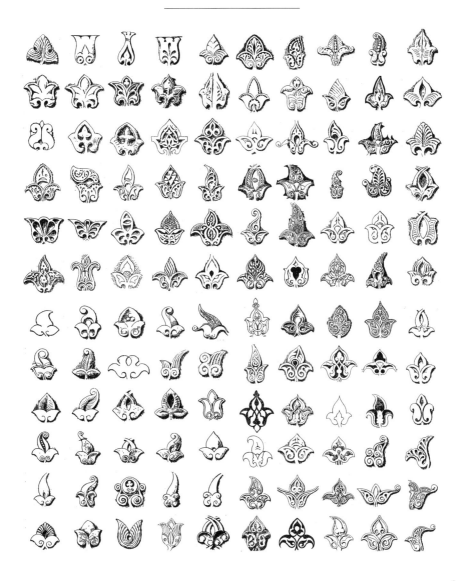

CLASSICAL CURVY BORDERS

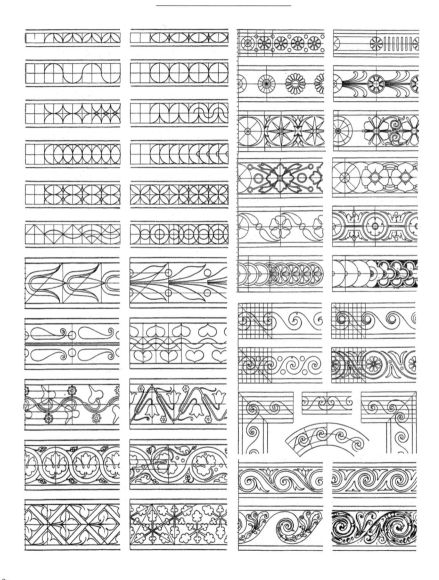

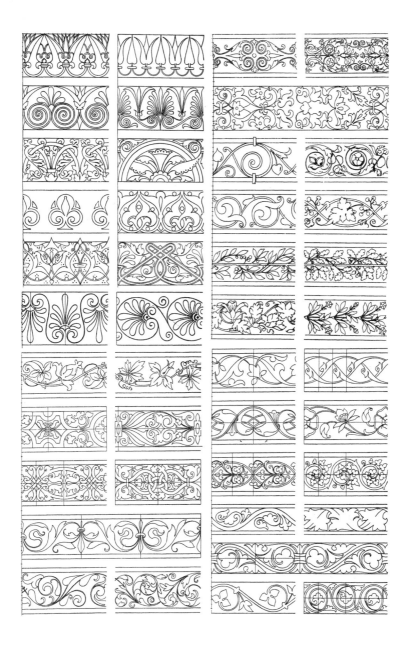

383

MATHEMATICAL CURVES

Many of the common two- and three-dimensional mathematical curves are shown here.
Bezier curves are today widely used to produce smooth curves in computer applications.

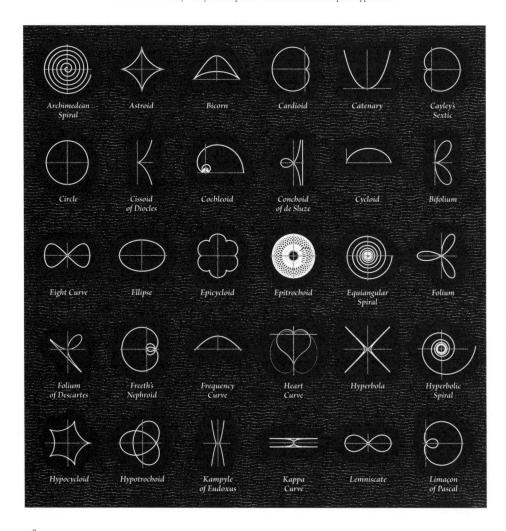

Archimedean Spiral · Astroid · Bicorn · Cardioid · Catenary · Cayley's Sextic

Circle · Cissoid of Diocles · Cochleoid · Conchoid of de Sluze · Cycloid · Bifolium

Eight Curve · Ellipse · Epicycloid · Epitrochoid · Equiangular Spiral · Folium

Folium of Descartes · Freeth's Nephroid · Frequency Curve · Heart Curve · Hyperbola · Hyperbolic Spiral

Hypocycloid · Hypotrochoid · Kampyle of Eudoxus · Kappa Curve · Lemniscate · Limaçon of Pascal

Lissajous
Curve

Lituus
Spiral

Logarithmic
Spiral

Neil's
Parabola

Nephroid

Parabola

Parabolic
Spiral

Plateau
Curve

Rhodonea
Curve 1

Rhodonea
Curve 2

Right
Strophoid

Serpentine

Spiral of
Archimedes

Talbot's
Curve

Tractrix

Tricuspoid

Trifolium

Witch of
Agnesi

Quadratic
Bezier Curve

Cubic
Bezier Curve

Cubic
Bezier Curve

Cubic
Bezier Curve

Cubic
Bezier Curve

Quartic
Bezier Curve

Circular
Helix

Conical
Helix

Cylindrical
Sine

Spheroidal
Sine

Hyperboloidal
Sine

Conical
Sine

Viviani's
Curve

Sici
Spiral

Fresnel
Spiral

Toroidal
Spiral

Spherical
Spiral

Rotating
Sine

385

SYMMETRY GROUPS

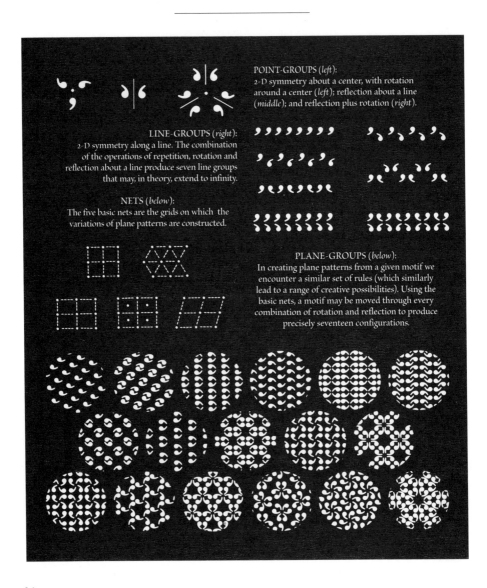

POINT-GROUPS (*left*):
2-D symmetry about a center, with rotation around a center (*left*); reflection about a line (*middle*); and reflection plus rotation (*right*).

LINE-GROUPS (*right*):
2-D symmetry along a line. The combination of the operations of repetition, rotation and reflection about a line produce seven line groups that may, in theory, extend to infinity.

NETS (*below*):
The five basic nets are the grids on which the variations of plane patterns are constructed.

PLANE-GROUPS (*below*):
In creating plane patterns from a given motif we encounter a similar set of rules (which similarly lead to a range of creative possibilities). Using the basic nets, a motif may be moved through every combination of rotation and reflection to produce precisely seventeen configurations.

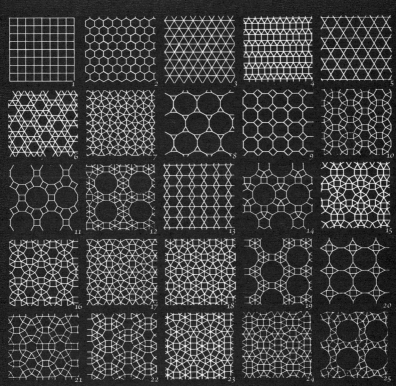

Similar constraints govern the regular division/ tiling of the plane. There are only three ways to do this using identical regular polygons; those with three, four and six sides (the square, equilateral triangle & hexagon) fill the plane by themselves, but five-siders (pentagons) do not. As well as regular divisions (1–3, above), there are eight semiregular tilings, sometimes known as Archimedean tilings (4–11), demiregular tilings (e.g. 12–25), and other variations not shown, which form a hierarchy of plane-division classification.

Mineral and Vegetable Li Patterns

Images on these and the next two pages are taken from *Li—Dynamic Form in Nature*, by David Wade (Wooden Books, 2003). The Chinese concept of *Li* falls between the idea of 'pattern' and 'principle', so that similar *Li* may appear via quite different circumstances and processes. (*See too pages 276–277*).

Irish Moss Seaweed

Fragmented liquid convection rolls

Agate

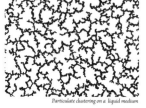

Particulate clustering on a liquid medium

Kerr magneto-optic effect in thin section of barium ferrite

Malachite

A positive Lichtenburg figure

Hairline cracks in ceramic

Magnetic maze-domain patterns in silicon-iron polished crystal

Cracks in parched earth

Cracks in dried out paints and gels

Magnetic domain pattern

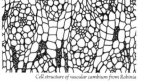

Cell structure of vascular cambium from Robinia

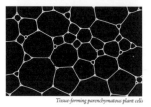

Tissue-forming parenchymatous plant cells

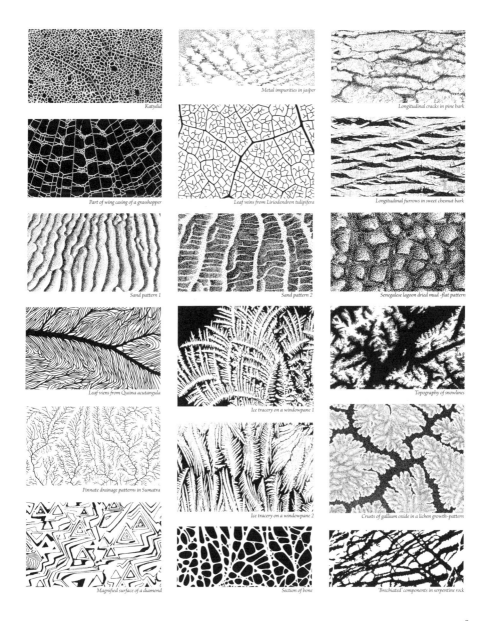

Katydid

Metal impurities in jasper

Longitudinal cracks in pine bark

Part of wing casing of a grasshopper

Leaf veins from Liriodendron tulipifera

Longitudinal furrows in sweet chesnut bark

Sand pattern 1

Sand pattern 2

Senegalese lagoon dried mud - flat pattern

Leaf viens from Quina acutangula

Ice tracery on a windowpane 1

Topography of snowlines

Pinnate drainage patterns in Sumatra

Ice tracery on a windowpane 2

Crusts of gallium oxide in a lichen growth-pattern

Magnified surface of a diamond

Section of bone

'Brechiated' components in serpentine rock

389

ANIMAL LI PATTERNS

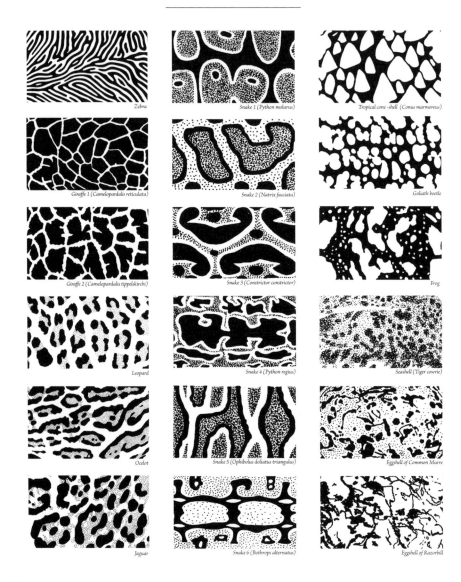

Zebra

Snake 1 (Python molurus)

Tropical cone -shell (Conus marmoreus)

Giraffe 1 (Camelopardalis reticulata)

Snake 2 (Natrix fasciata)

Goliath beetle

Giraffe 2 (Camelopardalis tippelskirchi)

Snake 3 (Constrictor constrictor)

Frog

Leopard

Snake 4 (Python regius)

Seashell (Tiger cowrie)

Ocelot

Snake 5 (Ophibolus doliatus triangulus)

Eggshell of Common Murre

Jaguar

Snake 6 (Bothrops alternatus)

Eggshell of Razorbill

Li patterns on Lizards, Frogs, Cuttlefish, Shells and Fish.
For more information, please refer to *Li, Dynamic
Form in Nature* by David Wade (Wooden Books, 2003).

TRAJAN TRICKS

The inscription on Trajan's column in Rome, made circa 112 AD, is widely regarded as the high point of Roman lettering (a modern typeface based on it is used on the cover of this book). Work by leading calligrapher Tom Perkins has revealed that the Roman letterforms are all derived from simple 'golden' geometry. Using high-quality rubbings and line drawings published by E.M. Catich in 1961, Perkins was able to describe six simple rectangles:

1) The square, used for M, O, Q and W.
2) The double-square, used for K, L, S and X.
3) The root five rectangle, used for B, E, F, J, and P.
4) The double golden rectangle, for A, T, R, H, U, Y & Z
5) The double root five rectangle, for C, D, G, N, and V.

Shown to the right are constructions for i) a √5 rectangle from a double square; ii) a double golden rectangle from a √5 rectangle; iii) a 3:4 rectangle (also sometimes used) from a √5 rectangle; iv) a √5 rectangle inside a square; v) a golden rectangle from a square. See too page 404.

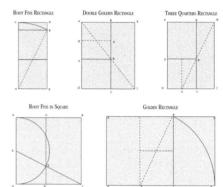

ROOT FIVE RECTANGLE · DOUBLE GOLDEN RECTANGLE · THREE QUARTERS RECTANGLE

ROOT FIVE IN SQUARE · GOLDEN RECTANGLE

Above: The construction of important designer's rectangles, used in the formation of letterforms from the Trajan Column in Rome (below). J, U, and W (as a separate letter) are later additions to the Latin alphabet so do not appear on the column.

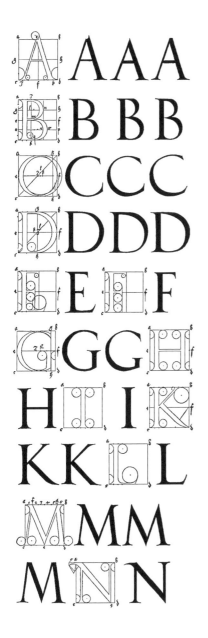

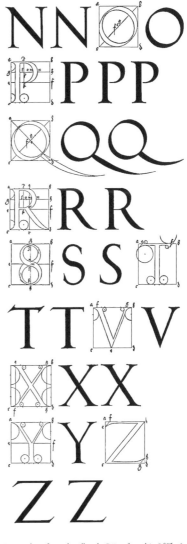

Roman letterforms by Albrecht Dürer from his *Of The Just Shaping of Letters*, in *The Art of Measurement* (1525).

TAJ MAHAL GOLDEN GEOMETRY

The Tah Mahal in Agra, Uttar Pradesh, India, was built between 1632 and 1653 by Mughal emperor Shah Jahan in memory of his third wife, Mumtaz Mahal, and is widely recognized as one of the finest buildings in the world. The geometrical analysis shown here (*by Russian architect* *Dymtro Kostrzycki*) clearly demonstrates the deliberate use of the golden section by the principal designer, generally thought to be Ustad Ahmad, in key elements of the design. Notice how the overall elevation has the same golden proportions as the great pyramid (*top left on facing page*).

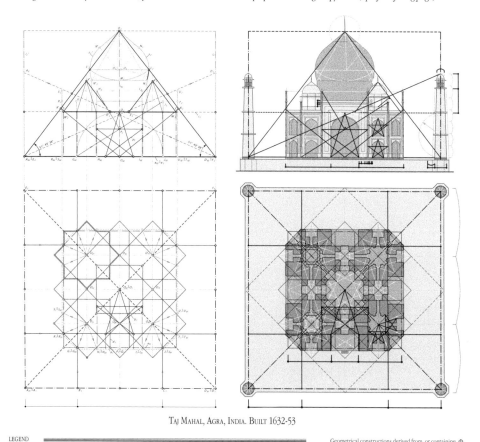

TAJ MAHAL, AGRA, INDIA. BUILT 1632-53

Golden Constructions

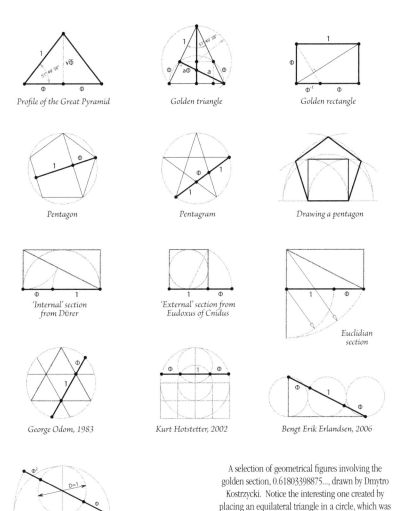

Profile of the Great Pyramid

Golden triangle

Golden rectangle

Pentagon

Pentagram

Drawing a pentagon

'Internal' section from Dürer

'External' section from Eudoxus of Cnidus

Euclidian section

George Odom, 1983

Kurt Hotstetter, 2002

Bengt Erik Erlandsen, 2006

Dmytro Kostrzycki, 2011 (after Dürer)

A selection of geometrical figures involving the golden section, 0.61803398875..., drawn by Dmytro Kostrzycki. Notice the interesting one created by placing an equilateral triangle in a circle, which was only discovered in 1983 by George Odom, and its close relationship to Hotstetter's adjoining construction.

RULER & COMPASS CONSTRUCTIONS

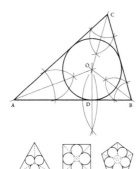

1. Incentre & incircle of a triangle:
1. Bisect ∠CAB, ∠ABC, ∠BCA (O);
2. Perp. to BC through O (D); 3. Circle O-D

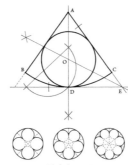

2. Circle in a sector:
1. Bisect ∠BAC (D); 2. Perpendicular
to AD on D; 3. Extend side AC (E);
4. Bisect ∠AED (O); 5. Circle O-D

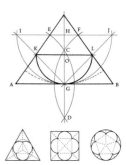

3. Semicircle in an isosceles triangle:
1. Arcs centers A, B (C to F); 2. Line CD (G);
3. Line EF (H); 4. Arc G-H (I, J); 5. Lines IG,
JG (K, L); 6. Line KL (O); 7. Arc O-KGL

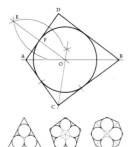

4. Circle in a kite:
1. Line AB; 2. Bisect ∠ACB (O); 3. Arcs
A-O, D-O (E); 4. Line OE (F); 5. Circle O-F

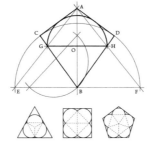

5. Semicircle in a kite that has two right angles:
1. Line AB; 2. Perpendicular to AB on B;
3. Arc B-CD (E, F); 4. Lines AE, AF
(G, H); 5. Line GH (O); 6. Arc O-GH

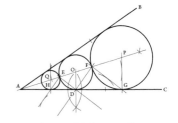

6. Tangent circles between two lines:
1. Bisect ∠BAC; 2. Perpendicular to AB through
any point O on bisector (D); 3. Circle O-D
(E, F); 4. Lines ED, FD; 5. Parallel to ED
through F (G); 6. Parallel to FD through E (H);
7. Parallels to OD through G, H (P, Q);
8. Circles P-G, Q-H;

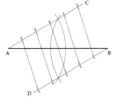

7. Dividing a segment into equal parts:
1. Arcs centers A, B (parallel lines AC, BD);
2. Mark off n equal partitions on AC, BD
(in this case five); 3. Join partitions as
shown to cut AB in n+1 equal divisions

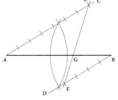

8. Dividing a segment into a given ratio:
1. Arcs centers A, B (parallel lines AC, BD);
2. Mark off lengths in given ratio on AC, BD,
in this case 7 & 4 (E, F); 3. Line EF (G);
AG:GB = AE:BF (in this case 7:4)

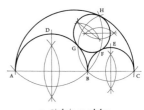

9. Circle in an arbelos:
1. Perp. bisector on AB (D); 2. Perp. bisector on
BC (E); 3. Arcs D-AB, E-CB (F, G, H);
4. Circle through F, G, H to complete

396

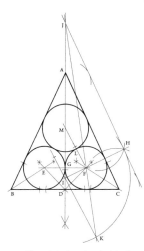

10. Three circles in an isosceles triangle:
1. Perpendicular on BC (D); 2. Bisect ∠ABC, ∠ACB; 3. Bisect ∠ADB, ∠ADC (E, F); 4. Line EF (G); 5. Circles E-G, F-G; 6. Arcs centers on AC, through F (line HI); 7. Parallel to AC through H (J); 8. Arc G-H; 9. Line JF (K); 10. Line IK; 11. Parallel to IK through F (L, M); 12. Circle L-M to complete

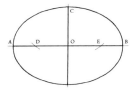

13. Gardener's method ellipse:
1. Arc radius OA center C (D, E); 2. Place pins at A, B and tie string tautly between them; 3. Move pins to D, E; 4. Pull string taut with pen to trace curve

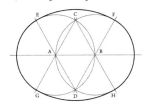

16. Simple fixed aspect ratio four-arc oval:
1. Circle center A on a line (B); 2. Circle B-A (C, D); 3. Lines DA, DB, CB, CA (E, F, G, H); 4. Arcs D-EF, C-GH

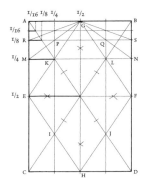

11. Geometric division of a rectangle:
1. Lines AD, BC; 2. Find midpoints of AB, CD, AC, BD (line EF, G, H); 3. Lines EG, EH, FG, FH (I, J, K, L); 4. Lines IK, JL; 5. Line KL (M, N); 6. Lines MG, NG (P, Q); Line PQ (R, S) ... and so on

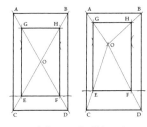

14. Similar rectangle within another:
1. For any point O within the rectangle, lines AO, BO, CO, DO; 2. Line EF parallel to CD; 3. Lines EG, EH parallel to AC & BD; 4. Line GH

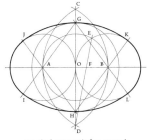

17. Fixed aspect ratio four-arc oval:
1. Circle center O on a line (A, B); 2. Arcs A-B, B-A (line CD); 3. Circles A-O and B-O (E); 4. Line ED (F); 5. Circle radius AF center O (G, H); 6. Lines GA, HA, HB, GB (I, J, K, L); 7. Arcs A-IJ, H-JK, B-KL, G-LI

Images & text from Ruler & Compass by Andrew Sutton, Wooden Books, 2009

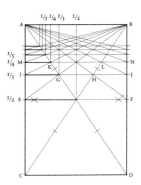

12. Harmonic division of a rectangle:
1. Lines AD, BC; 2. Find midpoints of AC, BD (line EF); 3. Lines EB, FA (G, H); 4. Line GH (I, J); 5. Lines IB, JA (K, L); 6. Line KL (M, N) ... and so on as needed

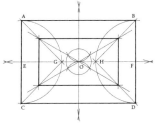

15. Rectangle of given ratio within another:
1. Bisect AB, CD & AC, BD (E, F, O); 2. Semicircles E-AC, F-BD (lines AG, CG, BH, DH); 3. Diagonals of inner rectangle centered on O (in this case a √3 rectangle) & complete

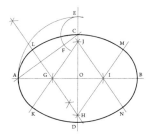

18. Flexible aspect ratio four-arc oval:
1. Extend CD if needed; 2. Arc O-A (E); 3. Line AC; 4. Arc C-E (F); 5. Perp. bisector on AF (G, H); 6. Arc O-G (I); 7. Arc O-H (J); 8. Lines JG, HG, HI, JI; 9. Arcs G-A & I-B (K, L, M, N); 10. Arcs H-LCM & J-NDK

397

HUMAN PROPORTION

Grids have been used to map human proportion at least since ancient Egypt where the height was divided into 19. Traditional arts around the world each have their own canon. Vitruvius reckoned the body at 10 faces or 8 heads in height (used by Da Vinci). Schemes of 7½, 8½, 9½ are common. More heads in the height emphasizes the body (useful for superheroes/models).

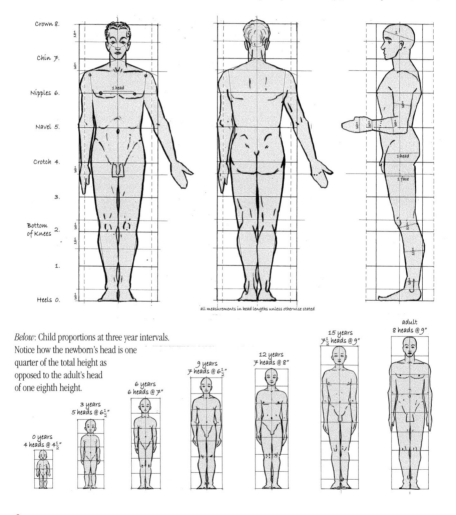

Crown 8.

Chin 7.

Nipples 6.

1 head

Navel 5.

Crotch 4.

3.

Bottom of Knees 2.

1.

Heels 0.

1 head

1 face

all measurements in head lengths unless otherwise stated

Below: Child proportions at three year intervals. Notice how the newborn's head is one quarter of the total height as opposed to the adult's head of one eighth height.

0 years
4 heads @ 4½"

3 years
5 heads @ 6½"

6 years
6 heads @ 7"

9 years
7 heads @ 6½"

12 years
7 heads @ 8"

15 years
7½ heads @ 9"

adult
8 heads @ 9"

398

Think of these schemes as 2-D 'mannekins'. Once memorized they can be used with little setting out and manipulated to fit the geometric proportions required. Any scheme must take into account fixed realations such as the elbows, navel, wrist and crotch as well as the widths at key parts of the body. The difference between male and female proportions is crucial to correct appearance. A women's navel sits lower by about 1/6th of a head, as do the nipples and knees. Men's shoulders exceed hips by about 1/3rd of a head, women's hips and shoulders tend to be equal width. *From an unpublished work by Adam Tetlow.*

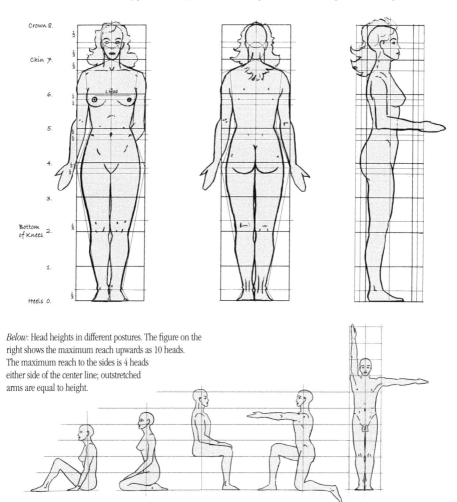

Below: Head heights in different postures. The figure on the right shows the maximum reach upwards as 10 heads. The maximum reach to the sides is 4 heads either side of the center line; outstretched arms are equal to height.

THE HUMAN HEAD

The Human head is drawn using regular divisions, subdivided into 1/3rds and 1/4rs, by drawing one circle radius 1/4 head for the lower head. Line AB is divided into 8 to give the eye width. Eye widths are then used to place mouth and width of nose. *Images and text on these pages taken from an unpublished work by Adam Tetlow.*

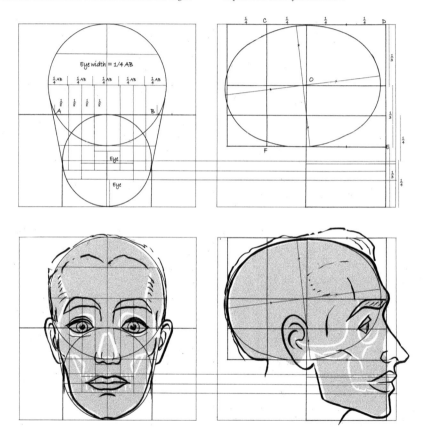

At its widest point the head is a little under 5 eye widths. The ears sit between the top of the eyelids and the bottom of the nose. The hairline for Vitruvius was at 4/5ths of a head, here it is at 5/6ths. A lifetime's study will reveal ever more relationships.

To construct the head in profile, first draw square CDEF, then divide into 3 vertically. Next add 1/3rd to the left side, divide CDEF horizontally in half, and add one half to the bottom edge for the jaw. The skull is drawn with a tilted ellipse (center O).

MEASURED DRAWING

MEASURED DRAWING allows an artist to draw accurately from life, a highly useful skill, and these days a rare one too. Drawings of this sort may not always be called for, but there are often times when knowing these methods can be invaluable. Of the many ways of measuring, the three most common techniques are *sight-size*, *comparative* and *relational* drawing. These are essentially formalisations of natural investigative processes.

SIGHT-SIZE DRAWING allows a very precise description of value and colour to be made as it records exactly what the eye sees (*see right*). By setting up an easel next to the object, the artist draws at exactly the same scale as the object, transferring horizontals with a straight edge and verticals with a plumb line.

COMPARATIVE DRAWING uses a standard measure taken from the subject and applies this to measure the placement of features. A thin straight rod (some people use their drawing pencil or paintbrush) is held at full arm's length to take a measure (*shown left*). Distances within the drawing can then be compared using this measure. When drawing the human figure knowledge gained from a study of proportional grids (*see previous pages*) can be tested against the drawing. This method is fast and well-suited to quick sketching—it gives a macro-view of the subject. However, certain problems can arise with comparative drawings, especially when measures are not taken very accurately. Cumulatively, these can lead to a 'skew' in the drawing.

RELATIONAL DRAWING is a useful technique on its own, or can be employed to correct problems in comparative drawings. Relational drawing gives the artist a micro-view of the subject. The method involves a straight edge, and plumb lines are then used to map distances and angles between points, weaving a web of interconnections, that all correct each other as the drawing reaches completion (*right*). This technique is more time-consuming but it allows unparalled opportunities to explore form, and was much favoured by DaVinci and Cezanne. It is a philosophical tool for understanding the world, whereas the sight-size method is more suited to precise replication of optical effects

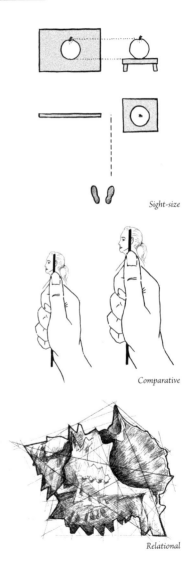

Sight-size

Comparative

Relational

PAINTING GRIDS

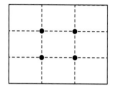

THE RULE OF THIRDS
Divide a canvas into thirds.
Place keys elements on the dots.

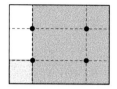

RABATMENT
Place a square in a rectangle to
get key lines and focal points.

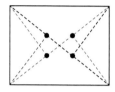

OCCULT CENTERS
Draw diagonals and their
perpendiculars to find centers.

Painters have long used geometrical techniques and rules of thumb to arrange elements in their paintings. For example, a horizon may be placed halfway up a painting. The most famous and widely-used technique is the so-called *Rule of Thirds* (*above, left*) where a canvas is divided into thirds horizontally and vertically. To do this accurately, use the 'starcut' technique (*shown right, after Malcolm Stewart*). Key elements may then be placed at the four focal points. Another widely-used technique is *rabatment* (*above, center*), where the largest possible square is placed in a rectangle, and then again, to give four focal points. A rarer technique is to use the *occult centers* of the rectangle (*above, right*).

Of couse, 1/2 (0.5) and 2/3 (0.666) are simply the first two approximations of the Golden Section, with the next being 3/5 (0.6) (*construction shown right, lowest*). Some artists simply prefer to go straight for the golden 0.618 division of their canvas, both vertically and horizontally, or even use a golden rectangle right from the start. A good example of this approach is Sandro Botticelli's 1486 Birth of Venus (*opposite top*). Because Botticelli uses a golden rectangle, the golden divisions are the same as the rabatment lines——a feature unique to golden rectangles.

A probably less deliberate but nevertheless highly instructive use of golden divisions and the Rule of Thirds may be observed in Claude Monet's 1868-69 series of paintings of the cliffs at Etretat in the Caux, Normandy, France. Opposite are shown four of his paintings, which all display elements arranged in accordance with the general idea expressed by the rules outlined above.

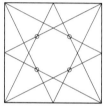

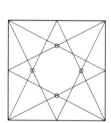

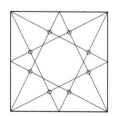

1/3   1/3   1/3

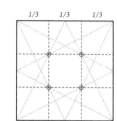

1/4   1/4   1/4   1/4

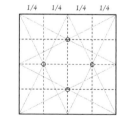

1/5   1/5   1/5   1/5   1/5

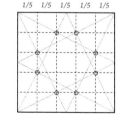

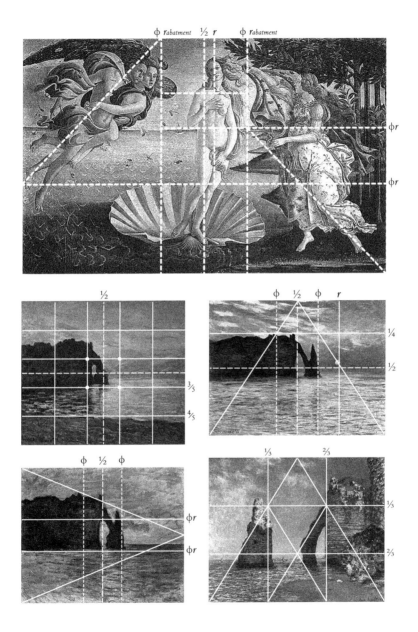

403

Designers' Rectangles

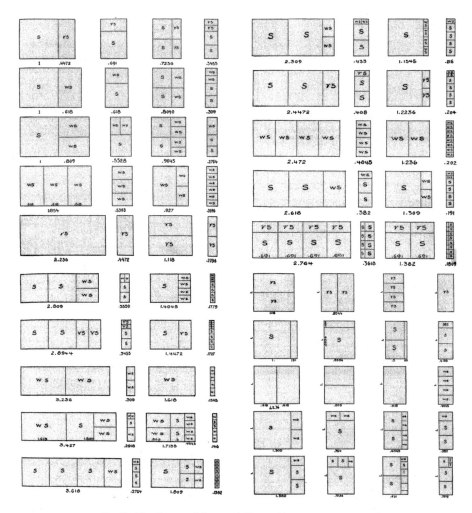

From Hambidge. Key: ws = whirling square (golden rectangle), s = square, v5 = root 5 rectangle

INDEX

A

Acanthus, 134-5, 162
Amaringo, Pablo, 344
Allen, George Romilly, 30
Arabesque, 1, 61-62, 74-75, 90, 92, 94-95, 136-7
Arrays, 216-19, 238-9
Arches, 156-9
Ark of the covenant, 326
Art, sacred, 54, 61, 161, 324, 338, 360, 379; Celtic, 7-55; Islamic, 61-111; biomorphic, 115-169
Artistic impulse and expression, 282, 284, 364
Arcs, in Celtic art, 12-13, 15-17, 24-27, 36; in Islamic art, 68-71, 92-93, 374-5
Arrowhead shapes, 32-33
Asymmetry, 237, 274-7; and the golden section, 322, 332, 346
Asymmetrical, grids, 40-43; patterns, 88-89, 148-9, 153, 234; ornamentation, 144
Avebury, 10-11

B

Bain, George, 26
Balmaclellan collar, 20-21
Battersea Shield, 18
Bifurcation, 268-9
Biomorphic design 115-169; precepts of, 126, 128-9, 134-5, 138-9, 158-9, 168-9
Background and foreground, 124-5, 142, 202-7
Book decoration, 52-53, 74, 92, 131, 160-1, 364, 380
Book, of Durrow, 52-53, 131, 365, 367; of Kells, 363, 368
Bonnet, Charles, 308
Borders, 17, 42-5, 66, 130-1, 154-5, 274; braided, 380; curvy, 382-3
Botticelli, Sandro, golden section analysis of *The Birth of Venus*, 332, 403
Braids, 356
Bravais, lattices, 254, 308
Break lines, 40, 52
British insular art, 18-21
Bronze, age 12; objects, 12, 17-18, 20

C

'C' shapes, 8, 30-31, 120-1, 132-33, 136
Calligraphy, 61, 72-73, 162-3, 392 see also Kufic
Calyx, 138, 140, 381
Camera obscura, 176-7
Cannon of Polyclitus, 316
Carnac (France), 10, 368
Castlerigg stone circle, 11
Çatal Hüyük, 28
Catich, E.M., 392
Celtic, pattern, 7-55; imagery, 16-21; keys, 24, 28-29, 30-37, 46, 48, 55, 361-5; knots 8, 23, 24, 38-51; spirals, 13, 17-19, 24-30, 37, 49, 161, 362-365; society, 10-13
Center, perspective, 190-1
Chaos theory, 271, 278, 318
Chain stitch, 357
Charcoal, making, 372
Chevrons, 8, 28-9
Chirality, 260-1
Christian art (early and Celtic) 7, 22, 24, 28, 54, 160-1, 330, 368
Clay, 369
Clarendon barrow, 11
Clement of Alexandria, 330
Colombe, Jean, golden section analysis of *The Baptism of Jesus*, 332
Critchlow, Professor Keith, 92-3, 338-9, 362
Cross shape, 8, 354
Crystals, 254-5
Cup and ring (in Prehistoric art) 8, 352-3
Curves (decorative), 116-169; in architectural ornamentation, 156-7, 159; in Baroque and Rococo ornament, 145; in Celtic pattern, 1, 11-13, 16, 20-21, 24, 35, 38, 46, 50, 361; how to draw, 120-3; in decorative plant form, 134-7, 140-1; in ironwork, 132-3; mathematical 262-3, 384-5; in pen and brush work, 162-3; primordial, 118-119; to turn corners, 154-5; visual detection of, 216-9; symmetries of, 262-3; spiral and helix, 264-5, 320-1, 364-5
Curvilinear, 117, 122-3

D

Depth, in perspective drawing, 176-7
Dendera Zodiac, 326
Desborough mirror, 20-21
Designers' rectangles, 404
Diaper patterns, 34
DNA double helix, 366
Dodecagons, 66-67, 76-79, 105
Dorsiventrality, 258-9
Drawing machines, 188-9
Druid, 7, 22, 54, 360
Dürer, Albrecht, 54, 178, 188-9, 286, 316, 392-3, 395
Durrow, Book of, 52-53, 131, 365, 367
Dyes and dyeing, 373

E

Elevation, 138-141, 162, 176, 178-9, 182-3, 190, 194-5
Enamel, 12, 131
Enantiomorphy, 260-1
Entoptic phenomena, 8
Erugenia, John Scotus, 48
Escher, 206-7
Euclid, 298
Euclidian section, 395

F

Fibonacci series, 244-5, 264, 266-7, 306-13, 316, 318-22, 326, 332, 334, 336, 342, 344, 360
Flourishes, 131-2, 142, 162-3, 164
Folding processes, 364
Fractalization, 318; and the golden ratio, 322-3, 344
Fractals, 26, 90, 125, 270-1, 276, 278-9, 376

G

Geometry, 7, 12, 14-15, 52-54, 72, 88-91, 96-97, 104, 142-3, 297; in architecture, 286-7, 326-7, 330-1, 394; dome, 106-7; fractal, 270-1, 278-9; golden section, 297, 304-5, 326-7, 330-1, 334-5, 344-5, 392, 394-5; of ice halos, 228-9; of muqarnas, 108-9; of perspective, 186-7; projective, 178-9; sacred, 286, 334-5, 338, 344, 360
Girih, 76-77, 94
Glass, 12, 188-9, 200, 272; making, 369-70
Glaze, 369
Glide symmetry, 130, 136, 146

Golden angle, 310
Golden section, 96, 100, 298-347; in 3-D space, 340-1; in architecture, 326-31; in cells and consciousness, 344-5; of the human body, 316-17; Lucas and Fibonacci numbers, 312-13, 318-19; in music theory, 334-5; in nature, 314-15, 346-7; in painting, 332-33; pentagrams and rectangles, 304-7, 324-5; in product design, 336-7; in sacred geometry, 338-9; in spirals and helices, 264-5, 308-11, 320-1; *see also* phi
Grids, 120-125, 150-1, 158, 386-7; ancient Egyptian, 326-7; in Celtic pattern, 8, 26-27, 36-37, 40, 42, 52, 360-5, 367-8; in Islamic pattern, 64, 80-85, 374-7; ; painting, 402-3; subgrids, 92-93, 104-5, 378

H

Hakoris chapel, Karnak, 327
Hallstatt culture, 12
Halos (atmospheric), 226-9
Hambidge, Jay, 328-9, 404
Harburg gospels, 368
Harmony, 61, 104, 286, 297; musical, 52, 334
Harry Potter, 336
Helices, 260-1, 264-5
Heraclitus, 318
Herringbone patterns, 192-3, 359
Hexagon, 52, 64-67, 70-71, 76-80, 82-87, 92-95, 98, 102, 116, 123, 148, 250, 363; Sierpinski, 271; tessellation, 62-3, 105, 387
Hilton Cadboll Stone, 49
Hogarth, William, 175

I

Illusions, context, 210-1; tonal, 200-1; optical, 212-17; perceptual, 206-9, 218-9; motion, 220-1, 223
Iona, 22
Ink, types of, 373
Iron (pigment), 370; gall, 373
Ironwork, 20-21, 24, 132-3
Islimi, 74; see also Arabesque
Iznik, 75, 116, 128, 143

J

Jamnitzer, Wenzel, 296, 340,
Japanese brush compass, 26, 368

K

Kells, Book of 363, 368
Kepler, Johannes, 252, 262, 308, 340,
Keys (Celtic patterns), 24, 28, 30-37, 46, 48, 55, 361-5
Knots, figurative,128, 242; fabric, 356-357; Celtic, 8, 23, 24, 38-51; Islamic, 76-77, 94
Kufic, 72, 379

L

Language of the birds, 7
La Tène culture, 12, 14, 17-20
Leonardo Da Vinci, 281, 286, 298, 308, 316, 340, 398, 401; golden section analysis of *The Annunciation*, 332
Leaf forms, decorative, 116-117, 120-121, 124-131, 138-141, 150-3, 160; acanthus, 134; Arabesque, 61, 74, 90, 136-7; in early Celtic art, 12-13
Leather, making, 372
Leaves, arrangement in phyllotaxis, 264-7, 308-311; classifications of, 134-5, 258; cellular structure of, 364; radial symmetry of, 246-7
Li patterns, mineral and vegetable 388-9; animal, 390-1
Liminal space, 18
Lindisfarne gospels, 161, 368
Line, the, 7, 50-51, 54, 62, 120, 303, 76, 94; golden cut/division of, 96, 298, 302-3, 346
Lines, 14, 50, 62, 65, 76, 118, 120, 122, 134, 152-3, 162, 238, 298, 304, 328, 339, 365, 366; ancient, 2; break, 40, 52; center, 38-9; diagonal, 30, 32-5, 38, 252; filigree 224; ; in grids, 402; guide, 324; horizontal, 68; incommensurable, 328; matrix of, 360; mirror, 240-1; parallel, 192, 264; perspective 190, 194-5; radial, 80, 94; of reflection, 240-1, 386; spiral, plant and animal, 14, 18, 28, 50, 320, 362; straight 24, 46, 50, 122, 132, 144, 156, 158, 218, 362; ; of symmetry 25, 238-7, 240-1, 251, 386; termination 194; vertical, 224; whizz, 220
Logos, 300, 330, see also ratio
Lucas, Edouard, 306, 312
Lucas numbers, 306, 312-13, 318-9; see also Fibonacci series, Phi and golden section

M

Machiayao, 119
Maes Howe, 10
Manuscripts, illuminated, 22, 26, 52-53, 154; grids in, 336, 368
Maori, 118
Marbled papers, 164-5
Martineau, John, 342
Mazes and Labyrinths, 354-5
Meanders, 8, 24, 28-9, 364; in mazes, 354; riverine, 263, 276
Media, artist's 371
Menkaure, bust of, 327
Metallurgy, 12; La Tene 14, 132 see also ironwork
Metrology, ancient, 10
Michell, John, 211, 322-3, 360, 410
Miniaturization, 14
Mitres, 34
Monet, Claude, golden section analysis of cliff paintings, 403
Morris, William, 135, 149
Mushrooms, shapes in Celtic art, 8, 13, 24, 363; radial symmetry of, 246

N

Newgrange, 8, 350-1
Number, 7; sacred, 330-1

O

Ohm, Martin, 298
One-point perspective, 184-5
Oort cloud, 248
Opposites -*see enantiomorphy*
Optical, illusions, 212-17; flipping, 206-7; see also illusions
Origin (point) 120
Orkney, 10
Orthographic projection, 178-83
Osirian temple, 327

P

Pacioli, Luca, 298
Paint, types of, 371
Painting grids, 402-3
Paisley, 13, 124-125, 166-7
Palladio, 331
Paper, making, 372
Path (lines in pattern), 7, 8, 30-35, 38-43, 44, 46, 48, 64-

65, 78-79, 98-99, 244, 262, 276, 363, 364-7
Parchment, 372
Paths, in mazes, 354-5
Parthenon, 298, 331-2
Peltae, 21
Penrose tiling, 272-3, 344-5
Pentagonal tiling, 272-3 344, 376-7
Pentagons, 35, 94-97, 98-99, 105, 250, 272-3, 387; in architecture, 331; and the golden section, 304-5, 314-5, 326-7, 395; in nature, 308, 314-5, 345
Pentagrams, 96-101; and the golden section, 304-5, 314-5, 320, 338-9, 342-3, 395
Perkins, Tom, 392
Perspective, 172-231; center, 190-1; one-point 176, 184-7; and projection, 176-83
Petrie crown, 17
Petroglyphs, 350-1
Phi, 266, 278, 287, 298, 304, 316, 324, 332, 342 - *see also golden section*
Phidias, 298
Pictish proportions, 360
Pigments, artist's, 370
Plaits, 356-7
Plan and elevation 138-141, 162, 176, 178-9
Plane, 61-63, 123, 158, 272-3; inclined, 190-1; use of in perspective, 184-5, 195; in symmetry, 197, 244, 250-1, 262-3; vanishing, 202; dividing the, 252-3
Plato, 52, 230, 262, 318, 338; and the golden section, 297-303, 324, 334
Platonic solids, 106, 340, 362
Point symmetries, 240-1, 244-5, 251, 386
Point, 62, 72, 110, 120, 128-9, 138-9; termination, 195; vanishing, 176-7, 184-7, 190-3, 195, 197
Polygonal subgrids, 378, 387
Polygons, 11, 24, 46, 242
Polyhedra, 10; golden section, 340-1
Proportion, precepts of, 286-7, 300-3; human, 10, 398-401; in Celtic art, 52-53; in calligraphy, 72-73, 392-3; rosette, 96-97, 100-1; divine (*see also* golden section), 96-97, 298, 314-15, 324-5, ; in tiling, 146-7; in nature, 314-15; in gnomonic growth, 320-1; from asymmetry, 322-3; in art and architecture, 326-31; 394 in painting, 332-3; in music, 334-5; continuous geometric, 300, 302, 336

Proportional symmetry, 286, 314, 322, 332, 346
Proportionality, 290
Prehistoric art, 8 118-9, 350-3, 356
Pythagoras, 248, 286, 297-8, 334
Pythagorean geometry, 300-1

Q
Quadrivium, 334
Quark, 26, 256

R
Rabatment, 305, 324, 332, 402-3
Rainbows, 226-9
Ratio, in Celtic art, 52; definition of, 300, 330; golden, 266, 272, 298, 300-3, 314-17, 322, 324, 336-7, 340, 342-5, see also Golden section, Phi, divine proportion; Fibonacci, 306-7, 312, 326, 328; in Music, 334-5, 368; Pythagorean, 286; in Zillij design, 88
Reflection, in pattern, 32, 130, 146-9, 154-5, 239, 282-3; symmetry, 240-1, 244, 251, 262
Reflections, in nature, 198-9; in perspective drawing, 196-197, 200-1
Repeat, units and patterns, 14, 26-7, 37, 46-7, 62-5, 66-95, 102-3, 106, 122-3, 146-153, 238, 240, 254, 284
Rhombs, 8, 30, 64, 148, 205, 360-1
Rosettes, 70-71, 80-81, 83, 88-89, 98-101, 105-7, 130, 138, 140-1, 161; Venusian, 342-3, 345, 361, 365, 376
Rotation, 146-7, 243, 244, 251; angle of, 310; spiral, 328; symmetry, 82-85, 130-1, 140-1, 240-1, 282-3, 367; viewing, 214-5
Roundels, 26-27, 274, 363
Rule of thirds, 402

S
'S' shapes, 8, 30-31, 120-1, 132-3, 136, 365; elemental, 126
Salvador Dali, 332
Sawtooth shapes, 32-33
Seal of Solomon, 62
Self-coincidence, 239-241
Self-similarity, 26-27, 90-91, 242-3, 264-5, 270-1, 314, 322-3, 328
Sense perception, 230-1
Set square, 64
Shadows, 190, 194-5, 198, 200-1, 230

Shipobo art, 364

Socrates, 322

Space (in design), positive and negative, 124-5; *see also background and foreground*

Spirals, 130-133; Arabesque, 74, 114, 124, 136-7, 140-1; in early art, 8, 118-9; Celtic, 13, 17-19, 24-30, 37, 49, 161, 362-365; genetic, 308; and helices, 261, 264-5; Fibonacci and phyllotaxis, 266-7, 320-1, 367; square 30-1;

Square root, 300

Square, double, 62, 392; knots, 357, 367; grids, 32-35, 39, 52-53, 70-71, 78-79, 80-82, 88, 120, 150-1, 361, 363, 365, 374-5, 379; pattern and motif, 86-87, 154-5; spirals 30-31, 364; tiling, 66-67, 76-77, 84-85, 123

Squares, 8, 108, 114, 144, 250, 387; in ancient architecture, 326-7, 331; arrangements in space, 252; in Celtic pattern, 28, 30, 34-36, 44-5, 361, 365, 367; as basis for curvilinear design, 123; in Islamic design, 66-71, 76-77, 80-81, 84-87, 105; drawing knots in, 44-45; in painting grids, 402-3; to show perspective, 190-1, 204-5; ; in rabatment, 324-5, 332-3; ; and golden rectangles, 304-5, 314-15, 328-9, 331, 336, 339; drawing spirals in, 28-31; tessellating, 68-69

St. Columba, 22

St. John and St. Peter, 22

Stereogram, 176-7

Stonehenge, 10-11, 368

Symmetry, 20, 61, 104-5, 126, 130, 236-291; animal, 258-9; architectural, 286-9; atomic and sub-atomic, 256-7; crystalline, 254-5; dihedral, 241, 244; dilation, 243; radial, 24, 40, 94-5, 102-3, 116-7, 140-1, 244-8; reflection, 76, 130, 240-1; rotational, 82-85, 130, 24, 240-1; three dimensional, 248-51, 254-5; spiral, 266-7

Synesthesia, 224-5

T

Tablet of Shamesh, 299, 324

Teardrops (decorative), 12, 116, 124, 162

Tetraktys, 312

Tiling (geometrical), 66-69, 76-79, 82-87, 92-95, 123, 387; spherical, 106; Penrose 272-3, 344

Tracery, 124-5, 156, 158-9, 389

Trajan calligraphy, 392-3

Tree of life, 168-9

Triangles, 14, 25, 32-35, 44, 105, 116, 123, 210, 365; 3-4-5 Pythagorean, 52-53, 76, 78-79, 84-85, 360; in architecture, 326-7, 331, 394-5; double, 62-63; equilateral, 66-67, 82-83, 92-93, 242, 250, 387; golden section, 304-5, 338-9, 394-5

Triskeles (interlocked spirals), 12-13, 15, 19-21, 24-7, 362

Trumpet shapes (peltae) 12-13, 21, 25

Trypillian, 119

U

Urnfield culture, 12

V

Vanishing points, 176-7, 184-7, 190-3, 195, 197, 202

Viewpoints, 176-181, 183, 189, 194-5, 214,

Vinca art, 29

Vincent Van Gogh, golden section analysis of *The Beach*, 333

Vitruvius, 286, 398, 400

W

Warp thread, 357

Waves, 262-3, 362

Wallpaper, 135, 146, 148-9, 254

Weaving, 356-7

Weaves, 358-9

Weft thread, 357

Wood, 200; blocks (printing), 148; carvings, 55, 96-97, 108, 156-7, 168-9; charcoal, 372; making paper from, 372; varnishes, 371

X

Xenophanes, 248

Y

'Y' shapes, 364

Yangshao culture, 119

Z

Zigazgs, 8-9, 78-79

Zillīj design, 88-91

Zoomorphics, 16-17 24, 48, 55, 214

FURTHER READING & REFERENCES

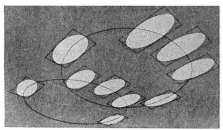

Perspective analysis of clouds, by John Ruskin, from Modern Painters, London 1856

CELTIC PATTERN

M. Gimbutas, *Language of the Goddess*

D. Lewis-Williams, *Mind in the Cave*

C. Nordenfalk, *Celtic and Anglo-Saxon Painting*

R. Stevick, *The Earliest Irish and English Bookarts*

D. Harding *Archaeology in Celtic Art*

K. Critchlow, *Time Stands Still*

J Michell, *Sacred Geometry*

R. Graves, *The White Goddess*

R. & V. Megaw, *Celtic Art*

C. Bamford, *The Voice of the Eagle*

K. White, *Open World*

ISLAMIC DESIGN

K Critchlow, *Islamic Patterns*, Thames & Hudson
Paul Marchant, *Unity in Pattern*
J. Burgoin, *Arabic Geometrical Pattern and Design*
M. Lings, *Splendours of Qur'an Calligraphy and Illumination*
J. M. Castéra, *Arabesques: Decorative Art in Morocco*

CURVES

L. Day, *Pattern Design*

S. Durant, *Ornament*

Meyer, *Handbook of Ornament*

F. Shafi'i, *Simple Calyx Ornament in Islamic Art*

O. Jones, *The Grammar of Ornament*

D. Wade, *Crystal and Dragon*

J. Trilling, *The Language of Ornament by J. Trilling.*

SYMMETRY

L. Lederman & C. Hill, *Symmetry and the Beautiful Universe*

M. Livio, *The Equation that couldn't be Solved*

I. & M. Hargittai, *Symmetry, a Unifying Concept*

PERSPECTIVE

R. Gregory, *Eye and Brain*

M. Kemp, *The Science of Art*

F. Dubery & J. Willats, *Drawing Systems*

R. Ornstein & P. Ehrlich, *New World, New Mind*

THE GOLDEN SECTION

P. Hemenway, *Divine Proportion*

G. Doczi, *Power of Limits*

M. Schneider, *Golden Section Workbook*

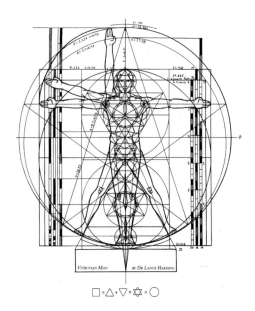

VITRUVIAN MAN   BY DR LANCE HARDING